LIVE · LOVE
LEARN

Endorsements

Wow! You had me hooked just from the title. From the introduction to the conclusion, this "book for life" resonated with my soul. It is definitely a bedside book to refer to on a regular basis. Living authentically and with gratitude towards a greater purpose is everyone's right and duty, and this book contains simple, effective, practical and timeless advice to do just that. The anecdotes further embed the lessons for the reader. The structure of the book also provides easy reference. Thank you for making my heart sing and for sharing your wisdom with the world.

Parusha Gajathar – Chief Financial Officer, BankServ

When reading *Live • Love • Learn. The power of authenticity*, it is easy to recognise yourself in the book. It is such a rich tapestry of wisdom that not only gently takes you inside yourself, but also provides you with the tools to understand and respond. I would urge anyone who wants to be a better person tomorrow than they are today, to work with this wisdom.

Steve Teasdale – Group Head of Organisational Development, Change & Transformation, Discovery People

This book will transform your life. This powerful read is essential for anyone seeking to unleash their personal sense of purpose and potential by defining who they really are, what their true values are, and how to put an action plan in place to achieve deep personal growth, fulfilment and build the confidence to thrive. This book will enable you to positively progress your relationships, your health, your happiness. It is brimming with tips, tools, strategies and reflections to enhance your self-development journey, to improve your quality of life, to equip you for the challenges and pressures of daily living, and to build inner confidence and courage so that you might excel in a sustainable way.

Shirley Zinn – Non-Executive Director of Boards; Former HR Director (Nedbank, Standard Bank, Woolworths); author of Swimming Upstream

Life does not come with a manual, so we often find ourselves searching for the beacons and the guiding lights to help us traverse this tricky thing called 'Life'. Ashnie Muthusamy's book IS the manual we are all looking for. Her work is insightful, enlightening and extremely helpful in navigating the emotional environment around us. She equips up with the tools and gives us a systematic understanding on how to make our Human experience a kinder and more meaningful one. This is a wonderful guide to life with real life examples and 'how to' exercises in the hope that we all learn to Live, Love and Learn and realise the power of authenticity.

Sureshnie Rieder – award-winning radio host on 5FM on the Roger Goode Show weekdays 6am until 9am; MC; voice over artist; motivational speaker

Live • Love • Learn is a book I will recommend to everyone. It's a simple, well put together book that highlights all the things we need to focus on if we want to live our most fulfilling lives, which everyone deserves to and is capable of doing. I mentor youth who are transiting from high school to tertiary education and then to the workplace. I will be giving every one of my mentees a copy of *Live • Love • Learn* so that we can use it as part of our mentoring and coaching programme. Thank you Ashnie, for taking time to put your experiences on paper and sharing this with us.

Kele Mazwai – Group Executive, Wesbank

This book is not only a relevant subject for the leaders of our time, but a vital and well-structured handbook to discover what depicts your inner self through a lens of multiple perspectives. It brings context and relevance to your own definition of meaning and sustains your ongoing journey through authentic thinking at the core.

Tony Christodoulou – CIO (EMEA) for American Tower Corporation; Adjunct Faculty at the Gordon Institute of Business Science

First published in 2019.

ISBN: 978-1-86922-808-8 (Printed)
eISBN: 978-1-86922-809-5 (PDF ebook)

Published by KR Publishing
P O Box 3954
Randburg
2125
Republic of South Africa

Tel: (011) 706-6009
Fax: (011) 706-1127
E-mail: orders@knowres.co.za
Website: www.kr.co.za

Printed and bound: HartWood Digital Printing, 243 Alexandra Avenue, Halfway House, Midrand
Typesetting, layout and design: Cia Joubert, cia@knowres.co.za
Cover design: Marlene de'Lorme, marlene@knowres.co.za
Editing & proofreading: Jennifer Renton, jenniferrenton@live.co.za
Project management: Cia Joubert, cia@knowres.co.za
Images: Shivanie Subramoney, geekonfleekorders@gmail.com
Index created with TExtract/www.Texyz.com

LIVE · LOVE LEARN

THE POWER OF AUTHENTICITY

ASHNIE MUTHUSAMY

kr
publishing

2019

Acknowledgements

To God, for blessing me with the knowledge, skills, fortitude and creativity to write this book and for always illuminating my path with light and opening doors of infinite possibilities.

To my husband, Justin, who continues to support my outrageous ideas and spurs me on to be the best version of myself. Thank you for your love and being my anchor.

To Darshna, my beautiful daughter who inspires me every day to be a better mother and teaches me to be a better human being. Thank you for being my light and mirror.

To my dearest mother, Lutchmee, who has been my role model of unconditional love, strength, independence and continuous growth and improvement.

In memoriam to my father, Krishna, who taught me the beauty of humility and that excellence is not about receiving thundering applause, but sometimes it is about making a silent difference in the lives of others.

To my siblings, Dinesh, Nevashnie and Dayan, for being my fellow travelers on this journey of life, and for providing significant life lessons for me to flourish. I am grateful for the companionship. Thank you for touching my life.

To Chiara, for always providing honest feedback and being authentically you. Thank you for your critical voice during the creative process and for validating my ideas.

To Shivanie, for creating beautiful visual connections to the key messages in the book. Your sketches confirm that a picture is worth a thousand words.

Table of Contents

About the author

Ashnie Muthusamy is an Author, Speaker, Coach, and currently Group Talent Manager at Sun International.

Ashnie's background is in Psychology. She is a Registered Counsellor with the Health Professions Council of South Africa in the field of Psychometry. She has a Masters Diploma in HR Management and a Master's Degree in Leadership. She is a qualified Masters Practitioner in Neurolinguistics Programming and an accredited change management practitioner. She is also a Masters Reiki practitioner and the author of the book *"Succession Management: Definite Do's and Detrimental Dont's"*

For the last 20 years she has worked in the field of Talent Management in various large scale organisations. She is a frequent speaker globally in the various fields of Human Resources and is passionate about optimising human potential and making a positive difference in the world. She is also a member of the Lightworkers Woman's Organisation, which focuses on assisting disadvantaged and vulnerable women and children in need.

Foreword by Lee-Ann Samuel – Group HR Executive, Implats

"There is an Indian proverb that says everyone is a house with four rooms, a physical, a mental, an emotional and a spiritual. Most of us tend to live in one room most of the time, but unless we go into every room every day, even if only to keep it aired, we are not a complete person" – *Rumer Godden*.

This proverb comes to mind after having read this beautiful book. We are integrated beings and a lack in one area affects every other area. This book is a toolkit that will help guide you through all the dimensions of your life, enabling you to become a whole being. The simple techniques and reflection exercises are very useful and actually quite fun to work through.

There are times when we may not feel at our best and brightest. At those times we can take a look at what we might do to let our inner light shine to the fullest. Because we are physical, mental, emotional and spiritual beings, we need to determine where our spiritual light is being filtered or blocked. We can work from the outside inward, knowing that we are the only ones with the power to dim our lights, and as we clear away the layers we can get out of our own way to feel the warmth of our own light shining again.

As vehicles for our mind and spirit, our bodies require proper maintenance. Caring for ourselves is like polishing – helping to clear away the accumulation of physical debris that keeps us from operating at our fullest capacity. A simple shift in our thoughts can positively affect our mental state, moving from complaints to gratitude and applying the powerful light of love to any shadowy thoughts. A change of scenery can allow us to see the world in new ways too.

Once we are free of our restrictions, we can become still and connect to the power at the centre of our being. It is always there for us, but when we forget to connect, or siphon our power in too many directions, we cannot make the most of our energy. Starting from the inside out may direct us to take the right steps for our journeys back to the light, but sometimes it can be difficult to find the stillness if our bodies and minds are in the way. As we practice steps to keep our energy flowing freely and without obstruction, we shine our light brightly, illuminating our own paths and making the world around us glow as well. This book offers the reader practical steps to keep our energy flowing freely.

The most powerful journey a man can go on is the one that leads him back to himself. This is what this book is all about – guiding one gently through the application of tools and understanding and appreciating Ashnie's own journey, experiences, extensive research and thinking, to allow you to reflect on keeping your eternal flame burning bright. This is one of the most amazing books I have read... profound in so many ways and yet so simple to understand and relate to. I will keep this book by the side of my bed as I continue to journey through life, knowing that whatever life throws my way, the important thing is how I respond. I have control over my life and I own my power, and when I act with the intention to serve my highest good I am also serving the highest good of others, for we are all connected. The book is a powerful reminder that we are all a culmination of our experiences, thoughts and actions, and that there is no right or wrong, good or bad, and that every choice we make will ultimately determine our destinies. Through free will you can change the course of your life if you remain true to yourself and open to change. You will absolutely love the poems. Enjoy your journey and the book!

Introduction

As a young child I had all the things that were necessary for me to flourish; I never found anything lacking in my life. I was too busy enjoying my childhood to worry about what was insufficient. I grew up in a family where I felt loved, nurtured and taken care of. I may not have had the luxuries, but I had the things that mattered most: a family who loved me, healthy food to eat, a safe place to sleep, friends to connect with and role models I could look up to. I was in a state of true contentment, with no worries. I was not aware of apartheid or the differences between people and cultures; it was just the way things were. I consider myself blessed to have had a healthy and functional childhood. I look at the past now through a different lens, and I am shocked that I held onto my ignorance for as long as I did. Who I am now is defined by the schools that I attended, the learners I made friends with and the teachers who helped shape my mind. I am grateful for the sum total of my experiences, as each encounter shaped my identity. All I remember is that my life was blessed with love, contentment and joy, and no regrets.

The influences in my life

This book is not an autobiography, but I could not in good conscience share the lessons and wisdom I have learnt without paying homage to the people who shaped the values in me. With this book I honour my father and mother and their teachings, which have helped me embrace the totality of life with wonder and joy, and reflect in awe at the countless blessings I have received.

I am grateful for the unconditional love of my parents, who always held a light in front of me to help me navigate my future; for my little sister who taught me the difficult lesson of sharing, which has become a fundamental belief that I revere; for my big brother, who allowed me to spend my early childhood in his shadow as an eager assistant in his adventurous escapades — his entrepreneurial spirit always showed me to think outside the box; and for my little brother, whose amazing sense of humour and wit always kept me grounded. I have a large extended family and I had the gift of lots of aunts, uncles and cousins growing up, who taught me about the importance of social support and relationships. I had great role models in people who lived their lives with purpose, and yet there was always time for laughter and fun. These are the memories that I look back on fondly.

What is this book about?

A disproportionate amount of time and energy is usually spent focusing on one's career, to the detriment of all other life areas. During this time, people grapple to find something to hold onto, and their energy is often focused on their careers or the work aspect of their lives. To truly live a fulfilling life, it is important to become fully aware and work on all aspects of one's life. This book focuses on the holistic development of people, and draws on simple psychological principles and neurolinguistic programming techniques which can be used to overcome common obstacles in one's life to reach one's optimum potential.

Just as light refracts through a prism into a spectrum of different colours, this book is intended to be a ray of light; each person will focus on a different colour which will have a specific meaning for them. This book strings together different philosophies and ideas and attempts to offer a framework to fulfil one's highest potential — it may be just one idea that can help you look differently at your own life.

We are shaped by our history and influenced by all the experiences that have brought us to where we are at this moment in time. We are the product of our achievements as well as our failures, of our loves and our losses. We spend our time nursing our fears, our inadequacies and build a throne for our self-limitations that we worship until we become a mere shadow of our true powerful selves. **This book is about how ordinary people can take a stand and create extraordinary stories by transforming their perceived limitations. This book provides simple actions on how to improve your life.**

Who is this book for?

I hope this book appeals to all people to create extraordinary lives by changing their focus and making different decisions about their lives. I want to contribute to building a better country and change the perspectives of young people by helping them reframe their personal challenges and optimise the potential in their lives. This book is written in a simple style that can appeal to all people, from the student in school to the employee in the last stages of their career. I have included reflection exercises so that it has a practical application, and have referenced my own stories and used anecdotal examples to further explain my points. I hope this book provides valuable insights that inspire you.

I have been reading motivational books for the last 20 years of my life. With each book I extracted the essence of the message, and I applied these lessons to enhance my life. **The intention of this book is for you to look into the mirror and appreciate yourself — the good, the bad and the ugly — and know that all parts of you serve a purpose.**

I suggest you read through the book once, then slowly read it again and choose the exercises that resonate with what you are going through at this moment in your life. I hope that the lessons from my book imprint positively on your life and that you find yourself in a better place than when you started reading.

This book is not going to change the circumstances of your life, but it will give you some basic tools to help you cope with your present circumstances. This book is not the solution to all your challenges; neither is it a comprehensive guide to wellbeing. What it is, is merely **a guide that will trigger your self-awareness** that something is amiss and that you need to further work on that life area. If, after reading this book, **you have expanded your perspective** and **changed the way you look at things**, then I will have been successful in my intention. I invite you to share this book with others who may benefit from some of its lessons.

Using this book

This book follows the personal mastery framework on page 5. There are seven main sections, which focus on all the necessary steps to bring your life into balance and to optimise your potential.

Each section has four main chapters or themes. The chapters are placed in a timeline from past to future.

Section one focuses on understanding the influence of the past on the present circumstances of your life.

Sections two, three and four examine different ways to optimise the present conditions of your life.

Sections five, six and seven focus on the future and give you guidance to plan your life purposefully to achieve a fulfilled and significant life.

Each chapter starts with a quote, short poem or story that provides a general introduction to the topic covered. This is followed by specific information that will assist you in your personal journey discovery.

Throughout the text, you will find:

- Quick Tips;
- some suggestions on improving your life; and
- anecdotal stories and poems to illustrate certain messages and reinforce these ideas.

Structure of the book

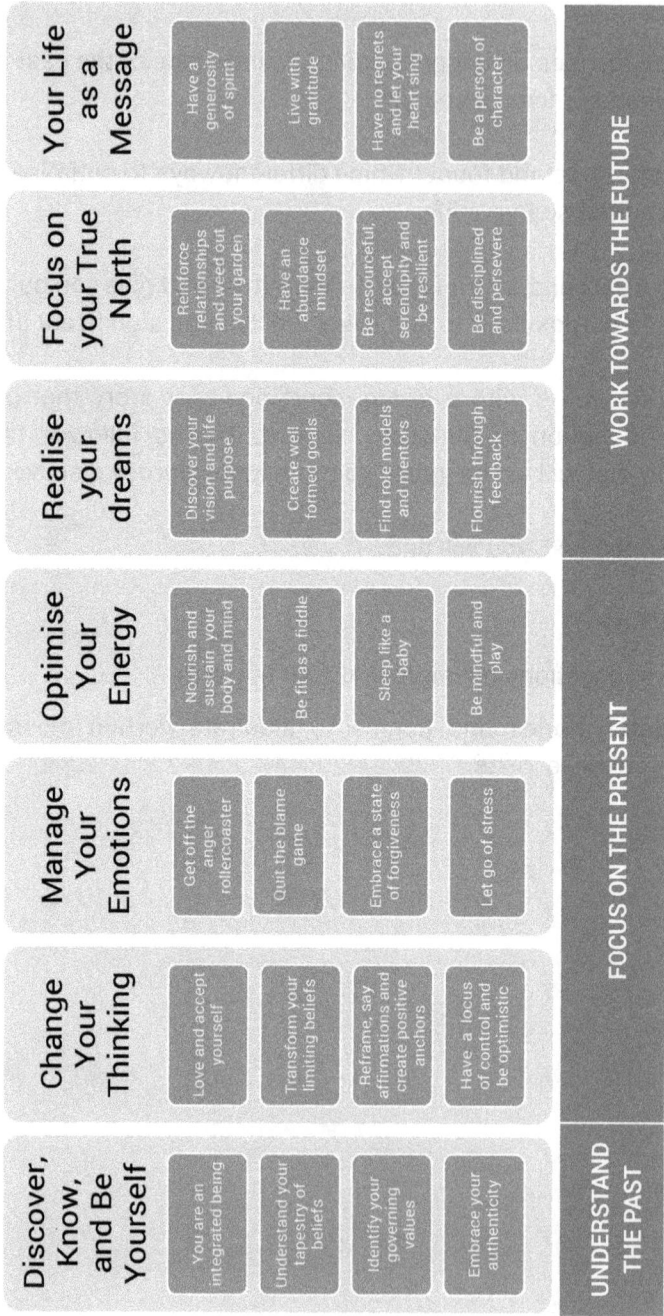

Discover, Know, and Be Yourself	Change Your Thinking	Manage Your Emotions	Optimise Your Energy	Realise your dreams	Focus on your True North	Your Life as a Message
You are an integrated being	Love and accept yourself	Get off the anger rollercoaster	Nourish and sustain your body and mind	Discover your vision and life purpose	Reinforce relationships and weed out your garden	Have a generosity of spirit
Understand your tapestry of beliefs	Transform your limiting beliefs	Quit the blame game	Be fit as a fiddle	Create well formed goals	Have an abundance mindset	Live with gratitude
Identify your governing values	Reframe, say affirmations and create positive anchors	Embrace a state of forgiveness	Sleep like a baby	Find role models and mentors	Be resourceful, accept serendipity and be resilient	Have no regrets and let your heart sing
Embrace your authenticity	Have a locus of control and be optimistic	Let go of stress	Be mindful and play	Flourish through feedback	Be disciplined and persevere	Be a person of character

UNDERSTAND THE PAST	FOCUS ON THE PRESENT	WORK TOWARDS THE FUTURE

Section 1

Discover, Know, and Be Yourself

- You are an integrated being
- Understand your tapestry of beliefs
- Identify your governing values
- Embrace your authenticity

The first section focuses on understanding that human beings are integrated beings and incidents in one area of life can have a ripple effect on other areas. Once we know this we can adequately prepare and deal with life's challenges holistically. We also need to understand what drives our behaviour so that we can be in greater control of our lives. By being yourself and focusing on discovering your authentic self, life is more fulfilling. You need to understand what is important to you in terms of your values. If you can live an authentic life aligned to your governing values, your life becomes more meaningful.

Chapter 1

You are an integrated being

"The whole is greater than the sum of its parts." (Aristotle[1])

Scenario 1

"Mummy save me." Sarah woke up with her clothes drenched in perspiration, her mouth dry and her heart beating rapidly. Another night with a variation of the same dream. She drank a glass of cold water and reassured herself that everything would be fine. She tiptoed into her daughter's room to check up on her. After watching her daughter for a few moments she returned to her room. She knelt down to pray that her appeal for funds got the response she hoped for. Sarah felt guilty since she, herself, had never been the most generous of people. Only an operation could save her daughter's life. With very little sleep she went to work the next day, but a day later her manager called her in and gave her a written warning. Sarah had made a huge mistake and paid a supplier an exorbitant amount of money. Sarah was scared of losing her job as she needed the medical aid for her daughter. She apologised and promised to be more careful. Sarah had been so focused on her daughter that she neglected eating. She had lost a significant amount of weight and barely had the energy to survive the day. Her finances were exhausted. **Sarah's wish was for her daughter's operation to be a success so that they could be a normal family again.**

Scenario 2

Michael still had to pinch himself to check if he was dreaming. It had been almost a year since the day he discovered that he had won R30 million in the lotto. He woke up every morning in a beautiful mansion, went down to breakfast and saw a room full of extended family. They had moved in when they found out about Michael's good fortune. Michael was happy but he had become arrogant with his new wealth. One year later and his winnings had halved, but he felt he still had so much more. He had neglected his real friends and found new friends at the country club that he had joined. He had put on 20kg from the expensive restaurants he frequented. His health had diminished, he had started drinking excessive amounts of alcohol, mainly expensive champagne, and had started smoking expensive cigars. Michael hardly slept and partied with his new friends early into the morning. He resigned the day he found out about his fortune so he did not have any work to do. He had seen wealthy Hollywood stars donate large amounts of money to charities so he started supporting an orphanage. **Michael's wish was that he was respected in his newfound status as a millionaire.**

Scenario 3

Chris loved his job. After many years he decided to take his wife on an overseas holiday. Even though his wife appealed to him for a longer holiday, he was reluctant because he was needed back at work. He saw great value in being a person of responsibility, so he kept his holiday to a week. One week after he returned to work, Chris was told the company was downsizing and his role was being made redundant. He was devastated as his work was the foundation of his life. This news was an emotional blow to his self-esteem. Chris avoided telling his family the bad news and for the next two weeks he continued his routine so his family would not find out that he was unemployed. He started avoiding family functions and stayed away from his friends; he was not able to face them. Chris lost weight and started drinking to deal with his depression. He started to spend evenings in the pub and usually returned home intoxicated. His wife separated from him as she could no longer tolerate his mood swings. One night he was so drunk that he drove to an unsafe neighborhood where he was beaten and robbed. **Chris' wish was to turn back the clock so he could make better life choices.**

Scenario 4

Rika was so happy and content. She had been married for six months and it was the best time of her life. She was enjoying every moment of her married life. She was so happy that she found herself singing most mornings going to work. She loved spending time with her friends and sharing the daily events of her life. Her friends started to call her "Roundika' because she had put on so much weight. She was dining out almost every night and had put on a few kilos due to the rich food she was eating. Rika constantly thought of her husband and waited to see him every evening. Rika loved her job, and was positive and engaged in what she was doing. She still had her wedding loan to pay off, but she was confident she would pay that off over time. **Rika's wish was for all her friends to get married and be as happy as she was.**

The above stories are anecdotal and each one illustrates the principle that we are integrated beings. When something happens to us in one life area it affects us in other life areas. We are multi-dimensional beings, which means that we are made up of many dimensions. There are different views on this but I prefer the following categories: your inner dimensions, such as your spiritual, mental, physical and emotional elements, and your outer dimensions, such as your social, career, financial and environmental elements.

I often hear people refer to work life balance – what they are doing in their mind is expanding the importance of their career life to 50% of their focus, and all other areas they categorise as "life" in the other 50%. There is nothing wrong with this view, but what I have experienced is that when most people feel stuck in their lives, they cannot seem to understand the reason for their dilemma. They do not know where to start looking for the cause. Just understanding that there are multiple dimensions in one's life beyond work and life gives you more options to reflect on.

When my daughter started playschool at the age of two, it was very easy for me to pack her daily snack in her two compartment lunchbox. I would include a variety of fruit and nuts. One day my husband bought her a new lunchbox with three compartments. Suddenly I found myself needing to fill the third compartment with a third snack. This sudden empty space brought in a new awareness that something was missing. An empty space was not acceptable to me; I needed to fill it with some food item. Similarly, by my expanding your awareness of the different areas of your life. I offer you a container with eight compartments.

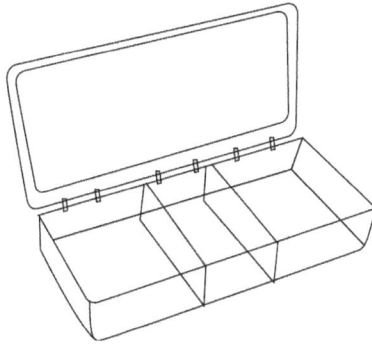

It is important that you are aware that you have these different life areas so that you can manage them all effectively. Allow me to explain each of these areas as I see them.

Emotional dimension

The emotional dimension includes your capacity to manage your thoughts, feelings and behaviours; the ability to be independent; and the ability to cope effectively with life's stressors. Emotional wellness is being self-aware about how to effectively manage your emotions with yourself in relation to the external world, as well as other people.

Mental dimension

The mental dimension refers to your thoughts and mental state, and is about expanding knowledge, learning from challenges and experiences, creating networks, and continually seeking mental stimulation.

Social dimension

The social dimension refers to your ability to interact with the people around you. It involves using good communication skills, having meaningful relationships, respecting yourself and others, and creating a support system that includes family members and friends.

Spiritual dimension

The spiritual dimension involves seeking meaning and purpose in your life. It is an active process of getting in touch with your inner self in order to integrate and find meaning in personal experiences and beliefs. Pierre Teilhard de Chardin said that, "We are spiritual beings having a human experience, and not humans seeking a spiritual experience".[2] Spiritual wellness allows peace and tolerance of those around us and is demonstrated by living each day in a way that is consistent with one's values and goals.

Physical dimension

The physical dimension refers to your physiological functioning, fitness and health. It includes participation in appropriate physical activities and exercise, nutrition, sleep, mindfulness, play and healthy eating habits, and the avoidance of harmful substances like tobacco, alcohol and drugs.

Environmental dimension

The environmental dimension of wellness involves accepting the impact we have on our world and doing something about it; it is about being part of creating and sustaining a healthy, safe and nurturing environment in which to live with others. Environmental wellness includes respecting the value of our physical and social surroundings.

Career dimension

The career dimension refers to our work life and the level of engagement, interaction and job satisfaction we gain from it. It considers how effective we are in structuring our career plan and goals, and engaging in continuous learning to achieve these career plans.

Financial dimension

The financial dimension is about having an understanding of your financial wealth and taking care of it in a way that allows you to meet your short- and long-term personal goals, regardless of your actual level of income. It is about maintaining balance and understanding the consequences of personal choice and responsibility regarding where and what you have the financial means to do.

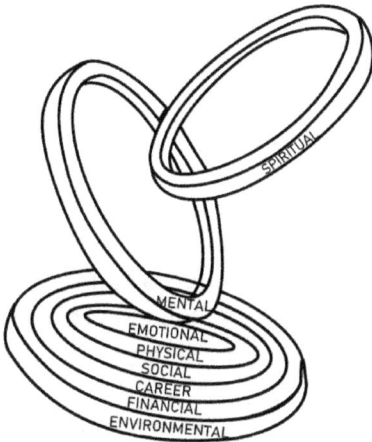

We experience life challenges in each of these life dimensions. Examples of social challenges are events such as divorce; career events such as being fired from work; environmental events such as minor violations of the law; spiritual events such as a crisis of faith; physical events such as personal injury or illness; emotional events such as coping with the death of a close family member; and financial events like a change in financial status. However, what is important to understand is that a challenge in one life dimension will affect the other life dimensions, as these are integrated. Imagine that each of these life dimensions cover one another like an onion. When I cut a slice of the onion, I see all the rings at the same time. Similarly, as we engage with life and experience a challenge in one area, all the other areas are affected simultaneously. It is therefore important to address the source of the problem rather than to let it start filtering through the other areas of your life.

Just imagine you have been working diligently to get ahead in your career and you are passed over the third time for a promotion. This happens in your career dimension. You are angry and depressed, which starts to affect your emotional dimension. You cannot sleep and you lose your appetite, which affects your physical dimension. You withdraw from your family and friends, which impacts your social dimension. You lose focus and cannot concentrate on anything, which impacts your mental dimension. You stop going to your regular hangouts, which impacts your environmental dimension. You do not have a bigger future income, which affects your financial dimension. You start questioning your bigger purpose in life, which affects your spiritual dimension. Similarly, if you read through the four scenarios presented in the beginning of this chapter, you will see that people demonstrated changes in other areas of their life after a significant event occurred.

You can take any life challenge and you will see that it affects other areas of your life. It is important to understand this so that you can better manage yourself when these challenges arise. Understand that this is normal and there is nothing wrong with you. At the same time it is important for you to understand that since life challenges are going to affect all these different areas, it is essential for you to make sure that each of these compartments are properly maintained. Remember that a chain is only as strong as its weakest link. You may think you are a successful person, but if there is one area of your life that is out of alignment then the balance in your life is affected. You never know when life will throw you a curve ball and when you will need to be prepared to handle a challenge. Start preparing for that eventuality by reinforcing the areas in each of your life dimensions.

Albert Einstein said that, "We cannot solve our problems with the same thinking we used when we created them"[3], so when you experience a challenge in one of your life dimensions, the solution may lie in some other life dimension. For example, you could lose your job which is in the career dimension, but may be surprised that your strong relationships with others will assist you in finding another job. This is why it is important to fortify all your life dimensions.

Please complete the Life Dimensions Survey Questionnaire in Annexure 1 to determine which area of your life you need to start giving attention to. Sometimes by just being aware that there are gaps in certain areas, your mind can start to think of ways to address them. Once you complete the questionnaire you will have a better sense of where you stand in each of the life dimensions. The different life dimensions are covered through the rest of the book and are closely integrated with each other, just as your life dimensions are in your daily life.

Reflection exercise		
What are your scores on the different life dimensions? Rate yourself out of 10.		
Mental	How would you rate your ability to continuously challenge yourself to learn new skills?	
Physical	How would you rate your physical stamina and fitness?	
Spiritual	How would you rate yourself on living your life aligned to your purpose and with meaning?	
Social	How would you rate the relationships you have with the people you love?	
Emotional	How would you rate your ability to have fun and live with joy?	
Career	How do you rate your level of fulfillment presently in your career?	
Environmental	How do you rate your commitment to causes in the external environment?	
Financial	How do you rate your financial preparation for the short- and long- term?	

In the life dimensions that you perform poorly in, try to understand what is stopping you from improving in those areas. For example, if physical fitness or being overweight is a challenge, you need to understand some of the negative beliefs that you have about losing weight that are limiting your progress in that area of your life. We will discuss beliefs in the next chapter, as it is the fundamental aspect of ourselves that we need to understand to master and change our behaviour. Now that you know what areas of your life you need to work on, let's explore the next step in the journey.

summary

- We are multi-dimensional beings, which means that we are made up of many dimensions. There are different views on this but I use the following categories: your inner dimensions (spiritual, mental, physical and emotional) and your outer dimensions (social, career, financial and environmental).

- Human beings are integrated beings and incidents in one area of life can have a ripple effect on other areas of life.

- Understand which life area is your weakest so that you can address it.

- It is important for you to understand that since life is going to affect all these different areas, it is essential for you to make sure that each area is properly maintained.

Chapter 2

Understand what drives behaviour

"The garden is a symbol for the mind. If you care for your mind, if you nurture it and if you cultivate it just like a fertile, rich garden, it will blossom far beyond your expectations. But if you let the weeds take root, lasting peace of mind and deep inner harmony will always elude you." (Robin Sharma[4])

Picture a beautiful apple tree growing in your mind that is just starting to bear delicious fruit. Wrapped around it is an aggressive weed that is wound so tightly that it is stealing its water and draining the energy and life force of the tree. The apple represents your contribution to the world. It is difficult for your apple tree to bear fruit when your energy is being sucked out by a weed. This aggressive weed comprises all your bad habits; separate strands build on one another until it becomes a rope that chokes out your essence. Every time you chop one branch of the weed, it starts to weaken and slowly releases its hold over you. You start to flourish and bear more fruit. You need to learn to remove the weeds which are your negative thoughts.

Human beings can constantly grow and expand their self-awareness; it is never too late. Some people may say you cannot teach old dogs new tricks, implying that it is difficult for old people to change their habits, but fortunately this statement no longer holds true. Recent research on the neuroplasticity of the brain demonstrates that it can actually adapt, and mental conditions which were thought of being unchangeable before, are now treatable.

How do we create our behaviours?

"Your life story is not a series of events. It's a series of your reactions to events." (Alan Knott Craig[5])

Between an activating event or stimulus and your choice of behaviour, your mindset acts as a processing filter or modifier. Your mindset (your set of beliefs, values, educational and authoritative influences, attitudes, assumptions and experiences) is made up of fixed mental patterns that act as a filter through which the world is interpreted.[6] Stephen Covey best explained this when he said, "We see the world, not as it is, but as we are — or, as we are conditioned to see it".[7] This idea is further reinforced by Marcus Aurelius, who once said: **"Our life is what our thoughts make it."**[8] This simply means that when we interact with the world, our mindset determines how we see and respond to the world and determines our relationships with other people. There is a great neurolinguistics programming principle which states that the map is not the territory. As people we have different mental maps of the same world based on our perceptions. We respond to how things work in the world based on our perceptions and not the world itself. If you ever asked different witnesses to relate what they saw at an accident, they would give you different accounts based on their perceptions of what they saw. It is therefore important to understand that as individuals we carry different maps of reality in our heads. These maps are influenced by our mindsets, which we have developed over time. When we talk to each other, we communicate using our own maps of the world and that is why conflict arises, i.e. people view the same issue from different perspectives based on their mindsets.

There is usually an activating event, stimulus or trigger that creates behaviour. For example you are driving to work and suddenly a taxi driver tries to cuts in front of you. You interpret the action through your belief system. If your belief about taxi drivers is that they are rude and obnoxious and should not be allowed to drive on the road, then when this happens you get highly frustrated and extremely angry. You deliberately accelerate so that there is no space in front of your car. The result is that you go too close to the vehicle in front of you and you crash into it. This accident starts another cycle. You blame the taxi driver and begin to get more agitated. You start to act irrationally and fail to take accountability for your part in causing the incident. This results in the other driver being rude to you.

Now imagine the same scenario, but this time your beliefs are different. Imagine that your belief is that taxi drivers are a critical part of providing a service to society. You know that when the taxi cuts in front of you, he is transporting 20 passengers who cannot afford to be late and lose their jobs. You think about the families that they support and suddenly you allow the taxi driver to cut in front of you as you are now feeling more empathetic. It is exactly the same scenario, the only difference is how you have internalised and interpreted the same event, resulting in different behaviour. Have you ever driven when there was a police car or ambulance behind you? You immediately move out of the way as you understand there is an emergency. Just by understanding their intention, your behaviour changes.

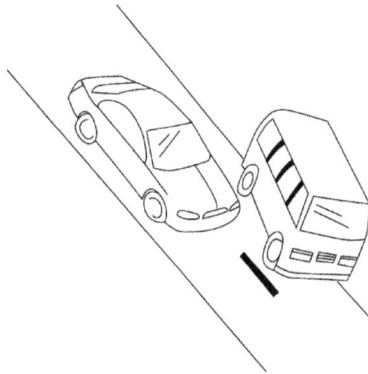

Every single day we respond to events in our lives. Most of the time we think that we are powerless, but actually **we always have the power to choose our response**. We need to always challenge and change our beliefs if we want to change our emotions and our behaviour. We always have the choice of how we react. If you stop reading this book after this chapter, I would be happy because you have learnt one of the most important tools to change the quality of your life. Just as financial people are generally better at accumulating wealth because they have learnt the principle of compound interest, this model of how you interpret the world is of equivalent importance in psychology.

How we interpret and react to the world

Activating event/ stimulus

Impact

MINDSET
TEMPERAMENT
BELIEFS
VALUES
PERSONAL NEEDS
ASSUMPTIONS
EXPERIENCE
EDUCATION

Interpret the stimulus and create meaning

Behave

Feel/ Experience emotion

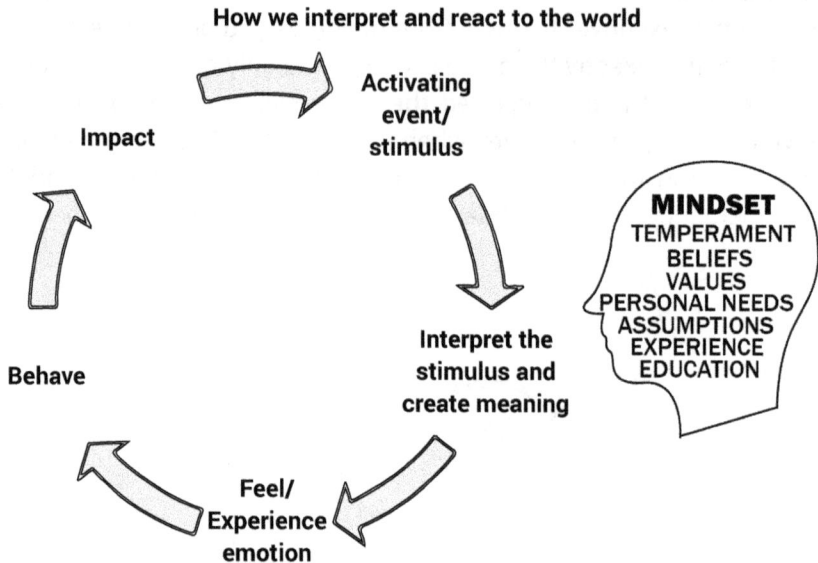

"Your living is determined not so much by what life brings to you as by the attitude you bring to life; not so much by what happens to you as by the way your mind looks at what happens." (Khalil Gibran[9])

Brian Tracy argued that you can tell what a person thinks most of the time by looking at the fruits of his or her life. He added that happy and prosperous people with good friends and family are people who think about their lives in positive terms, so his message is simple – use your thoughts to create the life that you want.[10]

Your outer world tends to be a mirror image of your inner world; what is going on outside of you is a reflection of what is going on inside of you. Our reality is a result of our inner most dominant thought. If you are presently unhealthy, you have certain thoughts about the food that you should eat. You could be thinking that in a stressful time junk food is a good reward to feel better about yourself, yet over time your thoughts about junk food could create serious health conditions within you.

If your life is filled with sadness or loneliness, it is because you may be feeling negative thoughts such as people are out to get you. These negative thoughts programme your external reality so you stay away from people, which in turn damages your relationships and leaves you without people and friends you can trust. This makes you more lonely and depressed, i.e. it becomes a self-fulfilling prophecy.

If you are feeling stuck in your career, it could be because you believe that you are not clever enough to volunteer for projects or extra work. You subsequently do not get exposure to new ideas, knowledge and skills, and do not get any recognition. All because your thoughts sabotaged your success.

It is within your control to choose your thoughts wisely, as they determine the direction your life will take. Using your responses from the Life Dimension Questionnaire that you completed, look at the dimensions where you scored the lowest. Ask yourself what your specific thoughts or beliefs are about these life areas. Next, try and understand where these thoughts come from. For example, did you hear other people complain about taxi drivers or did you watch your father's or mother's behaviour when a taxi tried to overtake their car?

Tapestry of beliefs

"You are the books you read, the movies you watch, the music you listen to, the people you spend time with, the conversations you engage in. Choose wisely what you choose to feed your mind." (The Minds Journal[11])

What truly makes every one of us authentic is that we each have a unique set of beliefs. There are certain principles such as the earth rotates around the sun, so if I believe that the earth rotates around the sun, my belief is based on that principle. We also have other beliefs that have formed throughout our lives that are not based on principles but on our feelings, experiences or advice received from the authority figures in our lives. All of us have our own sets of beliefs that shape our lives. These sets of beliefs affect what we think about ourselves, others and the world at large. They also greatly influence our emotions and actions, and consequently affect our success and happiness. This is the reason we need to understand the way our beliefs are formed and how they influence the choices we make.

Beliefs are generally formed in two ways: by our experiences, inferences and deductions; or by accepting what others tell us to be true. Most of our core beliefs are formed when we are children. When we are born, we enter this world with a clean slate and without preconceived beliefs. We start to make sense of the world by observation and through modelling our parents. Our parents and environment play a big part in shaping our beliefs from a very young age. Our teachers, our lessons, our school environment and our friends also play an important role. For example, when we are little we listen to the wisdom of our parents, such as "Don't talk to strangers". We start to create an idea that strangers are a threat to us. Years later we are sitting in a conference in a room full of strangers and we cannot understand why it is so difficult to make small talk. Could it be the belief that we should not talk to strangers is unconsciously influencing our behaviour?

A belief is simply a feeling of certainty about something or an issue. For example, if you believe that you are beautiful, all you are really saying is, "I feel certain that I am beautiful". The basic building blocks of beliefs are ideas. Another way of looking at beliefs is to think of them as a table top. As you build references and experiences, you add legs to your table top. When your idea feels definite, it becomes a belief which is a full table. So let me explain further on the "beautiful" example. How did you form the belief that you are beautiful? It could be that as a child you were complimented on your looks. Perhaps in school you were the most popular girl and all the boys liked you and close friends commented on your beauty. You won beauty contests, which provided further evidence and reinforced the belief that you are, in fact, beautiful. This may seem like a silly example, but this is how easily we form beliefs in our lives. We first get an idea about something, and then when we get further evidence that supports the idea, we start to accept it until we create a belief about it. It is important that you understand how easily beliefs are formed, because these beliefs are the programmes that run our main operating system – our mind. As beliefs form from the time we are babies, these single strands form an integrated tapestry as we grow up.

All our experiences help to either reinforce or dispel certain beliefs. As we journey through life we are continually adding to this tapestry, therefore each tapestry is totally unique based on all the programming we receive from various sources.

Whatever you believe with absolute certainty and conviction becomes your reality. Who is running your program and who is pushing your buttons? Have you ever watched old spy movies where people have been brainwashed? They suddenly hear a secret phrase and they start to do something uncharacteristic. We may not realise it, but we are all subjects of programming. From the time we were born we received feedback from our parents and the external environment, which we have formed beliefs around. These beliefs have become so integrated with our being over time that we respond to external stimuli based on our filters, which comprise our mindset. Have you ever had the experience when you are busy doing something and you hear a voice in your head? It could be the voice of your boss, your husband or your wife. Sometimes that voice is filled with encouragement and other times it is filled with doubt.

The surrounding environment programmes children as they grow up. This programming is called conditioning, which forms our beliefs. Due to the emotional attachment, dependency, and love they have for their parents, the messages (both positive and negative) that a child receives in their early years have a much higher probability of being processed and accepted as beliefs, without question or reservation.

My four-year-old daughter believes in Santa Claus because she saw a man dressed in a red Santa outfit who told her that if she was good he would bring her presents on Christmas morning. She discussed this with her young cousin, who confirmed that Santa had brought him presents the previous year, and assured her that he would definitely come on Christmas and she needed to put out milk and cookies for him. She then watched a movie where she saw Santa Claus driving a sleigh with reindeers and leaving presents under a Christmas tree. To reinforce this belief and preserve her excitement, I was happy to provide further evidence. On Christmas Eve I placed milk and cookies on the kitchen counter, and being an overachiever, a carrot for the reindeer. We wrapped her gifts and placed them under the Christmas tree. On Christmas morning, she rushed into the lounge and was very excited to see that the milk was half drunk and the biscuit and carrot were eaten. There were also presents placed under the Christmas tree, so she was convinced that Santa Claus does exist. I am fully aware that this belief will last for about two more years until she learns from friends that Santa Claus does not exist and that her parents have been buying the Christmas gifts all along.

Another example of programming beliefs is as follows. You do poorly on a maths test in Grade 8 and the teacher tells you that you are not good at maths. The teacher gives feedback to your parents that you are weak at maths and that you should not pursue it as a subject. You go to the shop and do not pay attention and the shopkeeper does not give you the correct change, so your father tells him that you are bad at maths. The teacher has planted the seed of the belief, which becomes reinforced by feedback from the external environment. You begin to believe the teacher that maths is not your strong point, so you stop trying to improve the skill and accept the evidence that you will never improve. You start becoming anxious when there are maths lessons and maths homework. Decades later you get promoted into an executive job which manages a million Rand client portfolio. You start to feel stressed and incompetent because you know that you are not good with numbers. This has become a self-limiting belief in your mind, which places constraints on your potential.

Your beliefs shape your attitudes about life and often determine how you think about things, how you process the events of the world around you, and how you make decisions. We are continually looking for evidence to validate our beliefs. Sometimes a conversation, reading a book, watching a documentary, engaging with people, or listening to an expert can reinforce an idea that will form a belief. The beliefs we have can either serve us or they can limit our potential.

Here is poem that is inspired by the true story of a teenager whose relationship with his older brother had deteriorated, and he had been acting out, much to the disappointment of both his parents. They could not understand what was driving his behaviour.

> *My brother is so perfect,*
> *Why should I even try?*
> *Everyone thinks he is so awesome,*
> *Oh what an awesome guy.*
> *My parents try to shower me with love,*
> *But deep inside I know I am just not enough.*
> *I walked in his shadow all these years,*
> *Silently watching all the applause and cheers.*
> *My mother lovingly dusts my brother's trophies on the shelf,*
> *"There is no place on that pedestal for me, I say to myself."*
> *They say, "Stop acting out and just come along,"*
> *I feel the sadness in me whispering "you will never belong".*
> *If they truly loved me, they wouldn't have left me at the hospital alone,*
> *They probably don't miss me, they have my brother at home.*
> *I am just a sickly child, how can I compete,*
> *When both my parents worship at my brother's feet.*
> *My brother is so awesome, Oh such an awesome guy,*
> *My parents say I'm special too, what an absolute awesome lie.*

One of my friends, Jane, is an amazing mother who has always encouraged and supported her kids to achieve their very best. Her eldest son is quite talented, both academically and in different sports. He is always bringing home awards and is generally recognised for his achievements. Recently he lost some of his drive and she was worried about his lack of interest in school and sports. Jane sat down and thought about her influence on her son and thought that maybe she was driving him too intensely. When Jane reflected, she realised that in fact it was her own personal need and belief to be successful and gain recognition. When she asked her son whether he was motivated to achieve and win trophies, he responded that he was only doing it to make her happy; it was not something he wanted to strive for. So Jane asked herself where the need for achievement and recognition stemmed from. This resulted in great insight for her; she realised that growing up she had a very successful brother who excelled at everything he tried. Jane felt inadequate and wanted to share some of the attention that her brother was receiving, so she strived for perfection and recognition.

Years later this childhood belief was influencing the way she reared her children. Jane used this insight to change her parental approach.

Women have traditionally been brought up in environments that place cultural limitations on them, creating self-limiting beliefs and defining them in relation to men rather than in their own rights. Many people refer to the corporate glass ceiling that restricts the progression of women to senior roles and positions in organisations. What most people do not realise is that there is a second glass ceiling that is different for each woman, as it is crafted by an intricate web of years of conditioning. Conditioning is what experiences girls have been exposed to growing up, and the beliefs that they have developed about their worth and potential to be fully successful human beings. Most women are not aware that the second ceiling exists, they are so busy throwing stones at the corporate glass ceiling. The second glass ceiling has become part of who they are — almost like a second skin. You cannot change your behaviour and dispel your beliefs if you are not aware of what is running your operating system.

Let me offer anecdotal examples of the way what I am describing plays out in the workplace:

- Sally lived through her parents' messy divorce, which destroyed her sense of self-worth and left her desperate for external validation. She does not question the status quo and is unable to make unpopular leadership decisions; she is a people pleaser.

- Milly was brought up in a traditional patriarchal family, where respect to elders was ingrained. She has learnt not to question authority and defers all decisions to the men in her department.

- Susan was emotionally traumatised as a child, having been brought up by dysfunctional parents who often blamed her for their problems. She has internalised this and has begun to blame herself for all the challenges she faces in her life. She becomes the sacrificial lamb in the office whenever things go wrong.

I have attended and spoken at many conferences for women, and what I have found is that sometimes it is not a sufficient intervention to reverse decades of cultural and societal conditioning. The women chosen to speak at or attend these conferences are amazing pioneers and successful icons in their own right. Women leave feeling positively charged by the testimonies they hear of tenacity and dedication. However, when they leave they turn to each other and say, "There is no way I can walk in her footsteps, my reality is different". At this point the evidence of the second glass ceiling becomes apparent.

It is difficult to liberate women from shackles formed by years of conditioning; each shackle is individually designed. These shackles are formed in the most innocent of ways — sometimes by parents who unknowingly subscribe to the traditional roles society dictates for women. I am guilty of this offence. I started to crochet the shackles for my daughter when the doctor announced, "It's a girl!" As I dress my daughter in another pink dress from meaning well-wishers, I cringe at this tangled web I am weaving. "Mummy I want to watch a princess movie." So harmless at first, but the seeds are already being planted that will shape my daughter's identity. As I hold my head in my hands, I wonder what I am doing. She is too small to make decisions for herself. As her trusted parent and guardian, I am contributing to and writing her narrative. I gently suggest to her the movie *Shrek*, as I know that Princess Fiona is not the typical mould of a damsel in distress waiting to be rescued. I am very aware of the beliefs I am embedding in her mind. I want to bring my daughter up as a strong-willed, confident and independent woman, who, when faced with opportunities, can run towards them. I want her to express her opinions and views with the same exuberance that she sings her nursery rhymes, without fear of condemnation.

The following is a personal example of how a limiting belief I formed in early childhood had to be adapted because it no longer served me. Last year I started learning self defence. I was a terrible student. I lacked hand eye coordination, I was out of shape, and my response time was dismal. The only cardio exercise I had done over the previous four years was jumping... jumping to conclusions.

I was so bad that I was an endless source of entertainment to Fabian, my instructor. I tell you this because as child I used to be asthmatic and stayed away from any form of physical exercise. When I was in primary school I was given the opportunity to learn karate, but instead I chose Indian classical dancing because I was terrified of being hit. Growing up I detested all forms of violence and totally supported Gandhi's philosophy of Satyagraha (passive resistance). Fast forward to 2008, and I was leaving work one evening traveling through the central business district in Johannesburg. Three men crossed the road, smashed my car window and proceeded to try and pull me out of the car by my hair. They tried to switch off the car and take the keys, but I managed to drive away. That 30 second encounter seemed to last for an hour. The experience created a fear and a belief that driving at night as a solitary woman is highly risky. This fear continued to fester until I avoided driving late at night; I had formed a belief that in a dangerous situation, I was powerless. Last year was a terrible year, with growing numbers of cases being reported of violence against women, so I decided that I needed to work on my fears and beliefs of helplessness. My motivating factor was that I needed to be able to protect my daughter in the case of a dangerous situation. I have no illusions of ever being a mixed martial arts expert, but that is not my aim. In a dangerous situation my aim is to be able to defend myself sufficiently so that I can escape.

I was overweight, out of shape and convinced I was beyond hope. Within the first five minutes of meeting my instructor, he said to me: "Drop down and do 10 push-ups, 10 press-ups and 10 squats". I looked at him to see if he was joking. From the expression on his face I could see he was not. As I struggled to go through the routine, complaining with every move, he stood over and watched with a stern expression on his face. I will never forget his next words, which were all the encouragement I needed to get into shape: "In a dangerous situation, the attacker is not going to wait for you to get into shape." What a wise instructor and brilliant self defence coach. I started weekly self defence classes and last year successfully completed my Level 1 grading. Just by changing my intention and my need to take back my power, I psychologically felt more in control.

Your choices and decisions over the years have determined the condition of your life at this moment. By changing your beliefs you can make different choices, which will determine a new direction for your life. Here is a popular story to illustrate the point about how assigning a different meaning to the same event can create different beliefs and realities.

Twin boys were brought up by an alcoholic father; one became an alcoholic and when asked what happened, he said he grew up watching his alcoholic father. The other son never touched a drop of alcohol his whole life, and when asked what happened, he said he grew up watching his alcoholic father. Both boys grew up in the same house and were exposed to the same influences, yet they turned out different because they internalised the experience differently. They assigned a different meaning to their experience and thus created different beliefs.

A list of my beliefs

The following are some of the core beliefs that I hold sacred. I share these beliefs with you so that when you read my book, you will understand how my beliefs shaped the content. This book is a reflection of my mental models of the world as I engage with it, and the lessons I have learnt.

- I believe that we are spiritual beings and that our physical existence is an opportunity to experience life and learn lessons that will expand ourselves and help us reveal our humanity.

- I believe that all lessons — both achievements and perceived failures — teach us and bring us closer to understanding ourselves and each other.

- I believe that each day we have an opportunity to positively impact someone's life and rekindle the fire within them through kind words or gestures.

- I believe that when we can love, respect and forgive ourselves unconditionally, it allows us to show the same courtesy to others.

- I believe in understanding my own intent and motives in life as a prerequisite before I try to understand others.

- I believe that there is always goodness in the world and that I have a responsibility to show kindness to myself and others.

- I believe that each person has an infinite capacity to grow and learn.
- I believe that we should not pass judgment on the behaviours of others, but rather try to understand the intent behind those behaviours.
- I believe that each person has a responsibility to keep their own inner light burning.
- I believe that simple words and actions of acknowledgement, appreciation and love are the greatest foundation I can lay.
- I totally subscribe to Einstein's view that one cannot solve a problem with the same level of thinking that created the problem in the first place.
- I believe that the choices I make determine and create the landscape of my life.
- I believe that one's perception of something is not the same as the actual situation.
- I believe that when you interact with people they leave imprints in your mind. Sometimes it is positive and improves the quality of your life, and sometimes it is destructive.
- I believe that just by changing my attitude I can change how I view a situation.
- I believe that respect for one's self is often a prerequisite to respecting others.
- I believe in the Law of Karma, which in essence means that I reap what I sow.
- I believe in being authentic, in line with Oscar Wilde's view: "Be yourself, everyone else is taken."

Reflection exercise
List your own personal beliefs
1.
2.
3.
4.
5.
6.
7.
8.
9.
10.

- Think about how you formed these beliefs.
- When did you first form these beliefs?
- What evidence do you have to support these beliefs?
- Is this belief enhancing the quality of your life or limiting it?

Reflection exercise
Think of three recent incidents in your life where you could have changed your behaviour by changing the beliefs you had about the incident.

summary

- Your mindset (your set of beliefs, values, educational and authoritative influences, attitudes, assumptions and experiences) is made up of fixed mental patterns that act as a filter through which the world is interpreted.[12]

- When we interact with the world, our mindset determines how we see and respond to the world, and defines our relationships with other people.

- Your outer world tends to be a mirror image of your inner world. What is going on outside of you is a reflection of what is going on inside of you.

- From the time we are born we receive feedback from our parents and the external environment, which we form beliefs around. These beliefs become so integrated with our being over time, that when we respond to external stimuli, we respond based on our filters.

- All of us have our own sets of beliefs that shape our lives. These sets of beliefs affect what we think about ourselves, others and the world at large. They also greatly influence our emotions and actions.

- We first get an idea about something and then when we get further evidence that supports the idea, we start to accept it until we create a belief about it.

- It is important that you understand how easily beliefs are formed, because these beliefs are the programmes that run our main operating system — our mind.

- Your beliefs shape your attitudes about life. They often determine how you think about things, how you process the events of the world around you, and the decisions you make. We are continually looking for evidence to validate our beliefs.

Chapter 3

Understanding your governing values

Father heard the children scream and shout,
So he scolded them and locked them out,
Saying as he pushed out the third,
"Children should be seen, not heard!"

Mother heard the children cry,
So she rushed out to find out why,
Kissing each one goodnight on their heads,
Don't mind your father, just go to bed...

The above poem illustrates how two parents have different approaches to parenting; their choices are driven by their values and beliefs. Have you ever asked yourself what the real influences of your decisions are? Why do you prefer one situation over another? The answer lies at the core of your character, of what defines you as a person, and that is your personal value system. Understanding your values and what you deem to be important is key to the decisions and choices that you make in your life. They provide clarity and build your self-awareness. If you can identify your values, difficult decisions are easier to make. Knowing your negative values, i.e. those you try to keep away from, is also very helpful. For example, if you need to change your job and you know that job flexibility is a high value, you can choose to work in organisations that can provide this level of flexibility. Mahatma Gandhi had two absolute values, which were truth and non-violence. Those values guided how he lived his life and made his choices and decisions.

Values are intimately related to our needs: Whatever we need — whatever is important to us or what is missing from our lives — is what we value. As our life conditions change, and as we mature and grow in our psychological development, our value priorities change. When we use our values to make decisions we focus on what is important to us — what we need to feel a sense of well-being. When you live by your values, you feel better about yourself and are more focused on doing the things that are important to you.

29

However, there are times when we make decisions in our life that are not aligned to our highest values and then we feel guilty. For example, if family is your highest value and then you accept a wonderful job opportunity that forces you to travel and be away from your family, after a while you will start to feel resentful towards your job.

Values matter because you are likely to feel better if you are living according to them, and worse if you do not. This applies both to day-to-day and bigger life decisions. It is therefore important to understand your values and the reasons these values are important to you. It is also important to prioritise your values, since prioritising can help you get even closer to defining what is important to you. Ideally, of course, you cannot live according to all the values on your list; your time and energy are limited. Prioritising helps you to ensure that you are spending them on the most important things that will have the biggest payoff in your life. What is a high value for one person may be low on the value list for someone else. For example, I place a high value on respect and when I am treated disrespectfully or I see others being treated disrespectfully, I become upset and I usually respond.

Dr Demartini has a wonderful tool called the Value Determination Process, which helps to identify your highest values. This simple, free questionnaire is available online and will assist you to determine your highest values. According to Dr. Demartini, "You value what you perceive as most missing". He added that one's values "arise from, and are therefore determined by, your conscious or unconscious voids (what you perceive as most missing). What you perceive as most missing (void) in your life therefore becomes what you perceive as your most important (value)".[13]

Your biggest void becomes your highest value. Have you heard of the success stories of struggling actors who were financially destitute, but become famous and financially prosperous? By growing up and not having sufficient money, money becomes the highest value. When I finished university I moved from Durban to Johannesburg to start my first job. Over the first few years, I could not afford to travel home very often and see my family as regularly as I would have liked. Those years were very lonely and depressing for me and I began to appreciate the value of family. As a result one of my top values presently is my family. Think about things you presently value and ask yourself why you value that particular characteristic. Another example of a void driving values is of a friend who grew up in a family without a car; all of their travel was done using public transport. She hardly travelled anywhere growing up and one of her highest values presently is to travel the world. Your values are not right or wrong, but they are things that are most important in your life.

Are you living according to your values in your life as a whole? Does your career choice reflect your values? How about your activities outside of work? Are you spending your time on things that matter to you? Sometimes we make decisions in our life that take us away from things that are important to us, so when we are feeling dissatisfied with our lives, we need to re-examine our values and find out which areas of our lives are out of alignment. I know of an executive who spent his life dedicated to his career in order to provide for his family. Sadly his daughter developed a life threatening illness and he suddenly realised that his choices were not aligned to his highest values.

Sometimes we fall into the trap of judging other people's actions through the filters of our own values. If family is your highest value, you are never going to understand how a businessman who travels extensively can spend time away from his family. If career success is important to you, you will not understand why someone would spend 10 years in the same job and has not climbed the corporate ladder. It is therefore essential to understand not only your values, but also the values of the significant people in your life. It is especially important if you are in a relationship or a marriage, as most conflicts arise due to differing values. One person may value career progression and success, while the other values family. Subsequently, a conflict occurs when there is a commitment such as a birthday party that clashes with an important business meeting.

Have you ever asked someone to do a favour for you and their response was they do not have time for it? What they are really saying is that it is not high on their list of priorities or values.

Success can sometimes be a lonely road to travel; you will need to make difficult decisions and sacrifices in the short-term to reap long-term rewards. It may mean standing out from the crowd and choosing a solitary, less travelled path. To be truly unique and create unique opportunities in your life, you may have to do things differently. People will not understand your choices because their values are very different from yours. You will always move according to the beat of your own drum. For example, my mother is over 70 years of age. She is still very active but is getting older. Her friends and family advise her to slow down and retire from all her activities, but these bring her pleasure. She loves what she does and finds great passion in her work. The view from society is that once you are over 60 you need to retire and take it easy. My mother has always been an entrepreneur and has lived each day of her life with passion and commitment. I am so proud that she maintains her zest for life and makes her own rules for how she lives her life.

When you are conflicted, make a decision based on your highest values. You need to know the governing values that you could not live without. For example, for vegetarians it may mean not eating meat, while for others it may mean not borrowing money. In the book, *Remains of the Day*, one of the main characters, James Stevens, is a butler. On the evening of a critical meeting he has to make a choice to render a service to his employer or spend time upstairs with his father who is on his death bed. He makes the choice to serve his employer as he reasons that his father, who was also a butler, instilled in him the value of service above all else. When we experience stress in our lives, we can cope more effectively when we focus on those values that are of the greatest importance to us.

Here is another example of conflicting values. In 2015, I had just had my beautiful baby girl and I was ecstatic. She was three months old and whilst my heart was overflowing, my mind was feeling rusty. With a little baby, I had insufficient time for myself, let alone time to do any reading or any other mentally stimulating activities. I saw a notice for a week-long Dr Demartini course, which only ran every two years in South Africa. I had previously committed to myself to attend this course when it next ran in South Africa, but could I leave my three month old baby to go on a course? Before I had my daughter, self-empowerment and development were two of my highest values, but to love and care for my baby suddenly became another a top value. What was the solution to this dilemma? My husband was very supportive and helped me see that my baby would be fine with

the nanny. He also reminded me of one of Dr Demartini's other principles, i.e. that there is balance in the universe and that nothing is missing. Even though I was not going to be there for my daughter during the day, she was still going to be taken care of competently by the nanny and my husband. So I attended the course and my daughter was perfectly fine.

Years ago, early in my career, I was facilitating a workshop and at the end I handed out feedback forms to all the participants. Feedback was usually anonymous but one of the delegates who was an older gentleman chose to write his name on the form and he gave me a poor rating on the course. He stated that I was guilty of blasphemy. I was perturbed and I asked his colleague for more information. She said that during the workshop I had exclaimed "Oh, my God" when I was surprised, and that I was using the Lord's name in vain. I was shocked; I had erroneously broken one of the 10 commandments. I apologised to the participant and made him aware that that was not my intention. What was just a figure of speech for me was a serious offence in the mind of the other person. This incident illustrated how important it is to be aware of other people's values so that you do not unintentionally trespass on them.

According to Brian Tracy, happy and prosperous people are those who have discovered the principles that govern their lives and have designed their lives so that they live in harmony with those principles.[14] Robin Sharma reinforced this point when he stated: "There can be no authentic success and lasting happiness if your daily schedule is misaligned with your deepest values."[15]

Summary

- Understanding your values and what you deem to be important is key to the decisions and choices that you make in your life. This provides clarity in your life and builds your self-awareness.

- Understanding your values helps you to make difficult decisions.

- The knowledge of your highest values can act like a guide for you.

- As our life conditions change, and as we mature and grow in our psychological development, our values and priorities change.

- When you live by your values, you feel better about yourself and are more focused on doing the things that are important to you.

- Your biggest void becomes your highest value, so understand why you place value on something over others.

Chapter 4

Embrace your authenticity

Be true to yourself

I looked in the mirror and what should I see,
A pitiful stranger staring blankly at me,
I searched for familiarity and what I found instead,
Was merely the shadow of my former self, standing by my bed.
A haunted expression, dull eyes in a weathered face,
Sadness, regret and years simply gone to waste.
Was I dreaming or was I wide awake?
When did I lose myself? What was my mistake?
I wish I could rewind time and try to reclaim,
My authenticity instead of this phony picture frame.

Sir Walter Scott[16] said, "O, what a tangled web we weave, when we first practice to deceive".

This quote beautifully summarises what happens to us when we stop acknowledging our true selves; we start to deceive ourselves regarding what our true nature really is. It is when we try to pretend to be something that we are not, that we end up creating challenges in our lives. We start attracting the wrong people into our lives who respond to the false selves that we are projecting. We get into relationships with other people, hiding our authentic selves, and years later, when our authentic self is revealed, our partners realise that we are not the people they married.

We follow the wrong career because we cannot admit what truly makes us happy. As a result of these poor decisions, we end up being unhappy and resentful. When we realise our true character and embrace it without shame or self-blame, only then can we stop deceiving ourselves. Just find the courage to be you. Stop wasting your life living other people's dreams.

Sometimes our lives become a reel of tangled cotton thread. All you need to do is focus on finding the one loose thread that can unreel the tangled confusion. When you feel you have control over a part of your life and you are taking action, then the rest of your life becomes easy. When you start to be authentic, you will find your life becomes more effortless and flows better.

"If everyone was cast in the same mold, there would be no thing such as beauty." (Charles Darwin[17])

People lose their life energy trying to be someone they are not. When we set goals aligned to our values then we live a life that is fulfilled. When we try to be someone we are not, it is exhausting as we are suppressing our true nature. We need to give ourselves permission to be our authentic higher self. We are so worried about whether people will like us and accept us that we focus on changing ourselves to fit in. It may have started as innocently as a Grade 3 wanting to wear the same clothes to fit into the clique at school, or carrying the same school bag to be recognised as a cool kid. Whilst this wanting to conform and connect may be great at first, when it starts to become a habit, then it becomes a risk as you start to lose your own identity. You start to subscribe to other people's ideas blindly without truly exploring your own beliefs. It is often difficult to remember who you are before the world told you who you should be.

My friend shared a story about a recent encounter he had with a new business acquaintance he was meeting for the first time. As he described the interaction, his voice became excited and his facial expressions told me it was a positive encounter. When I asked what was so great about the interaction, he said, "This guy was so genuine". In a society of false people who wear polite masks over their true characters, it is refreshing to meet someone genuine, so try to be a genuine person.

When you sacrifice yourself to take care of others, you place your life on hold. It is a noble deed to give of yourself and to take care of those who cannot take care of themselves, yet over time the scales are imbalanced and your generosity starts to drain you of your self-worth; you begin to lose your identity because you are so focused on others. I have a friend who put her life on hold to take care of her elderly parents. What a beautiful example of honouring them. When both her parents finally passed on a few years later, she could not remember who she was. The circumstances had swallowed her own identity and she needed to rediscover herself and remember the little things that she loved to do.

Stephen Covey stated that, "It is futile to put personality ahead of character, to try to improve relationships with others before improving ourselves".[18] This sentiment was also expressed by Kevin Cashman in his book, *Leadership from the Inside Out*, when he said that, "authenticity is the core of relationships around which synergy and trust grows".[19] If we want to be more effective with others then we must be more effective with ourselves. Authenticity is the essence of having fulfilling relationships with other people when you connect with your true self rather than the false image you project into the world.

How sad it is when we lose our true selves over time. We forget about what gets us excited, what makes us happy and what brings us joy. We spend all our time pretending to be something that we are not. We create a persona or image for the world and we start to believe more in that image than in our true selves. We expend so much of our energy acting a part, that over time that part becomes who the world sees. It is too late when we realise that we have sacrificed our happiness by living a lie. When you pretend to be someone that you are not, you create unnecessary stress in your life. You feel like you have to keep up this deception, and worry whether you will be found out. If your friends cannot accept you for who you truly are, then they are the wrong friends. Florinda Donner[20] best described this when she said, "Freedom will cost you the mask you have on, the mask that feels so comfortable and is so hard to shed off, not because it fits so well but because you have been wearing it for so long".[21]

As the character Polonius advised his son in Shakespeare's play, *Hamlet*, "To thine own self be true, and it must follow, as the night the day, thou canst not then be false to any man".[22] This describes how important it is to be true to yourself if you are to have a good character. The idea of authenticity is not a new concept and has been covered in literature as well as psychology textbooks. It is a concept that is still relevant today, however, because it remains a challenge for those who prefer the false persona they have created rather than embracing their authentic nature. They start to lie to themselves and very soon they start to lie to the world.

When writing this book I was unable to decide between creating a book with many research references that might appear as a textbook, or write a book without the research references so that more people could identify with it. In my first draft I had numerous research studies to provide evidence to support all my ideas, as I wanted to convince you, dear reader, that my ideas had a scientific basis. My husband reminded me that if I wanted to write a book that could change lives then I needed to reduce the amount of research I included. His exact words were, "Stop trying to show others how clever you are and focus on practical ideas that can enhance their lives".

The other risk I took was including actual examples from my life and allowing myself to be vulnerable. I am generally a person who values privacy and I do not easily share my personal life with people outside my close circle of family and friends. In the end I realised that if I wanted to demonstrate that I have incorporated these ideas into my life, however, I needed to provide real examples that you could relate to. I strive to be authentic by being honest about my strengths and weaknesses. One of my values is being authentic, and I appreciate other people who are courageous enough to be themselves. If I had a wish to be anyone in the world, I would choose to be myself. Herman Melville said it best when he explained, "It is better to fail in originality than to succeed in imitation".[23]

To know yourself, you need to understand yourself and have knowledge of who you are; what your likes and dislikes are. Once you understand yourself, you can accept yourself, and you will not feel compelled to compare yourself with others. Each of us has unique strengths and virtues that we are not aware of. You can take the VIA Signature Strengths questionnaire to determine your top three signature strengths: http://www.authentichappiness.sas.upenn.edu/Default.aspx (Note: you will have to register on the Authentic Happiness website first to take the test. This is a short form that should take only a few minutes to complete.)

Some of the questions you can ask yourself to gain more self-knowledge are as follows:

Self-reflection questionnaire	
Some questions for reflection and self-understanding	
What were your dreams as a child?	
What was your favourite thing to do as a child?	
What was your most treasured childhood memory?	
What do you miss about being a child?	
What are your hopes and fears for the future?	
What do you like to spend your time doing?	
How do you feel about yourself most of the time?	
What do you wish you had more time to put energy into?	
What do you like the most in your life: your appearance, your personality or your intelligence?	

In your view, what is your best trait?	
What are your greatest strengths?	
What is the skill you are most proud of?	
What makes your heart sing?	
What makes you angry?	
What do you dislike about yourself?	
What things make you sad?	
Which were the favourite days of your life?	
Thus far, what has been your life's proudest achievement?	
When did you do good deeds and make someone smile?	

Living through comparisons

"There is nothing noble in being superior to your fellow men; true nobility is being superior to your former self." (Ernest Hemingway[24])

People often fall into the trap of comparing themselves with others. Once you sign up for that race, you will never win. When you live your life constantly comparing yourself with others, you become miserable and depressed. Do you remember the story of the ugly duckling that kept being compared to the other ducks? The ugly duckling felt inadequate and was ostracised. It was only when the ugly duckling grew up that she realised she was a beautiful swan.

Your only competition should be with yourself. How have you improved yourself? If you benchmark yourself against others, the exercise will never end well, as you will find yourself actively competing with others. You may have innocently wanted to understand your relative spot in the world and compared yourself to others, yet an innocent comparison will turn into a hostile competition where you start to see the failures of others as your triumphs.

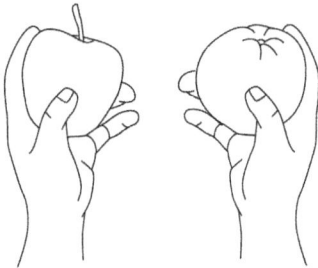

Researchers in one study showed that across different groups of people, the perception was that people believe that they spend more time alone, go to fewer parties, and are part of fewer social circles than other people, including their close friends. However, these researchers found that this happened because people compared themselves to highly visible and social people. This unrealistic comparison meant that people would always come up lacking.[25] These comparisons occurred in different areas, for example the fittest person or best dancer. What they found was that when people compared themselves to average people, the 'not being good enough' feelings went away. If we want to benchmark our skills and compare our achievements, then we should use realistic comparisons.

I have heard Robin Sharma tell people to run their own race. This simple phrase is extremely powerful and wise. It simply means that rather than competing with other people, focus on living your own life. We all have our individual journeys and we have an internal map that we need to follow. What would happen if you started following someone else's map? You would get lost and move away from where you were meant to be. So many of us wonder why we are stuck in our lives. We have lost our passion somewhere along the way. Somewhere in our life journey we became distracted because we looked up and saw someone else's journey and it seemed more exciting than the one we were following, so we took our personal map and squashed it and placed it in our pocket.

Sometimes this happens innocently enough. Some people decide to do subjects at school that they are good at, which their parents and teachers want them to pursue, even though other subjects bring them a greater sense of joy. Sometimes we get involved in relationships with others where we forget our own dreams and start to follow theirs, only to realise too late that we have lost our way. As parents we sometimes make choices to give our children the best opportunities and nurture their dreams, but that means we put our own dreams on hold. We stop following our own path and spend the rest our lives trying to find our way back. Only when we start to remember our own journey and find our own path again do we start to appreciate the blessings in our life. No matter how difficult your path may be to follow, remember it is your unique path.

The story of the golden Buddha

Centuries ago, a group of monks in Thailand cast a huge golden Buddha. Afraid that the Burmese were about to invade, the monks decided to cleverly disguise its worth by covering it with clay. The invaders probably saw the clay Buddha and left the statue behind. Nobody realised its true importance as it remained covered for centuries! Eventually, a new building was constructed for the statue. When the statue was being carried to its new home, the monks who were carrying the statue found it particularly heavy. It started to rain so the monks covered the statue. Later that night, the head monk went to check on the statue. As he shone his torch over it, he noticed a crack with a light coming through. He went to get a chisel and started removing the clay around the crack. Hours later, he found himself standing in front of the solid gold Buddha that had been there all along. The idea is that we all have our own version of "the golden Buddha" inside us. Throughout our lives, it gets covered until we finally acknowledge that it is still in there.

In Bangkok's temple of Wat Traimit you will find the seated, cross-legged Buddha statue known as Phra Phuttha Maha Suwana Patimakon. Standing at 3.91 metres tall and 3.01 metres wide, it is the world's biggest solid gold Buddha statue.

Recipe for finding your way back

RECIPE BOOK

So how do we begin this journey to self-discovery and how will we know that we have arrived and found our authentic selves?

- You have to acknowledge that you are unique. No one else has the same set of thumbprints as you. Even identical twins have different personalities.

- You need to acknowledge that you have certain specific gifts and a specific contribution to make to the world.

- You need to accept yourself. That means accepting all of you, including the parts you do not like.

- Demonstrate gratitude for all that you have in life. Reflect on all the great things you have done.

- Reconnect with your purpose by identifying the things that truly bring you joy. Show appreciation for these things.

- Follow your passion and act out your dreams.

We will explore these steps in more detail later on in the book.

According to Stephen Joseph, authentic people possess a number of common characteristics that show they are psychologically mature and fully functioning as human beings, i.e. they:

1. have realistic perceptions of reality (they have balanced expectations about life);

2. are accepting of themselves and of other people (they do not look to others for approval);

3. are thoughtful (they do not judge other people);

4. have a non-hostile sense of humour (their humour does not insult or hurt anyone);

5. are able to express their emotions freely and clearly;

6. are open to learning from their mistakes; and

7. understand their motivations.[26]

If we used the above list as a checklist, we would find that being authentic is not just knowing what we stand for, but also how we interact and engage with others. It gives us a sense of direction regarding what to aspire towards if we want to be more authentic individuals.

Another idea to identify your authentic self is to start a journal detailing one positive thing you like about yourself each day. By noting all the positive aspects of yourself you will appreciate the uniqueness that is you.

Stop auditioning for other roles when you have been cast in the most perfect role of your life; a unique role that has no comparison. John Mason captured the real reason to be authentic when he said, "You were born an original. Don't die a copy".[27]

Reflection exercise on authenticity	
When do you find yourself being inauthentic, i.e. when you are not being your true self?	
List all the recent situations when you were not yourself.	
What are you doing that is making you inauthentic?	
Why do you need to be inauthentic? What reward are you getting out of it?	
What would happen if you were authentic in those situations?	

How do people react to you when you are inauthentic?	
What percentage of your life do you spend being inauthentic?	
How much effort does it take to pretend to be someone else?	
What is inauthenticity costing you? Time, money, energy?	
What would happen if you chose to show up as your true self?	
Which people in your life would prefer you to be authentic?	
List three benefits of being more authentic in your life.	
Write down a situation that will occur in the near future where you can start practicing being more authentic.	
What will you be doing that will be different and more aligned to your true self?	

summary

Leo Bascaglia referred to a beautiful statement that resonates with me. He said that when you die and go to meet your maker, you are not going to be asked why you did not become a messiah or find a cure for cancer. All that you are going to be asked is why you did not become you; why you did not become all that you are.[28] George Elliot said that it is never too late to be the person you might have been. What do you have to lose?

- When we stop acknowledging our true selves, we start to deceive ourselves regarding what our true nature really is. It is when we try to pretend to be something that we are not that we end up creating problems in our lives.

- We create a persona or image for the world and we start to believe more in that image than in our true selves. We expend so much of our energy acting a part that over time that part becomes who the world sees.

- We start attracting the wrong people into our lives, who are responding to the false selves that we are projecting.

- Authenticity is the essence of having fulfilling relationships with other people when you connect with your true self, rather than the false image you project into the world.

- People often fall into the trap of comparisons with others. Once you sign up for that race you will never win. When you live your life constantly comparing yourself with others, you become miserable and depressed.

- A way in which you may like to identify your authentic self is to write in a journal every day about one positive thing you like about yourself. By noting all the positive aspects of yourself, you will appreciate the uniqueness that is you.

Section 2

Change Your Thinking

- Love and accept yourself
- Transform your limiting beliefs
- Reframe, affirm and create positive anchors
- Be proactive and drive optimism

This section focuses on learning to love and accept yourself. Once you accept yourself, you can work on those areas of your life that you need to improve. In these areas you have limited thinking, which you need to change to improve the quality of your life. There are different techniques you can use to change your limited thinking, such as reframing, anchoring and affirmations. Being proactive and having an optimistic attitude also helps you to create a positive mindset. Once you have changed the way you think, you will be able to deal with managing your emotions.

Chapter 5

Love and accept yourself

My Deepest Fear

My deepest fear is that I am not good enough.
How can I be? I am an empty shell without love.
Who can love someone so broken deep inside?
I swept the pieces under my heart and my vulnerabilities out of sight.

The external voices shout out, so accomplished, so talented, stand in your light.
How can I stand in the light, when I feel so ashamed and unworthy inside?

I hear the words 'I am not enough' echoing in the hollow chamber of my heart,
A shy voice whispers you are beautiful, you are gifted and you are smart!
I repeat stubbornly, I am not, I AM not, I AM NOT!
The voice responded, a bit louder, YOU are, YOU ARE, YOU JUST FORGOT!

At the height of my pity party, my inner child threw a tantrum of note.
"STOP IT", she shouted shaking me. "Yours is not the only vote!"
"Put the streamers away, close up the party, say no more."
She marched my guests, Pity, Shame, Sadness straight out the door.

"You are not broken, you are a beautiful soul.
Get back to the driver's seat, just switch off cruise control.
"Choose me, nurture me", she said... fill your heart with self-love.
Just know deep inside, that you are always more than enough.
Let your light shine radiantly so that you may see,
You are loved, blessed and most especially worthy.

The one belief that people seem to have is the fear that "I am not enough", which creates doubt and uncertainty, and erodes their confidence. No matter how brilliant and successful you are, sometime in your life these four words will be a hushed whisper in your consciousness, challenging everything about yourself – your confidence, your abilities and your knowledge. You start to question yourself. Am I clever enough to study? Am I beautiful enough to find a life partner? Am I wealthy enough? Your questions start to plant tiny seeds of doubt, which take root in your mind and rapidly grow until they undermine all your self-esteem. These words take a tenacious hold on your self-worth and all your confidence crumbles. Treat yourself like someone you once loved. Be kind and gentle with yourself.

We tend to compare ourselves with others and place others' achievements on a pedestal, and then look at ourselves and find ourselves wanting. Social media often fuels the fire of this pandemic. We see posts on social media of family, friends and work colleagues looking ecstatic and sharing their achievements and their holidays to far off places, and then we feel inferior. We feel as if we are not as successful or happy as they seem to be. Suddenly it seems in comparison that our lives are not as glamorous and exciting. This often leads to us becoming depressed with our simple existence, and we feel that our lives are not enough. We forget that people do not post the low moments in their lives; a bad hair day never shows up on Instagram or Facebook. Whilst social media is a great form of fostering social connections, it also has its flaws, and you must be realistic when using these social platforms. Not all that glitters is gold. We also forget that we all have our own individual and unique purposes and that we should not compare ourselves to others.

Over the years you become your own critic. You start to play the tapes in your head of the authority figures in your life who told you that you were not good enough, clever enough or pretty enough, and theirs become the only voices you believe. You start punishing yourself and allow these voices to direct your life. You anchor this experience and it becomes the repeat recording you play. It is only when you can break the hold of these limiting beliefs that you will be able to accept and love yourself. If you do not accept your idiosyncrasies then how can you accept the differences in others? When we judge ourselves it is easy to judge others. When we are so busy stereotyping and labeling, we lose track of what is important in our lives.

We need to forgive ourselves so that we can love ourselves. When we are busy judging ourselves and feeling guilt, there is no space for love. Guilt is an insidious disease that often plagues and destroys us. The greatest weapon against guilt is self-forgiveness and self-love. When we hold onto feelings of guilt, they manifest into illnesses. You must love yourself, not in a vain or arrogant way, but in a self-respecting way that authentically appreciates who you are. We often do not show this love to ourselves;

we feel guilty about things we did, did not do, or think we did. We punish our bodies by choosing junk food, abusing substances and nurturing bad habits, which creates stress in our bodies. We destroy our lives when we stop trying to live up to our potential.

Light your own fire

This year I threw a party for my daughter for her fourth birthday. She wanted a superhero party as she had a Super Girl outfit. As I prepared for the party, I realised that as little kids we also grew up idolising these superheroes, who had superpowers that they used for doing usually good deeds and defeating the "bad guys". The Avengers movies have done extremely well at the box office, confirming the view that people love superhero movies. As human beings, we have always held a fascination with the notion that someone with special talents is to be admired, yet we are so busy admiring others that we forget that we too have unique skills that are inspiring to others.

We are so busy praising others that we forget to praise ourselves. Not praise in an arrogant manner that places you on a pedestal, but praise from a humility perspective, where you know and appreciate your gifts. We all have a special gift – it may not be an extraordinary talent that allows one to compete on an international stage, but may be something as simple as the ability to make others feel special or cared for. Sometimes the consistent gentle crashing of the waves on rock is more powerful in wearing down the stone than any formidable force. There is power in gentleness like there is power in serenity and calmness.

In society we tend to focus on the most boisterous voices, forgetting that it is often the gentler people like Mahatma Gandhi, the Dalai Lama and Mother Theresa who carve their names in the history books. There is an incredible power in knowing and accepting yourself. We want to try and emulate others, but by doing so we suppress our own brilliance and unique, gentle strength. There is strength in being different. We need to stop hiding in the shadows and step out into the light. The light I refer to is not centre stage with adoring fans shouting your name, but your inner light. If you let it shine, it will transform you.

The Japanese philosophy of wabi-sabi encourages us to focus on the blessings hiding in our daily lives, and celebrating the way things are rather than how they could be. It is the true acceptance of finding beauty in things as they are. Mike Sturm explained that wabi-sabi is about accepting yourself and building on what you already have in life: "*embracing wabi-sabi is as easy (or as difficult) as understanding and accepting yourself — imperfections and all. It's about being compassionate with yourself as you are, and building on whatever that is — not feverishly trying to rebuild yourself in order to pose as something else entirely.*"[29] The Japanese find beauty in a chipped tea cup which they repair and continue to use. It is about acknowledging all parts of you with equanimity.

Recipe for self-love

RECIPE BOOK

Louise Hay's exercise for improving one's love for oneself involves people picking up a small mirror, looking into their own eyes, saying their names, and saying, "*I love and accept you exactly as you are*".[30] I have used this exercise as part of coaching and I was amazed at how many people are uncomfortable doing it. It is strange that many of us look at the mirror when we prepare for work on a daily basis, but as soon as you say connect with who you are, looking at the mirror becomes more difficult. When all is said and done, we are all three year old children pretending to live well-rounded lives as adults; we all crave acknowledgement that we are loved and accepted for who we truly are.

Self-love is important and so is self-forgiveness. What are the words you want others to tell you? Is it gratitude, is it feelings of love or understanding? We spend years waiting for other people to validate us and tell us what we mean to them. The reality is that it may never happen and as a result you will feel frustrated. Even when people do not give you this message, you can still give yourself the gift of these words.

Imagine the other person standing across from you verbalising the words. Now tell yourself the words you need to hear. No one is going to be able to say the words more perfectly than how you want to hear them said. You owe it to yourself to say these words to yourself. It does not have to be a speech. Imagine a line of people in your life who you interact with that you expect some gesture from. Now imagine them telling you the words that you want to hear. It could be simple phrases like: I am grateful for you, I love you, I forgive you, I accept you, I honour you, Thank you. It is these phrases that will feed your spirit and open your heart. Once your heart is open, you will be able to be present and engage in life. The more you love who you really are inside, the more you will let go of the need to look for external approval and validation. Be kind and gentle with yourself.

As part of loving and accepting yourself you need to change your beliefs about yourself. You need to let go of beliefs that are no longer serving you.

summary

- The one belief that people seem to have is the fear that "I am not enough", which creates doubt and uncertainty, and erodes one's confidence.

- No matter how brilliant and successful you are, sometime in your life these four words will be a hushed whisper in your consciousness, challenging everything about yourself, your confidence, your abilities and your knowledge.

- Over the years you become your own critic. You start to play the tapes in your head of the authority figures in your life who told you that you were not good enough, clever enough or pretty enough, and they become the only voices you believe.

- You must love yourself, not in a vain or arrogant way, but in a self-respecting way that appreciates authentically who you are.

- We need to forgive ourselves so that we can love ourselves. The greatest weapon against guilt is self-forgiveness and self-love.

- We are so busy praising others that we forget to praise ourselves.

- Wabi-sabi encourages us to focus on the blessings hiding in our daily lives, and celebrating the way things are rather than how they could be.

Chapter 6

Transform your limiting beliefs

Is that you dear friend?
I hardly recognize you, from the sadness in your eyes.
Don't look away, I am glad to see you.
What a lovely surprise.

As a child you were such a beautiful free spirit spreading your love.
I remember the laughter, the games. Time which was just never enough.
I remember your radiant flame, the twinkling smile in your eyes and the soft glow on your skin.
I noticed your effervescent personality shimmering as you drew it from within.

Dear friend, what has since happened? Why are you looking ashamed?
What has taken away your laughter, who has extinguished your flame?

"I couldn't stop the critical person. I was helpless. What was I to do?
I heard the taunting voice mock me each time I tried something new.
Each day the critical voice slowly dimmed my inner light.
As I saw the world grow darker, I stopped seeing my beauty inside."

With a saddened gaze, my friend slowly pointed her finger to me.
She whispered, "It was always you".
I stared at her in disbelief, not ready to be blamed.
When I looked at her eyes I knew, the words she spoke were true.

I will change I promise, my friend in the mirror. I slowly turned away.
My heart filled with remorse and regret, I knelt down to finally pray.

Please help me change my ways.

This poem demonstrates how we lose our lustre for life over time by allowing our inner critic to always undermine our true worth. We do not realise it until it is too late and the damage has been done to our self-esteem. Our self-confidence is eroded and we stop trying to be our best. We surrender all our dreams and potential and become bitter and negative people.

Self-limiting beliefs occur in all areas of your life. You need to challenge these limiting beliefs because they become the invisible chains that will restrict your growth and success in your life. The sad thing is that you are not aware that this is your operating system. You believe that this is how you are; a closed chapter. You are not open to improvement or new possibilities – you are comfortable with the rules you have defined for your life. In the next moment, when you hear of someone close to you achieving something great, you become bitter about their success. You do not question how the person achieved their success and the beliefs they had to challenge to be successful. Insanity is doing the same thing over and over again and expecting a different result, so why should the results in your life change when you have not changed your attitude about the way you approach things? Louise Hay's[31] advice is: "You have been criticizing yourself for years, and it hasn't worked. Try approving of yourself and see what happens."

Internal self-talk

"If you expect the battle to be insurmountable, you've met the enemy. It's you."
(Khang Kijarro Nguyen[32])

Sometimes we are our own worst enemy. We are so concerned about others who criticise us, that often we do not realise that we do a lot of the criticising of ourselves. Self-criticism is often more harmful than the criticism from others because we are not aware of it. It often happens in a microsecond in the daily rush of our lives, so that we do not even know it is there. The way to deal with self-criticism is to bring the shadow into the light by shining a torch on it. Miguel Ruiz, in his book *The Four Agreements*, stated that, "If you are not aware that your mind is full of wounds and emotional poison, you cannot begin to clean and heal the wounds and you will continue to suffer".[33]

Negative self-talk feeds negative belief patterns, which create unfavourable situations in your life which reinforces your negative self-talk. This vicious cycle is referred to as a 'self-fulfilling prophecy'. "The self-fulfilling prophecy is, in the beginning, a false definition of the situation, evoking a new behaviour which makes the originally false conception come true." (Robert K. Merton[34])

A commonly understood example of the self-fulfilling prophecy in psychology is what is known as the placebo effect (Isaksen[35]). This refers to improvements seen in patients' health even when the participants did not receive any meaningful medical treatment, i.e. it is caused by the participants' belief in the effectiveness of the "treatment" they received. The work in the area of self-fulfilling prophecy is so extensive that it demonstrates the power of your own thoughts and beliefs manifesting either positive or negative results in your life.

Recipe to quieten your inner critic

RECIPE BOOK

The best way to defeat your inner critic is to pay attention when things are going wrong in your life. Notice the messages you give yourself. For example, you could have forgotten to complete an assignment and then you say to yourself, "What a dumb thing to do" or "How could I have been so stupid?" Start noticing these phrases that you keep saying to yourself and decide to change them. Remember, as part of your life journey, you will make many mistakes in order to grow. These mistakes are necessary so that you understand that you are continuously growing as a human being. Research has found that animals learn from other animals' mistakes[36]; similarly, human beings can learn from mistakes to prevent themselves from repeating them. So, do not be so tough on yourself when you mess up; you and others are just learning from your mistakes. Each day you are growing and becoming better since we are all works in progress.

Once you notice the self-critic, the second step to addressing it is to give it a name so it is viewed as separate from you. The third step is to talk back to it and take some of your power back by telling it you are not listening or that it is wrong. Lastly, replace it with a kinder voice and try to talk gently to yourself.[37] When I make a mistake, I often say to myself, "You silly old Pooh!", which is a line from the book, *Winnie the Pooh*. My new voice is gentle and almost childlike. I use it whenever someone cuts in front of my car in traffic, when I accidentally spill something, or when I make mistakes like closing a document on my laptop without saving it.

We all experience moments of doubt. My own doubt crept in late one night whilst I was writing this book. I had written half of the book and was stressed about having writer's block and not meeting my deadline. What followed was an interesting dialogue between my internal critic and my appreciative self:

"So, you think you can write a self-help book huh?"
"It is not a self-help book, it is a book to create self-awareness", I responded.
"Do you know how many self-help motivational books there are in book shops?", my critical voice continued.
"Like a hundred, so what?"
"What makes you think you can write a book that people will enjoy?"
"I have already written a book that I have received positive feedback on. I even had a positive book review in Fin24."
"That's different, it was a niche topic. Who is going to read your book anyway?"
"A lot of people."
"Hmmm, sounds like wishful thinking to me. So, what if you write the book and only one person reads it, your editor?" My critical voice was becoming meaner.
"Then my editor would learn some interesting information."
"You are sacrificing a lot of time for only your editor to read your book."
"I know a few other people who might read it as well."
"Hmmm, how many?"
"Ten."
"Well I guess that is better than one. So why would people spend money on your book rather than on a book by Robin Sharma or Anthony Robbins?"
"My target market is different; my book is for people who want to change but do not know where to begin."
"News flash, so are theirs."
"I never claimed to be in the same league as Anthony Robbins or Robin Sharma. This book is meant to make a difference in someone's life. If someone's perspective changes because they read something in my book, I would have touched one person's life. So, bugger off and let me be so my ten people can one day read my book!"

And that is how I put my critical voice to sleep for the rest of the time I was writing the book.

Jennice Vilhauer[38] suggests that you keep a writing pad of paper next to your bed and every night before you go to sleep, write down three things you liked about yourself that day. When you wake up in the morning, read the list before you get out of bed. Keep adding three new things to your list every day to keep the list growing. She recommends that you do this exercise for 30 days. These can be little things like complimenting a co-worker on her dress and bringing a smile to her face, or helping carry the bag of an old lady.

Over the years your self-criticism has been gradually extinguishing your fire. This exercise is great to rekindle your brilliant fire within. You need to appreciate that you are a unique being and that you have beautiful gifts to offer the world. When you rediscover how amazing you are, you stop feeling depressed and start to feel more self-confident.

Letting go of the past

You cannot change the past, only the way you think and feel about it. All of us carry some regret of our past about something we did or did not do. We carry these memories, not as harmless pictures of the past, but often as prickly thorns that still have the power to prick us and pull us back to that moment in time. It is as if it is a chain that we are shackled with that jerks us back into the past.

Shakespeare wrote, "Nothing is either good or bad, but thinking makes it so".[39]

You have self-limiting beliefs in all areas of your life. How do you shift those beliefs and change your autopilot programming? It starts with a state of awareness; you cannot change what you are not aware of. If you look at the eight life dimensions we reviewed earlier, you will find that you have self-limiting beliefs in each of these dimensions. These self-limiting beliefs are holding you back from optimising your potential. You probably never thought about them before and took it for granted that that is just how life is. Understand your operating system and your programming, and be prepared to change your programme if it no longer serves you. Your circumstances will continue to change, and so should your priorities.

Table of self-limiting beliefs

Life dimension	Examples of self-limiting beliefs
Mental dimension	I am not clever like other people. I am too old to study further. When you finish school, you do not have to study further.
Spiritual life dimension	Spiritual people do not get angry. Spiritual people do not worry about money. Being spiritual is more important than being wealthy.
Emotional dimension	I am not good enough. I do not deserve to be happy. Only crazy people speak to counsellors.
Physical dimension	I do not have time to exercise. Only confident people go to the gym. My whole family is overweight.
Social dimension	You cannot trust people. People will always let you down. If you have close family you do not need friends.
Environmental dimension	Each one must worry about themselves. I will never have enough to share with others. Only rich people support charities.
Career dimension	I do not have the necessary qualifications. Only favourites get ahead. Only ambitious people have successful careers.
Financial dimension	Money is the root of all evil. Rich people are arrogant. I do not earn enough money to save.

Reflection exercise	
Life dimension	**What are some of your self-limiting beliefs?**
Mental dimension	
Spiritual life dimension	
Emotional dimension	
Physical dimension	
Social dimension	
Environmental dimension	
Career dimension	

	Reflection exercise
Life dimension	**What are some of your self-limiting beliefs?**
Financial dimension	

The impact of self-limiting beliefs on our lives

Psychoneuroimmunology is the study of the interaction between psychological processes and the nervous and immune systems of the human body. Psychoneuroimmunology has evolved in the last 40 years to include the study of the relationship between mind and body. Research in this field found that stress, which is caused by how you internalise events around you, has a significant negative impact on your body, especially your immune system.

Dr. Masaru Emoto is a Japanese researcher who studied the impact that the external environment has on water. He took a drop of water and froze it at a temperature of -13 degrees and took pictures under the microscope of the crystals that formed. His research demonstrated that the picture of the water crystals looked different in different circumstances.[40]   Dr Emoto's water crystal experiments consisted of exposing water in glasses to different words, pictures or music, and then freezing and examining the visual properties of the resulting crystals with microscopic photography. Dr Emoto made the claim that water exposed to positive speech and thoughts would result in visually "pleasing" crystals being formed when that water was frozen, and that negative speech and thoughts would yield "ugly" frozen crystal formations. The human body is estimated to consist of between 70% and 90% water, and each cell, organ and system of the body consists of some water. Dr Emoto's work thus demonstrates that our thoughts, emotions and actions have an impact on the molecular structure of water, which makes up 70% to 90% of the physiology of our body.

Recipe for changing limiting beliefs

RECIPE BOOK

Sometimes it is easy to transform limiting beliefs that are newly formed and thus not yet deeply embedded. You can provide counter evidence to demonstrate that the belief is, in fact, false. This is easier when your beliefs are linked to false facts which are easily disproved. To change deeply engrained beliefs, you have to use other techniques like affirmations, reframing and creating positive anchors.

Summary

Summary

- Self-limiting beliefs occur in all areas of your life. You need to challenge these because they become the invisible chains that will restrict your growth and success.

- Sometimes we are our own worst enemy. We are so concerned about others that criticise us, that often we do not realise that we do a lot of the criticising of ourselves. Self-criticism is often more harmful than the criticism from others, because we are not aware of it.

- Negative self-talk feeds negative belief patterns, which create unfavourable situations in your life which reinforce your negative self-talk.

- Understand your operating system and your programming. Be prepared to change your programme if it no longer serves you.

- The best way to defeat your inner critic is to pay attention when things are going wrong in your life and notice the messages you give yourself.

- Keep a writing pad next to your bed and every night before you go to sleep, write down three things you liked about yourself that day. When you wake up in the morning, read the list before you get out of bed.

Chapter 7

Reframing

"It's snowing still," said Eeyore gloomily.
"So it is."
"And freezing."
"Is it?"
"Yes," said Eeyore.
"However," he said brightening up a little, "we haven't
had an earthquake lately." (A.A. Milne[41])

Wayne Dyer best described 'reframing' when he said, "If you change the way you look at things, the things you look at change".[42]

Reframing is a technique used in therapy to help create a different way of looking at a situation, person, or relationship by changing its meaning. It is also referred to as cognitive reframing. It is a strategy that helps you look at situations from a slightly different perspective. When we change our point of view on any given situation, the facts remain the same, but our perspective of the situation changes. When we change our perspective and our thinking about our situation, there is a change in feeling and the meaning that we give to our life circumstances. You have been exposed to reframing most of your life without realising what it was. When someone is robbed of their cell phone, you will hear people provide comfort saying, "It is only a cell phone, I'm glad that you were not hurt". Or if someone is involved in an accident, people try to give comfort by saying, "You are so fortunate that you were not injured, it was only your car". We often reframe when we advise other people, but we rarely practice this on ourselves.

One example of reframing is redefining a problem as a challenge. Simply by viewing something as a challenge makes us feel as though we are in control of the situation, which moves us from a victim mentality to a victor mentality. Reframing requires seeing something in a new way, in a context that allows us to recognise and appreciate positive aspects of our situation. Another important principle in neurolinguistics programming is that every behaviour is useful in some context and every capability exists for some useful reason. For example, my four year old can be extremely feisty and stubborn when she wants her own way. If I had to reframe her behaviour, I can think of a future where my daughter's stubbornness may prevent other people from pushing her around.

Reframing is exactly as the word implies; it is about placing a different frame on an existing experience. By reassigning a different meaning to a belief or experience, you tend to look at it from a different perspective – you stop feeling like you are stuck and realise that there are alternative solutions.

An example of reframing is when your manager walks by without acknowledging or greeting you. Rather than make the assumption that he is upset with you, reframe the thought to: "He is preoccupied because he has a lot on his mind."

Brian Tracy says that whenever something happens and he is disappointed, he immediately interprets it positively. He says the affirmation: "Every experience is a positive experience if I view it as an opportunity for growth and self-mastery."[43]

Let me refer to the taxi example again. If the taxi cuts in front of you as you are driving to work, rather than get angry and worked up, reframe and think that they are carrying people who cannot afford to be late. When we change the meaning it shifts our perception and changes our emotional state. If we are angry with the actions of the taxi driver, it starts our day in a negative way, however once we reframe we become more tolerant and the anger dissolves into understanding.

Reframing is a skill that requires practice and it is important to start on daily occurrences to develop the skill. When life changing experiences occur, you are able to reframe the event. When my Dad died I was devastated. To help me cope with my loss I found myself reframing my experience. I reframed it into the spiritual growth I received through the six month period when we never knew one moment to the next whether he was going to survive. The emotional rollercoaster taught me resilience.

Byron Katie suggests that when you are going through different experiences, it is important to ask four questions that will assist in changing or reframing the way you approach life. She takes you through a structured process of first remembering a situation when you were upset with someone or something in your life. She recommends that you, "Travel in your mind to a specific situation where you were angry, hurt, sad, or disappointed with someone. Witness the situation. Be there now. Notice, name, and feel the emotion you were experiencing at the time. Find the reason you were upset". Secondly, understand what your thoughts were at that time. Find the dominant thought and ask yourself four questions. *Is it true? Can you absolutely know that it is true? How do you react; what happens when you believe that thought? Who would you be without that thought?* Lastly, turn the thought around and contemplate how each sentence turned around is truer in that situation.[44]

I have often heard people complain about their work because they feel obligated. By simply changing how they view their jobs and what value it brings to their lives, then their outlook will shift.

"Duty makes us do things well, but love makes us do them beautifully." (Zig Ziglar[45])

Choose your response

No matter what circumstances we find ourselves in, no matter how low we are in our lives and what is weighing us down, we can lift ourselves up, dust off the disappointment and regret, and move on. History is full of brave men and women who, despite overwhelming odds and torturous circumstances, were able to change their mindset from victim to victor. A great example of this was Victor Frankl, who wrote a beautiful book called *Man's Search for Meaning* in which he documented his experiences and life lessons. He was a Jewish psychiatrist imprisoned in the concentration camps of Nazi Germany. His parents, his brother and wife were killed in the gas chambers. He lived moment to moment, never knowing when it would be his turn to die. Frankl realised that despite the horrendous torture and circumstances, no matter what the soldiers did to his physical body, he could still retain the freedom of his mind. Frankl started to use his memory and imagination to picture himself giving lectures to his students or having conversations with his wife. He developed his mind so that he felt empowered. He realised that it was in his power to choose how he responded to his circumstances. Frankl made a critical discovery: between stimulus and response, man has the freedom to choose.[46]

Of all the lessons I have learnt over the years, this was the most fundamental in changing my behaviour. We grow up to believe that when something happens, we react, and this is a natural response to the triggers in the environment. However, over the years I have come to realise that the knowledge that we can choose our response to triggers is the most empowering tool. This is fundamental when we deal with life experiences.

Saying affirmations

> "As a single footstep will not make a path on the earth, so a single thought will not make a pathway in the mind. To make a deep physical path, we walk again and again. To make a deep mental path, we must think over and over the kind of thoughts we wish to dominate our lives." (Henry David Thoreau[47])

Affirmations are positive statements that can help you to challenge and overcome self-sabotaging and negative thoughts. When you repeat them often and believe in them, you can start to make positive changes in your life.

Brian Tracy referred to the Law of Subconscious Reality, which is that whatever thought or goal you accept in your conscious mind will be accepted by your subconscious mind as a command or instruction.[48] The view is that once your subconscious mind understands the instruction, it will start to draw in the people and resources you need to achieve it. Your subconscious mind starts to pay particular attention to things that might help you realise your goal; it influences your thoughts, ideas and body language in accordance with that instruction. As you interact with people your tone of voice and your attitude are impacted by new thoughts and beliefs. People will start to respond to your behaviour and this creates an almost self-fulfilling prophecy.

The mind cannot differentiate between real and make believe, therefore it is easy to trick your mind into believing certain ideas. Similarly, when you are told negative messages by others repeatedly, such as "You are not clever" or "You are so fat", your mind starts to believe it and it becomes entrenched as a belief. It is therefore difficult to work on a positive affirmation that you are brilliant when the negative belief keeps cancelling it out.

A large body of literature, however, has demonstrated that a class of interventions called self-affirmations have benefits across threatening situations. Affirmations can decrease stress, increase wellbeing, improve academic performance and make people more open to behaviour change.[49] Yet you need to understand that affirmations alone are not going to change your reality – they are not a magical solution to all your issues. I am 1.5 metres tall and no matter how many affirmations I say about my height, they will not change that fact. What affirmations will do is act as a constant trigger to remind you that you have all the skills and abilities to be the best version of yourself.

My husband and I have been doing affirmations with our daughter since she was three years old, which we have built into her daily ritual. In the car to school we start off with affirmations before we do anything else. These affirmations have helped as reminders for her when she is not behaving. For example, one of her favourite affirmations is that she is kind and generous, so when she complains about her day and one of the kids who did not share a toy, I remind her: "Remember that you are kind and generous." One morning I was driving her to school and in the car I was trying out a new affirmation: "I am a great mother." My daughter responded, "You are not a very good mummy." I was surprised so I asked her why she thought so. "You don't listen to me." I apologised and asked her for an example of when I do not listen to her and she said, "When I want to watch TV, you don't let me". I just smiled at the feedback. Affirmations will only work if there is some level of truth in them. If my daughter had given a list of valid concerns then my affirmation would have seemed superficial. I have used affirmations when I have been going through stressful times and needed to reassure myself that "I am resourceful". Affirmations help to create positive events in your life through the power of a self-fulfilling prophecy.

Recipe for affirmations

RECIPE BOOK

The important point to remember when creating affirmations is that they must be personal, emotional, positive, visual and stated in the present tense.[50] You cannot say, "I am going to stop eating junk food", but rather "I am eating nutritious food". Also, try not to compare yourself to other people when you are making affirmations. For example, "I am a better dancer than Susan".

There is much scepticism about the effectiveness of affirmations, and whilst many self-help gurus swear by them, there are others who have tried and did not get any positive results.

Some of the strategies to check whether your affirmations are working for you is to review them on a regular basis to determine whether there was any behavioural change. If they were not effective, then you should link your affirmation with a goal and action steps. Now when you are repeating the affirmations you will feel that they are more meaningful. If people are extremely negative then moving into positive affirmations may be too big a jump, so they should start with neutral affirmations. These neutral affirmations may be more palatable because they are less threatening. So, instead of saying that "I am a beautiful, successful artist", you could say "I accept the beauty within me". Once you are comfortable with neutral affirmations, you can start working on stronger ones.[51]

Ronald Alexander provided five steps to make affirmations work. He suggested firstly making a list of negative qualities and checking where in your body you are experiencing them. For example, anxiety could be sitting in your stomach when you do not feel good enough. Now look at a list of positive qualities that can better serve you. Secondly, write the positive affirmation in the present tense and make sure that the words you use are strong adjectives. Instead of "I am clever", you could say, "I am brilliant". Thirdly, rewrite the affirmation repeatedly in your notebook to reaffirm the belief. For five minutes each day −morning, noon and night − you should repeat the affirmation. Fourthly, you should breathe in the affirmation and place your hands on the part of the body where you were uncomfortable when experiencing the negative belief. Lastly he suggested that you get a coach to repeat the message to you or repeat the message in front of a mirror.[52]

Sometimes it helps to stick affirmation notes around your house where you will see them during the day. You can stick them on the mirror in the bathroom or on your desk where you are bound to see and remember them. When you see these stickers, read them out loud.

You can try these different approaches and check which one works best for you. I will leave you with a great idea for an affirmation that Brian Tracy proposed. Each morning you start your day with a positive expectation that sets the tone for great things to occur in your life. He suggested that you repeat the suggestion until you are positively charged. "I believe something wonderful is going to happen to me today."[53]

"People often say that motivation doesn't last. Well, neither does bathing – that's why we recommend it daily." (Zig Ziglar[54])

Some of my affirmations
I am the best version of myself.
I am my best every day.
I forgive myself for my mistakes.
Today is going to be an awesome and fulfilling day.
I am more than enough, I am me.

Reflection exercise
Write down five affirmations for yourself for a behaviour you want to change or a new behaviour you want to introduce into your life.
1.
2.
3.
4.
5.

Creating positive anchors

One of the best lessons I learnt in neurolinguistics programming was to understand the role of anchors in my life and to recognise and change anchors so that they inspire me in my daily life. Anchors can be kinaesthetic, auditory, gustatory or olfactory, and can influence us for years later. An anchor is simply a trigger that when you see it, hear it, feel it or smell it, it reminds you of something else. For example you walk into a restaurant and the fragrance of the food suddenly reminds you of your mother's pasta and you are transported back in time to her kitchen. You walk into a shopping mall and get the scent of a perfume and you are reminded of a good friend and you miss her. You are driving to work and hear your father's favourite song and you become emotional. All these triggers are referred to as anchors and if you are not aware of them, they can move you from one emotional state to another. If you recognise the negative anchors in your life you can change them by creating positive associations with them.

In 1995 I was asked to do two weeks' vacation work in Johannesburg as part of my bursary conditions. I was 20 years old and the furthest I had travelled from my Durban home was 80km away. Whilst I had spent holidays away from home with family, this was a huge deal at that time. I stayed at my mentor's apartment with another student, but the other student had family in Johannesburg so she was always away. In the two weeks I was lonely and miserable. I missed my family terribly. The lady I was staying with had an album collection of the music band, Air Supply. I enjoyed the music so I listened to these songs over and over again for the duration of my stay. Years later, whenever I heard any song by Air Supply, it immediately transported me back to that moment. I would suddenly experience those feelings of loneliness, sadness and general depression. I let it go since I rarely heard Air Supply songs, but one day I was in a shopping mall having a very nice outing with my family and I heard an Air Supply song. I felt someone put off my happiness switch. I thought this was absolutely ridiculous so I decided to change my negative association with the song. This is what I did. I created a new memory association with the song by playing it and dancing to it with my daughter. Whilst the song was playing we would dance but with exaggerated movements. Now when I hear the song the new association I have is of my daughter and I having fun. Do you have songs in your life that you absolutely despise due to the memories they trigger? Maybe it was of an emotional breakup or it reminds you of a lonely time in your life. The good news is that you can change the association and release the emotional hold it has on you.

If anchors are that powerful then you should use them deliberately in your life. I use the song by Michael Bolton, "I can go the distance", when I need to feel inspired. I first heard the song when I watched the movie *Hercules* about a hero's journey, and the words and music immediately resonated with me. Years later I was watching Michael Bolton singing the same song live and I knew that it was going to be my inspirational song. When I hear the song I am immediately reminded that sometimes a hero's journey is lonely, but in the end it is worth the sacrifice. If I ever feel stuck and uninspired, I play the song and immediately I start to feel more positive. If you want to change your emotions, music is often the easiest way to do it. You can choose a song that reminds you of a time when you felt happy and carefree. When you are feeling stressed and need to remember those carefree emotions, you can play your favourite song. Sometimes an anchor can be a photograph that you carry in your wallet that is a constant reminder of someone or something that inspires you. It can be a special fragrance that you use to boost your confidence. You can also create kinaesthetic anchors with your body.

Here is an example of a kinesthetic anchor. Think of a time when you felt really happy, optimistic and absolutely carefree. It was one of the happiest moments of your life. Try and remember what you were doing. Where were you? What were you wearing? Who were you with? Why was it a happy day? What were you feeling? Try and remember as much detail about that day as you can. Just relive the moment. After about 30 seconds reliving the memory, when you feel that you are at your peak of feeling good, take the thumb of your non-dominant hand and touch the top knuckle of your middle finger of the same hand. Now repeat the exercise and like before, when you are fully experiencing the moment, touch your knuckle with your thumb. Try this exercise again with another happy memory. What you will find is that when you are feeling sad, by touching your thumb to the knuckle of your middle finger, it acts as a trigger of happy memories and brings you back into a happy state.

You can continue to access your memories for more positive happy experiences and continue to stack these experiences together. What you will find is that it will make your anchor stronger. The next time you are feeling depressed, all you need to do is touch your thumb to the knuckle of your middle finger and you will be able to access these feelings. It is important that you really relive these positive experiences for the anchor to work, and you must use specific, concrete examples.

Summary

- **Reframing** is a technique used in therapy to help create a different way of looking at a situation, person or relationship by changing its meaning.

- When we change our point of view on any given situation, the facts remain the same, but our perspective of the situation changes. When we change our perspective and our thinking about our situation, there is a change in our feelings and the meaning that we give to our life circumstances.

- **Affirmations** are positive statements that can help you to challenge and overcome self-sabotaging and negative thoughts. When you repeat them often and believe in them, you can start to make positive changes in your life.

- The important point to remember when creating affirmations is that they must be personal, emotional, positive, visual and stated in the present tense.[55]

- An **anchor** is simply a trigger that when you see it, hear it, feel it or smell it, it reminds you of something else.

- Anchors can be kinaesthetic, auditory, gustatory or olfactory, and can influence us for years.

Chapter 8

Locus of control

Generally there are two types of people – those who have an internal locus of control and those who have an external locus of control. A **locus of control** is an individual's belief system and refers to the degree to which people believe that they have control over the outcome of events in their lives, as opposed to external forces beyond their control. If a person has an internal locus of control, that person attributes their success to his or her own efforts and abilities. A person who expects to succeed will be more motivated and more likely to learn. A person with an external locus of control, who attributes his or her success to luck or fate, will be less likely to make the effort needed to learn. People with an external locus of control are also more likely to experience anxiety since they believe that they are not in control of their lives. For example, if someone fails a test, a person with an internal locus of control will attribute the outcome to a lack of studying. A person with an external locus of control will blame the teacher for setting a difficult paper.

Your locus of control can influence not only how you respond to the events that happen in your life, but also your motivation to take action. If you believe that you hold the keys to your fate, you are more likely to take action to change your situation when needed. If, on the other hand, you believe that the outcome is out of your hands, you may be less likely to work toward change.

To create an internal locus of control, you can try the following ideas suggested on the *Motivation Mindset* vlog:[56]

1. Whenever possible, consciously make choices that demonstrate to yourself your sense of control over your life, and tie those choices to the broader effect they have on the direction and "results" of your life.

2. Take responsibility for everything that happens in your life, good or bad. Doing so helps you to shift your perspective from a victim mentality to a more proactive one. When you take responsibility for an outcome, it

naturally leads you to think about what you could have done that may have resulted in a more favourable result.

3. Identify people who have an internal locus of control and model them. Ideally, these should be people you know, but the most important thing is to find someone to model. Watch how they behave in situations that would upset or frustrate you and learn from them. If possible, ask them to walk you through their thought process after the triggering event happened.

4. When you notice yourself getting upset or reacting to something, do not focus on what is outside your control (like the traffic, the economy or another person). Instead, get in the habit of asking yourself a few questions:

- What feeling, specifically, am I reacting to?

- Is my reaction going to change anything or make the situation any better for me?

- Is my reaction going to prevent the situation from happening again?

- Could a different response produce a better outcome?

"Watch your thoughts, they become your words. Watch your words, they become your actions. Watch your actions, they become your habits. Watch your habits, they become your character. Watch your character, it becomes your destiny." (Lao Tzu[57])

Optimism

Rose-tinted glasses

Each morning I wake up, I have two choices,
To listen to calmness or to listen to Life's noises.
So I reach for my bag of accessories,
Hmm should I take my sword and shield?
My pair of rose-tinted glasses always held a greater appeal.
I deliberately choose to focus on the world of possibilities,
This decision leads to exploring different realities.
Rather than looking at the hopelessness and saying, "I can't cope",
With my rose-tinted glasses, my picture is framed in beauty and hope.

"You normally have to be bashed about a bit by life to see the point of daffodils, sunsets and uneventful nice days." (Alain de Botton[58])

Life is all about choices. No matter what your present circumstances or situation, it is within your control to either be happy or depressed. Often, all it takes is a one-second choice when you open your eyes in the morning, whether you are going to approach the day with resentment, or you are going to embrace the day with possibilities. When you choose to be happy, it forces you to look at the present situation in your life from a different perspective. This requires continuous persistence to find the answer to the question, "Why is this happening to me?"

One's 'explanatory style', which is the way you explain things to yourself, is critical in determining whether you have a positive or negative mindset. When you explain things to yourself in a positive way, you become more positive. When you explain things to yourself in a negative way, you become more negative. Dr. Seligman[59] found that positive people always explain an event to themselves as if it was a temporary, specific situation, rather than a long-term, general condition. When something goes wrong, a positive person will say, "It is just not my day, tomorrow will be better". A negative person with the same experience will generalise it and say something like, "Just great, this always happens to me".

A great poem to illustrate this point. "Two men look out the same prison bars; one sees mud and the other stars." (Beck)[60] The two men share the same experience, which is being imprisoned, yet the circumstances that brought them to this point in time is different. What they focus on when they look outside the prison windows is defined by their outlook on life and their life experiences. The person who sees only the stars might believe that prison may be a temporary experience, and there may be life lessons to gain from it, whilst the man who sees mud believes that there is no hope and may view his prison experience as the lowest point in his life.

Choose to focus on what is going well in your life. In different cultures there are unique words that refer to a similar philosophy or mindset. In Africa, 'Hakuna matata' means 'No worries'. In Thailand, 'Mai pen Rai' means 'Everything is going to be okay'. In the Philippines, 'bahala na' means 'Whatever will be, will be". My favourite is Winnie the Pooh's "Oh dear", which expresses so much. Just by using these phrases, one's view of the world changes.

"It never hurts to keep looking for sunshine." (A.A. Milne[61])

In his book, *Seven Habits of Highly Effective People*, Stephen Covey refers to people who either focus on circles of concern or circles of influence. When you place your attention on a circle of concern, you focus on events that you have no control over and you become pessimistic. When you focus on a circle of influence, i.e. on those things you can directly influence, you feel more in control and generally more optimistic. Have you met people who are so pessimistic in nature that no matter what is happening they permanently forecast storms and heavy rains in their lives? They generally focus only on the things that are going wrong for them. If you happen to be a pessimistic person, remember that where you focus all your thoughts and energy, manifests in your life. Practice looking at the rainbows in your life instead of the storms.

"There is freedom waiting for you,
On the breezes of the sky,
And you ask, "What if I fall?"
Oh but my darling,
What if you fly?"
(Erin Hanson[62])

Summary

- Generally there are two types of people – those who have an internal locus of control and those who have an external locus of control. A locus of control is an individual's belief system and refers to the degree to which people believe that they have control over the outcome of events in their lives, as opposed to external forces beyond their control.

- If a person has an internal locus of control, they attribute success to their own efforts and abilities. A person who expects to succeed will be more motivated and more likely to learn. A person with an external locus of control, who attributes his or her success to luck or fate, will be less likely to make the effort needed to learn.

- Your locus of control can influence not only how you respond to the events that happen in your life, but also your motivation to take action.

- One's 'explanatory style', which is the way you explain things to yourself, is critical in determining whether you have a positive or negative mindset.

- People either focus on the circles of concern or circles of influence in their lives. When you place your attention on the circle of concern, you focus on events that you have no control over and become pessimistic. When you focus on the circle of influence, i.e. those things you can directly influence, you feel more in control and generally more optimistic.

Section 3

Managing Your Emotions

- Get off the anger rollercoaster
- Quit the blame game
- Embrace a state of forgiveness
- Let go of stress

This section looks at the importance of managing your emotions and not letting them stop you from being successful. There are many emotions that can hinder one's success. This section covers the common ones such as anger, blame, stress, anxiety and forgiveness.

Aiden knew he was the best financial accountant in the organisation; his work was impeccable. He had received great reviews on the quality of his reports and everyone sought his financial insight. Aiden had been in the same role for three years and he was ready to move into the role of Financial Manager. A vacancy recently arose and Aiden was convinced that he was going to get promoted. He had made it known that he was interested in the position and even bought new clothes in keeping with his hoped for higher status. Aiden was having a great week until one morning he opened his email and saw an announcement of a new Financial Manager. Aiden was shocked and confused by this – he thought they were still going to advertise the role. He stormed into his manager's office and threw the printed email announcement on his manager's desk. By now he was furious and he banged the table demanding an explanation. The manager calmly listened to Aiden's ranting and continued to feel good about the appointment he made. Whilst Aiden was technically a strong candidate he lacked emotional maturity, which was demonstrated by his behaviour.

In my role as a Group Talent manager, I have sat in on hundreds of talent discussions where potential candidates are reviewed for promotions. The one consistent development area that always comes up is people's lack of emotional maturity. Most employees are technically brilliant in their roles but emotionally struggle to deal effectively with other people. Their low emotional intelligence often sabotages their success, therefore managing one's emotions is paramount to being successful in one's life.

Imagine you are building a house and the land has huge rocks and trees. You need to first clear the terrain before you can start laying the foundation. Similarly, before you start designing an amazing life, you need to excavate the rocks and trees first, which are all those habits that will sabotage your success.

Kryptonite is the fictitious rock that renders Superman powerless when he is in the vicinity of it. We all have our own version of Kryptonite in our lives, which derails us from discovering our passion and attaining success in our lives. A similar concept to Kryptonite is referred to as an Achilles heel, which indicates a person's point of weakness. According to Greek mythology, Achilles' mother dipped him in the river Styx when he was an infant, holding onto him only by his heel. He became invulnerable where the waters touched him — that is, everywhere except the areas of his heel that were covered by her thumb and forefinger.[63]

Some of the common characteristics that plague many people are anger, resentment, blame, a lack of self-confidence, a fear of failure, resistance to change, entitlement, self-pity, laziness, arrogance, poor self-discipline, not identifying goals and not living according to values.

You need to be prepared to improve your life. You should have the ability to recognise when being okay is no longer good enough when others are thriving and being the champions in their lives. How many wealthy people do you know who are attractive, charismatic and dynamic? Ignore supermodels, sports stars and general movie actors. So not all rich people are attractive? How many super intelligent people are wealthy? Do you think that you are cleverer than most politicians?

The bottom line is that not only the cleverest, most beautiful, most knowledgeable people succeed. Darwin said, "It is not the strongest of the species that survives, nor the most intelligent that survives. It is the one that is most adaptable to change".[64] What you need to do is change the circumstances of your life by identifying your personal Kryptonite or Achilles heel, and learn the necessary coping skills to manage these emotions when necessary.

Lori Deschene offered a beautiful message about moving past your painful experiences: "Be the person who breaks the cycle. If you were judged, choose understanding. If you were rejected, choose acceptance. If you were shamed, choose compassion. Be the person you needed when you were hurting, not the person who hurt you. Vow to be better than what broke you — to heal instead of becoming bitter so you can act from your heart, not your pain."[65] We often carry emotional baggage that continues to haunt us; most of the time we allow our past to influence how we behave in the present.

Self-awareness is the first step in managing your emotions – you cannot change your emotions if you are not aware of them. Self-awareness is your ability to perceive your own emotions in the moment and understand your tendencies across situations. Secondly, to manage your emotions effectively you need to be able to direct your behaviour positively. For example, if someone unfairly criticises you, you should become aware of your emotion which may be irritation, and reflect on the best way to respond, which may be, "Thank you for the feedback".

The Russian philosopher, Peter Ouspensky, wrote in *Search of the Miraculous* that the four basic causes of negative emotions are justification, identification, inward considering and blame.

- Justification focuses on all the reasons that you feel you are justified or right about reacting the way you are. You repeat all the reasons you have to be angry.

- Identification is when you take something personally and have an attachment to the person or thing.

- Inward considering is where you become overly concerned with how people are treating you. If your self-esteem is not high you will be sensitive to the actions and reactions of others.

- Blame occurs when you react with defensiveness when criticised and often deflect the issue and blame someone else. When you blame you generate anger which is a destructive emotion. To dissolve these emotions you need to take responsibility for your actions.

The next time you respond with a negative emotion such as anger, ask yourself which of the above reasons are the cause for your reaction.

The two wolves[66]

There is a popular Cherokee story where an old man is explaining life to his grandson.
My son, there is a battle between two wolves inside us all.
One is evil. It is anger, jealousy, greed, resentment, inferiority, lies and ego. The other is good. It is joy, peace, love, hope, humility, kindness, empathy and truth.
The boy thought about it and asked,
Grandfather, which wolf wins?
The old man quietly replied, "The one you feed".

This story highlights that we always have choices in how we respond to a life event. What we focus on grows. When we blame others for things that go wrong in our life, we are feeding the bad wolf. We think other people are responsible for our actions. Have you heard the phrase, "He makes me angry" or "She really irritates me"? What you learnt from the previous chapter about changing your thinking is that your thoughts create an emotional response. You need to change your language to, "I made myself angry" or "I irritated myself". When you rephrase it, it seems bizarre. Why would you deliberately make yourself angry or irritated? It sounds illogical but in fact that is what we do every moment of our lives. We create our own emotional responses. "People are disturbed not by things, but by the views they take of them." (Epictetus[67])

Chapter 9

Get off the anger rollercoaster

I am so angry, I can SCREAM!
What is this coming out of my ears, IS THIS STEAM?
How dare he crush my spirit, what does he know?
I was bound for the stars, that's how far I can go!
I want to shake him until he shivers with fright.
I am so worked up, not going to sleep another wink tonight.

Wait a minute, I am not letting him invade my peace of mind,
I am going to breathe in slowly and try to unwind.
I will not let him rob me of my precious sleep,
I am going to forgive the ass, going to count some sheep...

Do you fume when someone cuts in front of you in a long queue? Does your blood pressure go sky high when your toddler throws a tantrum? Anger is a normal emotion and it is important to deal with it in a healthy way.

Anger is always perceived as a negative emotion in society, yet it is important to understand that in moderation it also serves a purpose in our lives. Anger is necessary from a self-preservation perspective. During the Stone Age, man used it to protect himself from wild animal attacks. Anger has some other benefits. It is believed that anger can be a motivating force by allowing us to push towards our goals. Have you ever had an experience when someone underestimated your potential? You get so angry and your first response is, "I will show them". By expressing anger appropriately, it also helps the other person know and understand that something is wrong, so a solution can be found. I would rather my daughter express her anger than for her to go through life carrying unhealthy baggage of things we could have easily resolved. Anger can also give us insight into our own selves by understanding our own values that have been compromised. When we get angry we need to understand the value that the situation is touching on. By expressing anger, it reduces physical violence as the emotion is released through speech. Have you ever noticed how angry people get placated as people are more willing to accommodate their requests? Think of a customer who calmly complains versus one who is creating a scene in front of other customers. The one who shouts the loudest often gets attention first. The point is that anger has its benefits when used appropriately in the correct context. Frequent anger that is erratic and uncontrollable is dysfunctional and leads to the need to seek retribution, however. This vengeance leads to more anger. Remember the quote by Gandhi who said, "An eye for an eye makes the whole world blind".

"You don't get frustrated because of events, you get frustrated because of your beliefs." (Albert Ellis[68])

Feelings of anger arise due to how we interpret and react to certain situations. Everyone has their own triggers for what makes them angry, but some common ones include situations in which we feel threatened, attacked, frustrated or powerless. When you are consistently experiencing anger, the emotion becomes a dysfunction and can prevent you from enjoying your life fully. Uncontrolled anger can have a detrimental effect on your health, your relationships and your career.

Ann Landers described this best when she said, "Hanging onto resentment is letting someone you despise live rent free in your head".[69] It is important to deal with anger in a healthy way; stop being angry with the world and stop blaming others for things that go wrong or people who have let you down. Remove yourself from unnecessary stress and tension. The Buddha is quoted as saying: "Holding on to anger is like grasping a hot coal with the intent of throwing it at someone else; you are the one who gets burned."[70] Be willing to let it go.

The mind uses three strategies to cope when processing large amounts of information, i.e. generalising, deleting or distorting. The mind generalises information by cataloguing and referencing it to previous information that we have stored. Deletion occurs when we select and store only the information that is perceived as important at that time. Distortion is when we change details around a situation, for example we tend to embellish certain details when we are describing something. When we require calmness, we need to remember that our mind is capable of generalising, deleting and distorting the facts, and our version of the truth may be just that, a version of the truth. How, then, can we get upset with someone else about an event that happened in the past? Both individuals' memories of that event will differ due to their unique perspectives.

We all experience anger at some point in our lives, however we can choose to give anger free rein in our minds which will create chaos, or we can effectively manage the force of the anger through different techniques. If you are able to regulate your emotions effectively, you will have better quality relationships with others.

Recipe for dealing with anger

RECIPE BOOK

Timing

Eleanor Roosevelt was a wise woman who said, "No one can make you feel inferior without your consent".[71] In this she was referring to the way we think about and internalise our situations that causes us to be angry. When someone upsets you, you may immediately want to retaliate with an equally abrasive comment (directly or indirectly) to their face, or in a text or email. "Speak when you are angry, and you will make the best speech you will ever regret." (Ambrose Bierce[72]) We need to realise that when we are extremely emotional, it is difficult for us to think logically;

you do not want to say something that you will regret later on. Take some time to cool down, and you will see more clearly and communicate more effectively. Breathe, take a walk, distract yourself to allow yourself time to regain your composure and perspective.

Exercise

Exercise can help to reduce the intensity of your anger. Try going for a run, a brisk walk or some other enjoyable exercise that helps you to reduce the anger that you are feeling.

Relaxation

Relaxation skills are great for dealing with anger. Deep breathing also helps to bring a sense of calmness. Imagine a calming scene or write your thoughts in a journal. I write poetry when I am angry as I get so caught up in coming up with rhymes, it diffuses my irritation.

The power of words

Your choice of words has power. By choosing your words it can sometimes alter the intensity of the feelings you are experiencing at that moment. Think about when you had an argument with someone and you chose to use the words "furious", "spitting mad", "so angry", "in a rage". How were you feeling? Now choose milder words to describe the same state such as "cross", "annoyed", "displeased". Suddenly the level of intensity has dropped. The words you choose in a disagreement can either fuel the fire or allow for expression of your feelings. Words have an energy and vibration which impacts the brain in different ways, as illustrated by the water crystal experiments by Dr. Emoto.

Visualisation

Sometimes people will say things to you that are awful and atrocious, so you need to first transform that overpowering rage into something that can be contained and then forgiven. When you are angry with someone you need to release the tenacious hold that they have on your mind so that you can work on removing the power of the impact.

One way of doing this is by closing your eyes and thinking of the person who is consistently doing something to make you intensely angry. How angry are you on a scale from 1 to 10? Do the exercise and then measure your level of irritation. This individual occupies space in your mind and has become the dominant thought in your head. In your perception, this person is a huge, overwhelming force in your mind. All you need to do to release this preoccupation in your mind is to change the image in your mind. Most people have their memories in colour, so you can change the image of the person to black and white. Suddenly the person seems less threatening. Next, change their voice so it is less powerful. You need to diminish the power that this person has over your mind. I usually change the person's voice to the squeaky voice of Donald Duck. I then reduce the image to size until they are small enough to fit into a Coca-Cola bottle. I close the lid. By doing this exercise I have disempowered them in my mind and reduced the intensity of anger I was feeling towards them. **Please note that this is not in any way to physically harm the person, but merely to minimise the power of them in your mind.**

Your imagination is one of the most powerful tools you have. I have often taken my frustrations and blown them up in my mind. Depending on your sensory perception there are different methods of getting rid of anger or frustration. Auditory people may want to spend more time changing the auditory messages, while visual people may want to spend more time scrambling the image in their mind.

This is a beautiful and powerful exercise from Louise Hay for dissolving resentment. The exercise is to sit quietly with closed eyes, allowing your mind and body to relax. Imagine sitting in a darkened theatre in the audience. In front of you is a small stage with the person you resent most. This person could be past or present, living or dead. When you see this person, clearly visualise good things happening to them. Imagine the person happy and smiling. Hold this image for a while and let it fade away. Next, imagine yourself on the stage happy and smiling and letting good things happen to you. If you can learn to release resentment and allow forgiveness in your heart, you can become a lighter and happier being.

summary

- We all have our own version of Kryptonite in the form of unhealthy emotions in our lives, which derails us from discovering our passion and attaining success in our lives.

- Self-awareness is the first step in managing your emotions. You cannot change your emotions if you are not aware of them. Self-awareness is your ability to perceive your own emotions in the moment and understand your tendencies across situations. Secondly, to manage your emotions effectively you need to be able to direct your behaviour positively.

- We always have choices on how we respond to life's events.

- It is important to understand that in moderation, anger serves a purpose in our lives.

- Everyone has their own triggers for what makes them angry, but some common ones include situations in which we feel threatened, attacked, frustrated or powerless. When you are consistently experiencing anger then this emotion becomes dysfunction and can prevent you from enjoying your life fully.

- When we require calmness, we need to remember that our mind is capable of generalising, deleting and distorting the facts, and that our version of the truth may be just that, a version of the truth.

- When you are angry with someone, you need to release the tenacious hold that they have on your mind so you can work on removing the power of the impact.

Chapter 10

Quit the blame game

There is a funny story that Zig Ziglar tells about the origin of blame.

> The "blame game" goes back to the beginning. God told Adam and Eve when He placed them in the Garden that they could have it all, except they were not to eat the fruit of the tree in the middle of the Garden.
>
> However, they ate the fruit of that tree and in the evening, as God walked in the Garden, He called for Adam and Adam responded, "Over here, Lord." Then God asked the question, "Adam, did you eat the fruit of the tree in the middle of the Garden?" God already knew the answer but He wanted Adam to respond. Adam, however, did the "manly thing" and replied, "Lord, let me tell you about that woman you gave me!" and that's where the ball started its long, unending roll. God then asked Eve if she had eaten the fruit, and Eve passed the ball along and said, "Lord, let me tell you about that snake!" And, of course, the snake didn't have a leg to stand on![73]

It is human nature to want to blame someone for something not going right in your life. When unfortunate events happen to you, how do you react? Do you find someone to blame? Or do you take responsibility for what is under your control? If you are like most people you will choose the blame option, because we are brought up to accept that blaming is a natural part of life. It starts out innocently as a response to a question about why something happened, and we become so comfortable in assigning a cause that we generalise this to all our relationships. It becomes normal in our everyday lives. When you blame you become stuck; it squanders your energy and prevents you from moving forward towards your goals

"We don't blame your shadow for the shape of your body. Just the same: Do not blame others for the shape of your experience." (Gillian Duce[74]) Sometimes acknowledging that we are at fault is a difficult pill to swallow; we are so used to pointing fingers at other people. We are quick to pass judgement on other people's mistakes and yet when our own are pointed out to us, we cringe with embarrassment and feel as if we are being ridiculed. We learn this behaviour as children and if it is not corrected as we are growing up, it can become a second skin that we are not even aware of. I saw this blame behaviour with my four year old, who blamed the nanny for her toys being scattered on the floor, her teddy bears being coloured with crayons, and playdough stuck on the carpet. She insisted that, "It is Theo, Mummy. I try to tell her but she doesn't listen". I replied that maybe we should find another nanny who does not draw on the teddy bears. Immediately my daughter smiled and confessed.

When I got married my friend gave me great advice; he said you can either be right or happy. I chose right, my husband chose happy. Since I was always right, it stands to reason that my poor husband was perceived to be the one at fault. I am not proud of this, but when I first got married I fell into the trap of blaming my spouse for everything that did not go right. In one of our disagreements I distinctly remember my husband saying, "I see you watering the blame tree again". At once I had an overwhelming image of a tree growing between us and pushing through the roof of our house. That image was enough to make me realise how unfair I was being. Over the years my behaviour has significantly improved and both of us take turns to be right, and both of us are happier.

Whenever I fall into bad habits, I can trust my husband to sweetly ask me if I am watering the blame tree. When he falls into the bad habit of blaming and starts to blame me, I start singing the chorus from the old pop song by Milli Vanilli, *Blame it on the rain*. It short circuits the blame and creates immediate awareness of the negative behaviour. I know people who have a forest of blame trees that they are watering each day.

Do you have a blame tree in your relationships that you are nurturing and growing?

Recipe to break the cycle of blaming

RECIPE BOOK

1. Be aware when you start to blame

Awareness is always the first step. It usually starts with, "It is not my fault..." People who blame others either tend to use absolute statements such as, "You are always letting me down" or "You *never* do your share of the work". Become more aware of how you talk to others; this will help you realise if you are blaming (or not). Try using 'I' statements instead of 'blaming you' statements. Also provide specific examples. For example, instead of saying, "You did not show up for my award ceremony", you could say, "I was disappointed that you could not attend my award ceremony. This was an important milestone in my life".

Most of the time we grow up in a culture of blaming, such that it becomes almost second nature to everything that we do. Try adding coins to an empty jar every time you blame. As you see the jar fill up, you will realise that blaming has become part of your behaviour. You need to acknowledge that this blaming attitude will slowly erode your relationships unless you change. I did the jar exercise and it is extremely humbling when you see the coins start to accumulate.

2. Thank the other person for the lesson

Wayne Dyer suggested the following: "When you are inclined to think that someone else is responsible for your circumstances, take an instant to say a prayer of thanks for the lesson."[75] He added that we should be thankful since it makes us aware that we are experiencing feelings and therefore we have the ability to choose our response.

3. Demonstrate compassion

Show compassion to the other person; focus on understanding them and try to understand their intent. Was it just a mistake? To err is human, to forgive is divine. Understand you also make similar mistakes and be prepared to empathise and understand. Always act with grace and kindness with others, even when you are aware that someone else was responsible for not doing what was promised.

Wherever you are, whenever you feel strong emotions stirring in you and you notice yourself feeling the need to "be right", silently recite the following words from the Prayer of Saint Francis: Where there is injury, [let me bring] pardon.[76]

4. Take ownership

"He who blames others has a long way to go on his journey. He who blames himself is halfway there. He who blames no one has arrived." (Chinese proverb[77])

When you blame others without taking accountability, you start to disempower yourself and give your power away. Have an internal locus of control and understand how your actions could have contributed to the situation. There is a statement in neurolinguistics programming that says, "The perceived meaning of your communication is the feedback that you get". You need to take responsibility in the situation. Did you communicate your expectations correctly?

This principle has helped me become a better communicator because once you take responsibility for your communication, you cannot blame others when that communication is not properly received and understood. Sometimes it may be the fault of the other person who could have been preoccupied and not fully present during the communication, however I have found that a lot of times it was my oversight.

Brian Tracy suggested that as soon as something goes wrong, you say to yourself, "I am responsible". This removes the tendency to blame or to get angry. Even if it is not your fault, it will remind you to respond in an appropriate way.[78]

5. Do not let your emotions take you hostage

Zig Ziglar said that when you go into gold mining, you do not go looking for the dirt.[79] Similarly, you need to go looking for the positive when interacting with people. Remember that the incident is just a trigger of other issues in your life. You often overreact because it reminds you of another similar incident. It is important to look at each incident in isolation rather than thread it to all other situations and create a mountain out of what was merely a molehill. It always helps to look at situations through a different perspective, so take time to reflect on other possibilities.

Self-reflection

Stop and self-reflect before you start saying things you might regret later on; it is better to take ownership than to blame others. Focus on self-reflection and understand what lesson was learnt. If you focus on blaming you lose the lesson and then will be bound to repeat it in the future.

Every night before you go to sleep, review how you reacted to different situations and grade your behaviour. Did you get an A grade for taking full accountability for your actions, or did you fail because you were obsessed with blaming others? Remember to always ask yourself what you can learn from a lesson, rather than, "Why did that person do this to me?" When you get stuck in the game of blame, it is difficult to unglue yourself.

You need to be able to acknowledge your mistakes, make amends by correcting them, and apologise sincerely. When you blame, it says more about your behaviour than the other person. People who live in glass houses should not throw stones. We all make mistakes and we grow through the experience. Be willing to let certain things go without allocating blame.

Summary

- Most of the time we grow up in a culture of blaming, such that it becomes almost second nature to us.

- Be aware when you are starting to blame.

- As soon as something goes wrong, say to yourself, "I am responsible". This removes the tendency to blame or to get angry.

- You need to be able to acknowledge your mistakes, make amends by correcting them, and apologise sincerely.

- Try creating awareness for yourself about this by counting how many times a day you have blamed others.

- Always act with grace and kindness towards others, even when you are aware that someone else was responsible for not doing what was promised.

- When you blame others without taking accountability, you start to disempower yourself and give your power away.

Chapter 11

Forgiveness

Our Father, who art in heaven, hallowed be thy Name, thy kingdom come, thy will be done, on earth as it is in heaven. Give us this day our daily bread. **And forgive us our trespasses, as we forgive those who trespass against us.** *And lead us not into temptation, but deliver us from evil. For thine is the kingdom, and the power, and the glory, for ever and ever. Amen.*[80]

I remember saying this prayer in assembly during my school years. I recited it without really reflecting and absorbing the significance of the words. It was only years later that I realised what a powerful prayer it is. There are various benefits to forgiveness. It allows us to become emotionally healthier by reducing unhealthy emotions such as anger and frustration, which impact on our health in the long-term. Forgiveness provides us with a sense of freedom. Nelson Mandela explained, "As I walked outside the door towards the gate that would lead to my freedom, I knew that if I didn't leave my bitterness and hatred behind, I would still be in prison".[81] This powerful statement illustrates the debilitating effect that anger and resentment can have on our lives if we cannot learn to forgive. Mandela, who spent 27 years in prison, was able to transcend his anger into forgiveness and forgave and reconciled with his opponents. It was his ability to open his heart to forgiveness and compassion that set him apart as an exemplary leader and an authentic human being.

When you can forgive, it makes you feel that you have grown as a person in character, because you have overcome your own anger and chosen a higher path. Forgiveness is a worthy virtue that enables others to learn from your example. As Mandela said, "Courageous people do not fear forgiving, for the sake of peace".[82] We contribute our individual energy and optimism to the collective society in which we live. If we transform our negative energy from anger, resentment and revenge to forgiveness, the people we interact with will benefit. Another Mandela quote states that, "Forgiveness liberates the soul. It removes fear. That is why it is such a powerful weapon".[83]

"To forgive is to set a prisoner free and discover that the prisoner was you."
(Louise B. Smedes)[84]

Sometimes we are not aware that we are harbouring negative feelings towards someone. We may rationally think that whatever transpired was just 'one of those things', and that you were unlucky. You may lightly brush it off, only to realise that deep inside you are hurt and resentful of the situation or person. The easiest way is to dissolve these ill feelings before they start creating illness within you.

Sometimes someone will disappoint you. It may be a life partner or a child. What makes it especially cruel is that you never expected it. How do you forgive and move on? We all carry different levels of hurt and disappointment within us that have become holes in us that are seeping our life force. We cannot understand why we are so drained and angry with the world, because we fail to look within and actually realise that we need to be healed. The anger we feel towards others and towards the world is the same anger that becomes toxic within us.

How do we learn to forgive when we want to hold onto the injustices of the past? Often we are not ready to forgive, but the longer we take with this process the more drained and bitter we become. Forgiveness does not diminish the severity of the deed or justify it, but it allows you to let it go. Forgiveness is really more about our relationship with ourselves than the person or thing we are forgiving. "The truth is, unless you let go, unless you forgive yourself, unless you forgive the situation, unless you realize that the situation is over, you cannot move forward." (Steve Maraboli[85])

Do not live in the past – be present

When we find it difficult to forgive, it is often because we are not living in the present. Instead we assign more importance to the past, wasting a good portion of our energy and attention lamenting the good old days that are gone forever. When we keep looking in the review mirror of our life, we are unable to move forward.

Dealing with life's challenges in a creative way

We need to understand that our brain is the director of our lives and, like a movie script, you can change the direction of how your life plays out. It is within your power to rewrite your own script and steer your life in a different direction, you just need to be able to take the basic rules that your mind uses and use them to your advantage. You can change your memories and consequently change your emotions.

Malachy McCourt once said, "Resentment is like taking poison and waiting for the other person to die".[86] In addition to lower mortality rates, forgiveness is linked with better immune system functioning, lower cholesterol, lower blood pressure and a reduced risk of heart problems. Forgiveness is associated with fewer negative feelings (anxiety and depression), higher self-esteem, more feelings of control and freedom, an increased ability to cope with stress and trauma, finding meaning in suffering, and increased feelings of closeness to God and others.[87]

People with greater exposure to stress over their lifetimes have worse mental and physical health, but researchers have also discovered that if people are highly forgiving of both themselves and others, that characteristic alone virtually eliminates the connection between stress and mental illness. Therefore people who are able to forgive have better levels of mental health.

Recipe for forgiveness

RECIPE BOOK

Sometimes we may inflict pain on others and we need to be able to ask for forgiveness for our actions and apologise to the other person. It is important to firstly apologise by saying that you are sorry. Next you need to acknowledge and accept blame by admitting it was your fault. Lastly ask the question – what can I do to make it right? This is the most important part. Apologising alone is not sufficient; making amends is just as important.

I did the following exercise years ago with a healing specialist. I was going through a bad patch and I was feeling very victimised by my manager. I needed to release the negative emotions I was experiencing that were draining my energy.

Reflect on how you would rate the level of charge that you have towards a person on a scale from 1-10.

Now say, "It is an interesting point of view, that I feel anger and resentment towards _____ for doing _____" at least five times. Now examine what level of anger you feel. Continue this exercise until it is 0, and then do the forgiveness exercise.

"Sit quietly with your eyes closed and say, "The person I need to forgive is _____ and I forgive you for _____".

Do this over and over. You may have many things to forgive or maybe only one or two. If you have a partner, let them say to you, "Thank you, I set you free now". If you do not, then imagine the person you are forgiving saying it to you. Do this for at least five or ten minutes.

"Search your heart for the injustices you still carry. Then let them go." (Louise Hay)

All of us carry figurative baggage around for years. This baggage largely comprises grudges, resentment, anger and imagined slights (those acts we have never confronted people about but have never forgiven them for). Imagined slights are the funniest things because we go through our lives furious with others, expending much time and energy on our vendetta, only to realise later on that the person is unaware and is going through life fully engaged whilst we become bitter and jaded.

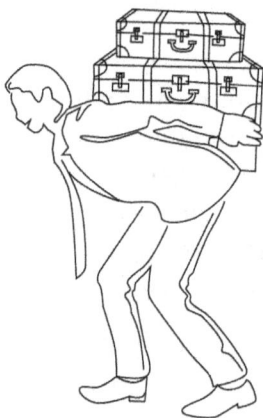

Years ago I attended a transformational workshop which taught me a great technique when confronting people around issues. You share with the other person what makes them great and then share the behaviour that stops them from greatness. I have found over the years that this simple conversation helps to focus on courageous conversations. For example you could say to a colleague, "What really makes you great is your willingness to share information/your commitment to hard work. However I really think that your willingness to spread rumours without validating information is stopping you from true greatness. Please understand the impact this is having on your brand and that others are not going to trust you easily".

Brian Tracy, in his book *Change Your Thinking, Change Your Life*, described four groups of people that must be forgiven.[88] Firstly, you must forgive your parents, living or dead, for every mistake, imagined or real, that they made whilst they were bringing you up. Tracy says that by not forgiving your parents, you remain forever a child and miss out on the chance to grow up and be a fully functioning adult. The second group of people includes those from your close relationships that did not work out. Accept that you were partially responsible for whatever happened in the relationship. He suggests you say, "I am responsible", and then forgive the other person with the words, "I forgive him/her for everything and I wish him/her well". Another idea is to write a letter of forgiveness that consists of three parts. First you say, "I forgive you for everything you ever did that hurt me". Second, you write a list of every single thing that you are still angry about. Third you end the letter with the words, "I wish you well". Then post the letter. Do not worry about how the other person reacts, as the goal is to free yourself. The third group you need to forgive is everyone else in your life who has ever hurt you in any way. Wipe each person out of your mind by saying, "I forgive him/her for everything, and I wish him/her well". The final person you need to forgive is yourself. Just say, "I forgive myself for every mistake I ever have made. I am a thoroughly good person and I am going to have a wonderful future".[89]

I will end with my favourite quote on forgiveness, which is a beautiful description of forgiveness.

"Forgiveness is the fragrance the violet sheds on the heel that has crushed it."
(George Roemisch)[90]

Summary

- There are various benefits to forgiveness.

- Forgiveness allows one to become emotionally healthier by reducing unhealthy emotions such as anger and frustration, which impact on one's health in the long-term.

- Forgiveness provides you with a sense of freedom.

- Forgiveness makes you feel that you have grown as a person in character, because you have overcome your own anger and chosen a higher path.

- People who are able to forgive have better levels of mental health.

- All of us carry figurative baggage around for years. This baggage is largely comprised of grudges, resentment, anger and imagined slights. Only when we are able to forgive will we feel lighter.

Chapter 12

Letting go of stress

Piglet: Supposing a tree fell down, when we were underneath it?
Pooh: Supposing it didn't. (A.A. Milne[91])

Wayne Dyer said, "It makes no sense to worry about things you have no control over because there's nothing you can do about them, and why worry about things you do not control? The activity of worrying keeps you immobilized".[92] Do not let the trivial things bother you; in the larger scheme of things they do not matter. Imagine you are on your death bed and you have enough energy for a last few sentences. What would they be? My boss did not acknowledge my efforts at work? Taxi drivers always cut in front of me in traffic? It sounds so ridiculous. A Cherokee proverb states, "Don't let yesterday use too much of today".

Manage these emotions to reduce stress…

- Anger – Let it go.
- Resentment and blame – Reframe the victim mentality and then learn to forgive; find other ways you triumphed.
- Lack of self-confidence – Focus on what you do well.
- Regret – Shift your energy from what went wrong to the future possibilities.
- Fear of failure – Take the opportunity to fly.
- Resistance to change – Focus on the benefits of change.
- Believing that you are not good enough – Reframe to thinking you are the best you can be.
- Entitlement – The world owes you nothing.
- Self-pity – Channel your energy to practice skills that can make you more confident.
- Laziness – Create a mindset of self-discipline. Build in penalties for not adhering to tasks.
- Arrogance – Demonstrate humility; people do not care how much you know until they know how much you care.

When you are in a constant state of anxiety, you cannot focus on anything else; one thing consumes your full attention and you feel out of control and helpless. Your heart is pumping. You feel fear. You do not want anyone to see anything out of the ordinary. You cannot sleep but you desperately want to so that your mind can rest. You lose your appetite and you worry. The same tape is playing over and over in your head. You want it to be finished. You pray for boredom and you look forward to a daily, mundane routine. You are not eating. You do not want to share this secret with anyone. You are not present. Your thoughts wander and you seem distracted to others. It seems like everything has lost meaning. You cannot remember when last you laughed. You need to find joy in something

Often it seems that life colludes to create circumstances that bring our lives into never-ending tumult. We feel bruised by the collective circumstances and become so obsessed with our pain that we cannot see any hope of a positive outcome. Mihaly Csikszentmihalyi spoke of human beings not being able to process more than 110 bytes of information in a second.[93] When we are stressed it consumes us, and just when we think we see light at the end of the tunnel, it becomes a mirage. We feel lost and out of control. Many of us have experienced this feeling at some point in our lives – in our personal relationships, finances, work lives, businesses or spiritual lives. When we are in a state of crisis it is difficult to see any glimmer of hope.

> Thomas cowered in fear at the corner of his bed. His father was in one of his drunken rages. He covered his head and tried to make himself as small as possible. He was grateful that his mother was working a night shift and was safe from the abuse. Thomas knew that to survive, he needed to stay out of the way and not say anything to make his father angrier than he already was. He repeated the prayer his mother taught him and remembered what his big sister had said before she left home. "Be brave, Thomas. Deep inside you there is a special place that he can never touch. It belongs to you. When he hurls insults at you, remember his words cannot get to the special place within you. So take care of that special place. When you treat yourself with respect and stay strong knowing you are special." His sister gave him a little angel pendant that he wore around his neck. As he touched the pendant, he remembered his sister and her words of wisdom. As his father shouted and banged the furniture, Thomas knew he could withhold the storm, because his father could never hurt his special space.

Imagine that in your mind there is a safe deposit box that holds your willpower. No one knows the combination, only you. No matter what happens to you, no one can get into your safety deposit box without you giving them the combination to your lock. In the safety deposit box is also the switch to controlling the vibrancy of your inner flame. Nothing can get to your inner safety box against your will.

Sometimes it seems that people carry heavy bags of problems, but make themselves lighter by offloading these onto your lap. You receive a bag of rocks that weigh you down and as you look up they are already turning away in a cloud of dust. Once the dust settles you take these rocks and start to fill your bag and carry it on your back. You become so weighed down by these rocks that you forget to look for the little diamond within that was covered up by the dust of the rocks. You should be picking up the diamonds and filling your pocket and letting the rest of the rocks slide to the ground. The only thing you will be carrying are the precious diamonds, which in this analogy refer to the life lessons that you are taking with you. In reality, what we do is allow people to dump their rocks on us and meekly start to add these to the rocks we have already accumulated in our lives.

We all try to achieve so much in all areas of our lives. It is exhausting and when we are trying to do too much, we are going to drop the ball on something. Earlier this year I was trying, as usual, to do too many things. Whilst I was writing this book during my evenings and weekends, I had a full time job during the day and still had my responsibilities as a wife and mother. As a result I neglected my garden, which was my responsibility. It gave me a sense of calmness to water and tend to my plants. I was so busy that I forgot and when I next looked, most of my beautiful plants were dried. I looked at my garden with regret; I had no one to blame except myself. I could have delegated this responsibility but instead I did not. The lesson for me was that we should never allow our responsibilities to consume us to the extent that we neglect our priorities. I have friends who are guilty of the same offense but in different areas of their lives. My acquaintance is a workaholic and neglects her marriage. When I say to her, "Do you realise what you are doing?", she nods and then continues her behaviour. It is her lesson to learn and she will learn it when the time is right.

Recipe for letting go of stress

RECIPE BOOK

As long as you are breathing, and there is a fragile glow of your energy, there is hope to resuscitate this glow into a glorious manifestation of a beautiful, robust life force flame. All you need are the right tools to bring this light into full force. Here are some different options:

- Count your blessings every evening. Focus with gratitude on the things that are going well in your life. Write three things to be grateful for. This will remind you that even though some things are not going well, there are other areas of your life that are bright.

- Picture yourself as a prism and allow the light from any area of your life to flow into you, fragmenting into different colours.

- Focus on laughter and spend time with people who make you laugh. Laughter is a great stress reliever.

- Sometimes in our minds we take our challenges and create Hollywood feature films with full scripts and special effects that would rival any Steven Spielberg blockbuster. However, when we start to talk about our problems we realise that they are often three minute commercials that are as interesting as an advertisement for washing powder.

- When we speak to others, we invite a different perspective about our issues. Share your experiences with someone you can trust. Some people share their problem over and over with other people and each time they do so, in their mind it becomes less severe and has less of a hold over them. There could be solutions we would never think of because we are spending the total attention of 110 bits of data on our problem.

- Take a 15 minute break and do something else like take a walk or make yourself a cup of tea. When you feel calmer, take your anxiety list and start to brainstorm ideas to deal with anxiety. You can also do this exercise with someone you trust like your life partner or friend. Once you feel you have a list of possible ideas, start looking at the most feasible ideas to address your anxiety. Next, put a timeline in place for addressing these fears.

Alternate nostril breathing

This is a technique I learnt in yoga which has helped me in times of stress to clear my mind, calm my anxiety and focus on my breathing. What I found is that I am so focused on my breathing that all other stress disappears. Alternate nostril breathing is a yogic breath control practice. In Sanskrit, it is known as nadi shodhana pranayama. This translates as "subtle energy clearing breathing technique".[94]

Alternate nostril breathing helps balance both hemispheres of your brain, which helps you to calm your thinking and be able to rest and relax much more easily. I once read that Hillary Clinton used alternate nostril breathing after her loss of the 2018 United States presidential election to manage stress and anxiety.

Alternate nostril breathing may be a useful method to help you lower your heart rate, which can help to promote cardiovascular health. If you feel any adverse effects, such as shortness of breath, while doing the breathing technique, you should stop the practice immediately. This includes feeling lightheaded, dizzy or nauseous. If you find that the breathing is bringing up feelings of agitation or that it triggers any mental or physical symptoms, you should stop the practice. Alternate nostril breathing is best done on an empty stomach. Do not practice alternate nostril breathing if you are sick or congested.

Next time you find yourself doing too many things at once, or you sense panic or anxiety begin to rise, move through a few rounds of alternate nostril breathing. It is a great way to hit the reset button for your mental state.

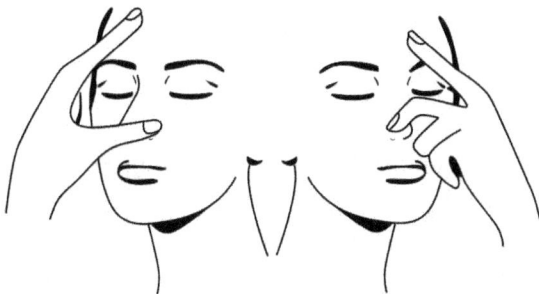

ALTERNATIVE NOSTRIL EXERCISE

1. Sit comfortably, making sure your spine is straight.

2. Bring your right hand just in front of your face.

3. With your right hand, bring your pointer finger and middle finger to rest between your eyebrows, lightly using them as an anchor. Take your thumb and ring finger and place them either side of your nostrils.

4. Close your eyes and take a deep breath in and out through your nose.

5. Close your right nostril with your right thumb. Inhale through your left nostril slowly and steadily.

6. Close your left nostril with your ring finger so both nostrils are held closed; retain your breath at the top of the inhale for a brief pause.

7. Open your right nostril and release your breath slowly through the right side; pause briefly at the bottom of the exhale.

8. Inhale through your right side slowly.

9. Hold both nostrils closed (with ring finger and thumb).

10. Open your left nostril and release your breath slowly through the left side. Pause briefly at the bottom.

11. Continue to practice this exercise until you can comfortably do it for five minutes at a time.

Steps 5-9 represent one complete cycle of alternate nostril breathing. If you are moving through the sequence slowly, one cycle should take you about 30-40 seconds. Move through 5-10 cycles when you are feeling stressed, anxious, or in need of a reset button.

Tip: Consistency is helpful, so try to match the length of your inhales, pauses and exhales. For example, you can start to inhale for a count of five, hold for five, exhale for five, and hold for five. You can slowly increase your count as you refine your practice.

At a time of intense stress, you need to build your stores of inner strength and confidence. For me this involved learning a new self defence skill. I am still a novice, but what it gave me was psychological preparedness. I would still be terrified if something happened, but the simple rules I was taught will act as a buffer. Similarly, there may be times when you will experience deep emotional stress that require you to depend on other people.

Financially, you may require money for unplanned events that place a huge financial strain on your resources. If you continuously and consistently save for a rainy day, you will be more prepared to deal with these events.

If you have neglected your health and not exercised or eaten healthy foods, you will weaken your body. If you suddenly become seriously ill, your health will quickly deteriorate, which is why it is important to create healthy habits in your life.

I was so stressed trying to complete this book according to my publisher's deadlines, on top of a full time job that I was committed to, a family who needed my attention, and a body that was taking strain, that I felt myself spinning out of control. Then, voilà, it hit me that the sweetness in my life had disappeared. I was filled with resentment; I needed to rediscover balance, but more importantly, joy. My daughter's consistent request to come and play with her suddenly made me realise that that was what I needed most. I needed to play and be in the moment. You forget that to experience joy you need to focus on the present. The one hour of play was enough to boost my inner battery. Like a car battery that runs flat, there is sometimes a need for an external force that can charge your inner battery.

Anxiety visualisation

Take all your confused and fearful feelings and draw them from your body into a ball of anxiety in front of you. Take this ball of anxiety and imagine throwing it into an active volcano. In your mind, follow it as you throw it into the mouth of the volcano. As it lands you hear a huge explosion and see lava ash being spat out. Keep doing this exercise in your mind as you feel yourself collecting every bit of anxiety from all parts of your body. Most people feel anxiety in the pit of their stomachs, but other people keep it in their necks or shoulders. Once you feel you have destroyed all your anxiety, take in some deep breaths and imagine with each breath that there is a ball of light entering your body and then dissolving as soon as it reaches your stomach. This light fills all the empty spaces that the anxiety once filled.

Positive self-talk

Give yourself positive feedback, such as: "Everything is going to be okay. You are safe. You are loved. Everything is going to be alright. You have a plan." Sometimes you feel anxiety when you feel out of control, so just coming up with a plan or talking to someone else about your plan reduces the anxiety in you.

Take control of your anxiety

Often you feel that you are spinning out of control; there are so many demands made on you that you feel overwhelmed and paralysed with fear. Steve Maraboli said, "Incredible change happens in your life when you decide to take control of what you do have power over instead of craving control over what you don't".[95] When you feel like this, the first thing to do is to make a list of your anxieties. Write down exactly the things that are making you feel helpless. This allows you to release some of the mental stress you were exerting on reviewing these problems over and over in your head.

There are many creative ways that people use to deal with stress. The actress Anne Hathaway is reported to set a countdown timer on her phone. She gives herself a specific time to write down all her anxieties, tears the page out of the book, lights a candle and burns the page. She sees all her anxiety go up in smoke.[96]

Sometimes there may be things that are outside your control and nothing you can do is going to change the outcome. You work yourself into a frenzy over things that you have absolute no control over. At this time, it is important to remember the serenity prayer.

"God, grant me the serenity to accept the things I cannot change, courage to change the things I can, and wisdom to know the difference." (Reinhold Niebuhr[97])

summary

- When we are stressed it consumes us. Many of us have experienced this feeling at some point in our lives – in our personal relationships, our finances, our work lives, our business, and our spiritual lives.

- Sometimes in our minds we take our challenges and create Hollywood feature films with full scripts and special effects that would rival any Steven Spielberg blockbuster, however when we start to talk about our problems, we realise that they are more like a three minute commercial that are as interesting as an advertisement for washing powder.

- Alternate nostril breathing is a yogic breath control practice that can assist with managing stress.

- When we find it difficult to forgive, it is often because we are not living in the present, and instead, we assign more importance to the past.

- There are many way to manage one's feelings of anxiety.

Section 4

Optimise Your Energy

- Nourish and sustain
- Be fit as a fiddle
- Sleep like a baby
- Mindfulness and play

"People often complain about lack of time when lack of direction is the real problem." (Zig Ziglar[98])

We all have the same amount of time each day, yet our choices determine how much of it we use in a fulfilling way. The reality is that we are never going to get extra time each day, so the only thing we can do is identify what we spend our time on. Most people who have 8 to 5 jobs cannot change this as it is part of their employment contract, which stipulates working time and work duties required. However, it is in our free time that we can design our time more effectively. The choices we make determine whether we are spending our time in a fulfilling and purposeful way. What I have learnt is that you cannot get more time in the day. This is fixed. The only thing you can do is change your energy levels so that you feel as if you have more time in the day.

We also need to use our time in a more enterprising way. Anne Dillard explained, "How we spend our days, is, of course, how we spend our lives".[99] I stopped watching television ten years ago. When I tell people I do not watch television, they look at me strangely, but it is a choice I made to live a fulfilling life. I grew up watching television as part of my daily routine; I was totally addicted to watching movies every evening right through university. My television became my companion when I could not sleep at night.

I was working full time when I did my master's degree, which was very intense. I could not study at night and still make time for television, so I slowly weaned myself off it. I still watch movies now and again, but it is once in a while. This is an easy habit to maintain as my husband also does not watch television. I do have a television that is only connected when my mother comes to visit. Since I have my evenings free, I have time to do other tasks like spending quality time with my family, reading, writing and learning. One's perception of time is a subjective experience. Research found that when people are enjoying the tasks they are doing they feel as if time goes quickly and the converse is also true; if you feel that you are not enjoying something, then the perception is that it takes longer for time to pass.

Imagine you are a cell phone. What percentage is your battery presently charged at? I always use this analogy to quantify my level of exhaustion. I used to say to my husband that I was so tired I was only 20% charged. This 20% mark was not improving no matter what I did. I had suffered from tiredness before, but this feeling was more enduring. I started to research and learn and changed my routine with new habits that increased my battery life to 80%.

What I learnt whilst focusing on improving my energy was that the management of one's emotions is not limited to psychology – there are other ways to manage your emotions such as nutrition, exercise and even breathing. By eating the correct foods you can be happier in your life; by doing some exercises like yoga and deep breathing you can reduce your stress levels. It is important to look holistically when looking at improving your energy levels. You have to look at your health, your eating habits, your sleep patterns, your stress levels and your physical fitness. Josh Billings' words are wise: "Health is like MONEY, we never have a true idea of its value until we LOSE IT."[100]

In this section I am going to share some of the things I do in my life to charge my battery. We never think about working on our energy level; we accept that it is the norm. I used to have that limiting mindset until I relooked at my life and the choices I was making.

The information that I share is based on my experience, so I encourage you to read more about these areas. Wayne Fields said it best when he described the six best doctors as sunshine, water, rest, air, exercise, and diet.[101]

Chapter 13

Nourish and sustain

"The food you eat can either be the safest and most powerful form of medicine... or the slowest form of poison." (Ann Wigmore[102])

Louise Hay provided great advice for staying away from processed and junk food. "If it grows, eat it. If it doesn't grow, don't eat it."[103]

"I am not feeling so great", I confided to my husband after eating a waffle with ice cream. "Really?", responded my husband sarcastically, rolling his eyes. "I have watched you eat absolute junk food in the last week and you wonder why you are not feeling so great." "Self-inflicted misery I have no time for", he added. I was silent. "What Ash, nothing to say?", he asked. I had no witty response. Probably as the large amount of sugar had resulted in brain fog. He was absolutely correct. Alas, I was my own saboteur.

Just like we develop our beliefs by listening and watching other people, similarly, our eating patterns are formed early in our childhood. The foods we grow up eating we often associate with the norm. I grew up in a traditional Indian family, so whilst we ate other types of foods, our regular meal was curry and rice. A salad was usually an accompaniment and never the main meal. My mother is an amazing cook so eating traditional Indian foods was absolutely delicious. It was only when I moved out and had to cook for myself that I started exploring other foods. Food not only has the capacity to affect our energy, sleep, skin, body, shape and size, but also our mood. Food can affect our energy levels and eating the wrong foods can drastically hinder our overall wellbeing.

Serotonin is a chemical produced in the body which is often referred to as the happy chemical. Serotonin is produced in your gut, so it makes sense that when your gut is out of balance it is going to affect your mood. I recently listened to an interview with the Hollywood actress, Charlize Theron, speaking about how much weight she had to put on for a movie role. She achieved this by eating an excessive amount of potato crisps. She said that she had never experienced depression before, but all of the junk food had a negative effect on her mood. This becomes a vicious cycle;

we are sad or disappointed so we look for comfort food that makes us feel better, but that is usually junk food which messes with our digestion and makes us feel far worse, so we eat more junk food to improve our mood. There are numerous research topics that talk about how the imbalance in your microbiome contributes to a host of illnesses such as a leaky gut and IBS, amongst others.

Just like a car which takes a specific fuel, or a tyre that requires the correct amount of pressure, your body requires specific food. Food is the material that feeds your life energy. What you feed your body either makes you flourish or makes you sick. The exception is some diseases that are genetically inherited or that are contagious. Even when people are extremely ill, nutrition plays a critical role in bringing the body back to a state of health. In my experience, after a huge operation, eating just hospital food is not sufficient to replace the nutrients the body has lost. I have often made a green soup for people who have gone through a long illness. The spinach, baby marrow, broccoli and garlic helps to boost the immune system. Sometimes medical science needs a gentle boost. The next time you feel that you have overindulged in too much rich food, try this soup to bring your body back into balance.

Nutritious green soup

RECIPE BOOK

Ingredients

6 big baby marrows
1 pack broccoli
5 big leaves of spinach
2 cloves of garlic
1/2 big onion
500ml water mixed with vegetable stock
Coconut oil
Salt and pepper to season

Method

Add 1 tablespoon coconut oil to fry the chopped onion. When onions are brown, add chopped garlic. Add the broccoli to the pot for 5 minutes and then remove the broccoli. (You do not want to kill nutrients by overcooking it.) Add the baby marrow to the pot. When it is almost cooked, add the chopped spinach (remove the stalks and use the leaves only). Add the vegetable stock to the marrow and spinach. When the baby marrow is cooked, add the broccoli for a few minutes. Blitz the soup with a blender until smooth. Add water if too thick. Season with salt and pepper.

I have an autoimmune condition related to my thyroid which I have struggled with for the last 15 years. Some of the symptoms include weight gain, a slower metabolism, extreme fatigue, insulin resistance and hormonal imbalance. There were two incidents that happened within a week of each other when my daughter was three years old that made me realise that I needed to address my underactive thyroid. The first occurred when I got home one afternoon and my daughter rushed to the door to greet me. She then turned and shouted to the helper, "Theo, the fat lady is home". What wonderful, innocent and honest feedback, and a wakeup call that I needed to take my health more seriously.

A week later I was running late when I was getting my daughter ready for school and she was not co-operating. I started to get worked up and became impatient with her. It was not the proudest moment in my life. I shouted at her and I said, "Clearly this relationship is not working out, you need to find another mummy and I need to find another daughter". As soon as I said the words I felt horrible. I am generally an even tempered person and I do not get angry easily. Fortunately my daughter was not paying attention to me. I immediately calmed down and I realised that I needed to do something to address my hormonal imbalance.

I was referred to a naturopath for my thyroid problem, who immediately placed me on a new eating plan. I was so determined to manage my condition that for six months I committed to the eating plan. In those six months, for the first time in years I was able to lose weight, but what was especially interesting is that I also had a huge amount of sustainable energy. I was exercising, dancing and doing yoga in addition to other extra activities I was involved in, as well as being focused on my job.

I had given up sugar, gluten, dairy and caffeine and focused on eating plenty of raw food in the form of salads. The naturopath also recommended drinking at least two litres of water per day to stay hydrated, however she was very prescriptive on when I should drink water; she suggested that I drink water at least two and a half hours after I eat. Now, when you are brought up in a culture to have a sandwich with coffee or tea and cake, breaking this habit can be difficult. When you walk into a restaurant the first thing the waiter asks is if can he bring you something to drink whilst you are looking at the menu. The rationale behind this is that when we drink liquids whilst we are eating we are diluting our digestive juices, thereby slowing down digestion. The digestive juices in the stomach are acidic so that they can break down food particles. Research shows that sipping a little water during meals is not a cause for concern, but drinking a glass or two may interfere with digestion. It is best to drink fluids half an hour before and two hours after meals, as this helps in the absorption of nutrients. It is okay to drink a little water if you are taking medication. Another suggestion is to eat fruit, but always half an hour before a main meal as fruit digests easier than meat. I was advised to chew my food properly so that it allows my brain sufficient time to send a message to my stomach that food is on its way and that the digestive juices must be ready. Before I went on this diet I used to have smoothies for breakfast. My smoothie usually consisted of spinach or kale, apple, carrot, blueberries or strawberries, cinnamon powder and other powders such as maca, turmeric and cayenne, depending on my mood. I was so proud of my healthy smoothie that I was quite miffed when my naturopath suggested that smoothies are for old or invalid people who struggle to digest food. She went on to explain that since the smoothie is already blended, it goes straight through your digestive system without giving your stomach an opportunity to properly absorb the nutrients.

I share this story with you because I want you to understand how sometimes we take for granted the eating habits we have as the norm. Since everyone is doing it, we do not interrogate whether it is the correct approach for our bodies. The new eating approach challenged my traditional belief system. I was so fascinated by this new approach that I spent days researching the validity of all these suggestions.

The following information is what I learnt. Hopefully you will be inspired to incorporate some of these ideas into your eating plan.

Improving digestion

If you want to optimise your energy, improving your digestion can assist in this process. We need to have a basic understanding of digestion since we will be using our bodies for the rest of our lives. Would it not be great to understand how it works? Digestion is the process of breaking down food so that we can absorb and utilise it for energy and maintain life. I have kept the explanation simple so that you understand why improving your digestion is important. Chewing your food is important to help the digestive process, as if food is properly chewed less work is required to break it down further. The chewing action also alerts your stomach that food is on its way. The hormones in your saliva are able to start digesting some foods.

Most of us are so busy that we are not mindful about eating. We eat dinner in front of the television or whilst working on our computers, so we do not spend time properly chewing our food. Chewing helps us to become more mindful as we taste the food when we chew. A dietician once told me to chew my food 30 to 40 times before I swallow. I am not even close to that number, but I have improved the number of times I chew. I also stopped eating my lunch whilst I work so that I can be more mindful of the experience.

Just as it is important to eat the right foods to help our digestion, it is important that we eat the correct portion sizes. Your stomach is usually the size of your closed fist without food in it. When you eat large meals and take a second helping of food, your stomach has to stretch to accommodate it. One of the ancient practices in Japan is Hara hachi bu, which refers to eating only two thirds of what you wanted to eat.[104] This can be achieved by eating off smaller plates or skipping dessert. Food usually sits for 30 minutes in the stomach to allow digestive juices to break it down. Have you ever noticed when you are on a diet that you do not consume as much food because your stomach usually reduces to its original size? When you eat carbohydrates such as rice, pasta, potatoes and bread it takes about 20 minutes for your brain to be notified that you are eating, whilst when you eat fats such as olive oil or avocados and proteins such nuts and meat, the brain is usually notified within five minutes of us eating. That is why it is important to include fats and protein with each meal so that you feel fuller.

Eat the correct food combinations

Sometimes when we eat we feel bloated, even though in our minds we had a highly nutritious meal. This can be due to the combinations of the food that we are consuming. Oils and other foods rich in fats such as avocado can be eaten with a meat-based meal or vegetable-based meal, however one should not eat any meat such as beef, chicken, lamb, or fish with a starch such as potatoes, pasta or rice; you should eat meat with vegetables. However, if you are eating a vegetable protein such as lentils, chickpeas or beans, then you can eat these with a starch such as potatoes, rice and pasta. Also, fruit is recommended to be consumed as your first meal as it often causes a range of digestive problems when it ferments in your gut. This is often difficult to adopt since most people are used to eating meat and potatoes. We are so used to restaurant menus that combine a meat and starch such as a burger and chips; it has become a widely accepted norm and lifestyle. People consider you strange when you talk about certain food combinations, yet I learnt years ago when I studied abnormal psychology that what some cultures consider the norm, very often would be defined as abnormal behaviour in other cultures. For this reason it is important that you understand the reason for your food choices. I try to eat the correct combinations of food at least three times a week.

Eat raw food in the form of salads

Advocates claim that raw foods are more nutritious than cooked foods because enzymes, along with some nutrients, are destroyed in the cooking process. It is important to properly rinse fruits and vegetables well to get rid of any bacteria and pesticides. When you consume food, digestive enzymes in your body help break it down into molecules that can be absorbed. The food you eat also contains enzymes that aid digestion. Enzymes are heat sensitive and deactivate easily when exposed to high temperatures. In fact, nearly all enzymes are deactivated at temperatures over 47°C. Raw foods may thus be richer in certain nutrients than cooked foods. Some nutrients are easily deactivated or can leach out of food during the cooking process. Water-soluble vitamins, such as vitamin C and the B vitamins, are particularly susceptible to being lost during cooking. Boiling results in the greatest loss of nutrients, while other cooking methods more effectively preserve the nutrient content of the food. Steaming, roasting and stir-frying are some of the best methods of cooking vegetables when it comes to retaining nutrients. Lastly, the length of time that food is exposed to heat affects its nutrient content. The longer a food is cooked, the greater the loss of nutrients.

One study found that cooking tomatoes reduced their vitamin C content by 29%, while their lycopene content more than doubled within 30 minutes of cooking. Also, the total antioxidant capacity of the tomatoes increased by over 60%. Tomatoes can therefore be eaten either raw or cooked and you will get health benefits. It is important to note that not all foods should be eaten raw as some foods have a greater nutritional value when cooked.

Foods that are healthier raw

- Broccoli – Raw broccoli contains three times the amount of sulforaphane, a cancer-fighting plant compound, than cooked broccoli does.

- Cabbage – Cooking cabbage destroys the enzyme myrosinase, which plays a role in cancer prevention. If you choose to cook cabbage, do so for short periods.

- Onions – Raw onion is an anti-platelet agent, which contributes to heart disease prevention. Cooking onions reduces this beneficial effect.

- Garlic – Sulphur compounds found in raw garlic have anti-cancer properties. Cooking garlic destroys these sulphur compounds.

Foods that are healthier cooked

- Asparagus – Cooking asparagus breaks down its fibrous cell walls, making folate and vitamins A, C and E more available to be absorbed.

- Mushrooms – Cooking mushrooms helps degrade agaritine, a potential carcinogen. Cooking also helps release ergothioneine, a powerful mushroom antioxidant.

- Spinach – Nutrients like iron, magnesium, calcium and zinc are more available for absorption when spinach is cooked.

- Tomatoes – Whilst tomatoes are great raw and do offer nutrients, cooking greatly increases the antioxidant lycopene in tomatoes.

- Carrots – Cooked carrots contain more beta-carotene than raw carrots.

- Potatoes – The starch in potatoes is nearly indigestible until potato is cooked. DO NOT EAT raw potatoes – they have toxins and anti-nutrients.

- Legumes – Raw or undercooked legumes contain dangerous toxins called lectins, which are eliminated with proper soaking and cooking.[105]

Eat foods that are high in antioxidants

To understand antioxidants, you first need to understand free radicals and oxidation.

Free radicals are oxygen molecules that have split into single atoms with unpaired electrons. As they seek out other electrons, they damage cells and DNA. Free radicals are created by a process known as oxidation. Oxidation happens naturally as your cells process the oxygen you breathe and convert it into energy. It is a chemical reaction that also produces free radicals. When there are too many free radicals, they overwhelm your body's natural repair processes and cause problems.

Free radicals are significantly increased by external factors like fried foods, alcohol, tobacco smoke, pesticides, pollutants in the air, and eating a poor diet. The build-up of free radicals in your body is known as "oxidative stress". Oxidative stress is thought to be a leading cause of deterioration and disease, including memory loss, the breakdown of organs, autoimmune disorders, heart disease, type 2 diabetes, cancer, and even wrinkles. Antioxidants are the good guys in the fight against free radicals; they neutralise them by giving them the electrons they need. While all foods contain some antioxidants, plant foods are the primary source. On average, plant foods contain 64 times more antioxidants than animal-based foods. It is important to try and incorporate some of the foods and spices below into your daily meals.

Here are some of the top antioxidant-rich foods and spices. Remember, it is important to eat organic as much as possible, because pesticides create free radicals in our bodies:

Clove; purple cabbage; curly kale; artichokes; oregano; peppermint; all spice; cinnamon; coriander; blueberries; dried apples, apricots and plums; dark chocolate; pecans and goji berries.

Reduce chronic inflammation

The term 'chronic inflammation' has become a new trend when explaining many health issues. Inflammation occurs as part of the body's response to harmful stimuli with the purpose of eliminating whatever is causing cell injury. There are many causes of chronic inflammation, some which are covered in other sections of this book. Some of these causes are food allergies (for example gluten in wheat or casein in milk), obesity, overeating (stomach acids struggle to digest food), chemicals (such as airborne irritants that we breathe in), stress (your brain creates inflammation to protect you), lack of sleep (your body produces higher levels of inflammatory proteins), excessive alcohol, clothing fibres that people are allergic to, an imbalance of hormones, pollution and bad air (creates more free radicals). You need to understand your body and your allergies, as by addressing the possible causes of chronic inflammation, you can live a better quality of life.

Maintain your pH balance

I have learnt that there are many healing foods that nourish our body, and that by including them in our daily diet we increase our supply of vitamins and nutrients. Your body should neither be too acidic or alkaline, but remain at the optimum level of pH balance. pH stands for the power of hydrogen, which is a measurement of the hydrogen ion concentration in the body. The total pH scale ranges from 1 to 14, with 7 considered to be neutral. A pH less than 7 is said to be acidic and solutions with a pH greater than 7 are basic or alkaline. Our ideal pH is slightly alkaline – 7.30 to 7.45. You can test your pH levels regularly by using a piece of litmus paper in your saliva or urine first thing in the morning before eating or drinking anything. When your body is too acidic, that is when you are more susceptible to illness.

Acidic environments are breeding grounds for some pathogens, however when your body has the correct pH balance it keeps bad bacteria inactive. The optimal pH of stomach acid is around 1.9, so when you drink water with your food, you are diluting the acid in your stomach making it more difficult for your stomach to digest your food.

To improve the pH balance of your body, reduce your intake of processed foods, fried foods, alcohol and dairy. Eat foods that are alkaline such as green leafy vegetables, including kale, chard, beet greens, spinach, etc., or other vegetables like mushrooms, tomatoes, avocado, radishes, cucumber, broccoli, oregano, garlic, ginger, green beans, cabbage, celery, baby marrow and asparagus. Drink water which has a low pH such as distilled water. Reduce exposure to drugs such as aspirin, toxins and coffee. I usually drink lemon in hot water as soon as I get up in the morning to help fight the acidity. Whilst lemon is acidic, once consumed it metabolises in the body and becomes alkaline. Remember it is preferable to drink lemon water through a straw so it does not damage the enamel of your teeth.

Drink sufficient water

Without water, a human being can survive for about three days. One of water's many benefits is an increase in brain power. Since your brain is made of 73% water, drinking it helps you think, focus, concentrate, and stay alert. As a result, your energy levels also improve. Water helps dissolve minerals and nutrients, making them more accessible to your body. It also helps remove waste products from your body. Water is essential for your kidneys to function; if they do not function properly, waste products and excess fluid can build up inside the body. To prevent dehydration, you need to drink adequate amounts of water. There are many different opinions on how much water you should be drinking every day, but health authorities commonly recommend eight glasses, which equals about two litres. Water is essential for the proper circulation of nutrients in the body; it serves as the body's transportation system and when we are dehydrated things just cannot get around as well. There is a view that suggests eating water is better than drinking it.[106] The idea is that the best possible way for the body to get water is out of fruits and vegetables. In this way, all the trace elements and vitamins are easily available. Water that is consumed in this manner reaches the blood more slowly and evenly, and at the same time that the minerals are absorbed.

Nutritional supplements

Due to our busy lifestyles, we often do not follow a healthy diet. Even when we do, our food's nutritional value is not the same as it used to be, since a lot of minerals and nutrients have been depleted due to pesticides in the soil. Nutritional supplements deliver nutrients that may not be consumed in sufficient quantities. Food supplements can take the form of vitamins, minerals, amino acids, fatty acids, and other substances delivered as pills, tablets, capsules or liquids. Talk with your doctor before taking any supplements, as some can change how medicines you may already be taking work. If you are taking supplements, please understand how to take them effectively. For example, iron supplements are best taken with vitamin C for absorption. You should not have an iron supplement if you are consuming dairy, since the calcium blocks the absorption of iron. Also, do not take iron supplements with tea or coffee. It is further advised to take iron supplements an hour before a meal or after a meal. Vitamin D is more effective if taken with a meal that contains fat, however it should not be consumed at night as it interrupts your sleep patterns. It is advised to take a vitamin B supplement in the morning as it boosts your energy. Take your calcium supplements with meals, rather than alone. The calcium needs the acid from stomach juices to break it down.

In Okinawa, an island in Japan, most people live longer than 100 years. When researchers examined the secret to their longevity, they found they followed a very different lifestyle to the Western world. At the core, they believe in a philosophy called 'ikigai', which in Japanese means "a reason for being". Héctor García and Francesc Miralles, in their book, *Ikigai: The Japanese Secret to a Long and Happy Life*, found that people who lived longer than 100 years had the following nutritional habits:[107]

● "Locals eat a wide variety of foods, especially vegetables. Variety seems to be key. A study of Okinawa's centenarians showed that they ate 206 different foods, including spices, on a regular basis. They ate an average of eighteen different foods each day, a striking contrast to the nutritional poverty of our fast-food culture."

- "They eat at least five servings of fruits and vegetables every day. At least seven types of fruits and vegetables are consumed by Okinawans on a daily basis."

- "Grains are the foundation of their diet. Japanese people eat white rice every day, sometimes adding noodles. Rice is the primary food in Okinawa, as well."

- "Eat fish an average of three times per week."

- "Tofu, Miso, Tuna, Carrots, Goya (bitter melon), Kombu (sea kelp), Cabbage, Nori (seaweed), Onion, Soy sprouts, Hechima (cucumber-like gourd), Soybeans (boiled or raw), Sweet potato, Peppers."

- "Okinawans drink more Sanpin-cha—a mix of green tea and jasmine flowers—than any other kind of tea...Okinawans drink an average of three cups of Sanpin-cha every day."

- "White tea, with its high concentration of polyphenols, may be even more effective against ageing. In fact, it is considered to be the natural product with the greatest antioxidant power in the world—to the extent that one cup of white tea might pack the same punch as about a dozen glasses of orange juice."

Now I am in no way suggesting that you drastically change your eating habits. What I am suggesting is that you be more conscious about the effect certain foods have on your health and energy levels. Each person's body is unique and one man's meat is another man's poison. Think about slowly stopping the amount of junk food that you consume in the form of chips, chocolates, cool drinks and energy drinks, and introduce some healing foods into your diet. Change your eating habits if you want more energy in your life. Remember insanity is doing the same thing over and over and expecting a different result.

Reflection exercise

What is the one eating habit you can change in your life that you can commit to?

summary

- Food not only has the capacity to affect our energy, sleep, skin, body, shape and size, but also our mood.

- Food can affect our energy levels and eating the wrong foods can drastically hinder our overall wellbeing.

- Even when people are extremely ill, nutrition plays a critical role in bringing the body into a state of health.

- If you want to optimise your energy, improving your digestion can assist in this process.

- Chewing your food is important to help the digestive process. If food is properly chewed, less work is required to break it down.

- Just as it is important to eat the right foods to help our digestion, it is important that we eat the correct portion sizes.

- It is critical to note that not all foods should be eaten raw, as some foods have a greater nutritional value when cooked.

- Free radicals are oxygen molecules that have split into single atoms with unpaired electrons. As they seek out other electrons, they damage cells and DNA.

- Your body should be neither too acidic or alkaline, but remain at the optimum level of pH balance.

- To prevent dehydration, you need to drink adequate amounts of water every day.

- Nutritional supplements deliver nutrients that may not be consumed in sufficient quantities.

- What you should be doing is eating foods that energise you. Each person's body is unique and one man's meat is another man's poison.

Chapter 14

Physical fitness and energy

"Exercise is a celebration of what the body can do, not a punishment for what you ate." (Women's Health UK[108])

We all know that exercise is important in our daily lives, but we do not know the full extent of the benefits. Our bodies are designed to be active, however we find ourselves in jobs which require long hours seated behind desks. Physical inactivity may contribute to anxiety and depression, as well as be a risk factor for certain cardiovascular diseases, diabetes, obesity and back aches.

There are many benefits of regular exercise and maintaining fitness, including:

- Exercise increases energy levels

  Exercise improves both the strength and the efficiency of your cardiovascular system to get oxygen and nutrients to your muscles. When your cardiovascular system works better, you have more energy.

- Exercise improves muscle strength

  Staying active keeps muscles strong and joints, tendons and ligaments flexible, allowing you to move more easily and avoid injury. Strong muscles and ligaments reduce your risk of joint and lower back pain by keeping joints in proper alignment.

- Exercise can help you to maintain a healthy weight

  The more you exercise, the more calories you burn. In addition, the more muscle you develop, the higher your metabolic rate becomes, so you burn more calories even when you are not exercising. If you are overweight this may help with weight loss.

- Exercise improves brain function

  Exercise increases blood flow and oxygen levels in the brain. This, in turn, boosts concentration levels and cognitive ability.

- Exercise is good for your heart

  Exercise reduces LDL cholesterol (the type that clogs your arteries), increases HDL (the good cholesterol) and reduces blood pressure so it lowers the stress on your heart.

- Regular exercise controls your blood glucose level

  Regular exercise helps to control blood glucose levels, which helps to prevent or delay the onset of type 2 diabetes.

- Exercise improves your immune system

  Exercise improves your body's ability to pump the oxygen and nutrients around your body that are required to fuel the cells that fight bacteria and viruses.

- Active people have a better night's sleep

  Physical activity makes you more tired so you are more ready to sleep. Good quality sleep helps improve overall wellness and can reduce stress.

- Exercise improves your mood

  Physical activity stimulates the release of endorphins, which make you feel better and more relaxed. These, in turn, improve your mood and lower your stress levels.

It is recommended by most health professionals to do 30 - 60 minutes of moderate intensity exercise five times a week, 20 - 60 minutes of vigorous intensity exercise three times a week, or a combination of both types. Examples of moderate intensity exercise include brisk walking (100 steps/minute), dancing, swimming, gentle cycling and volleyball. Examples of vigorous intensity exercise include running, power walking, cycling fast, aerobics, martial arts and skipping.

After the age of 30, we start to lose muscle mass, which is important for the generation of energy. Dr Libby Weaver explains that there are trillions of mitochondria in our cells whose primary function is to generate energy. She uses the example of imagining a mouse pedaling away, generating energy for us to use. Muscles contain the highest mitochondrial content of any tissue in our bodies, in order to provide sufficient energy for movement. During intense exercise, the mitochondria replicates itself and generates more energy.[109] Have you heard of people who say that once they started exercising they started feeling more energetic? It sounds counterintuitive but it's true; if you do not have energy, create more by exercising.

I do the five Tibetan yoga routine poses every morning. The Five Tibetan Rites is a system of exercises reported to be more than 2,500 years old. These exercises are great as you can do them even when you are on holiday. When I first started the Rites, I did each pose three times and gradually increased until I could do each 21 times. Sometimes if I am running late for work, I manage to at least do each pose 7 times. I found this routine improves my energy levels and helps with my flexibility. These exercises are easy to do.

Energy routines

One of the great energy routines that I do on a daily basis is designed by Donna Eden[110], who suggests a sequence of body movements and tapping of meridian points to activate your energy levels. There are great YouTube videos on this energy sequence. I do these every day as part of my morning ritual, and I really recommend it for those who struggle to get out of bed in the morning as it helps to boost your immune system.

In his book, *When,* Daniel H. Pink refers to various research that was conducted on understanding the perfect timing for being productive. One of the findings is that one's positive mood and energy rises in the morning, dips in the afternoon, and rises again in the evening. The implications of this research are that if you know that you are your best before 1pm, then focus on work activities such as having important meetings and making important decisions at this time; leave your administration work for the afternoon. In the night, when your energy levels peak again, focus on other activities. Pink suggests restorative breaks during the day to energise yourself. He refers to micro-breaks, such as every 20 minutes, take a break and look 20 feet away for 20 seconds to reset your brain. Drink water and stand up and shake your arms and legs for 60 seconds, rotate your core, flex your muscles and sit down. He also recommends moving breaks such as a five-minute walk every hour, preferably outside with someone else.[111]

When I reflect on my daughter's energy levels, it makes sense why she always has too much energy and wants to play at night rather than go to sleep. When writing this book I used the ideas of Pink by writing usually from 8 to 12 each night and in the mornings and evenings during the weekends. I found that I was most focused during these times. I also took constant breaks so that I could allow my creativity to be rebooted with new ideas.

Sometimes you need an energy boost to cope for the rest of the day. I usually make a turmeric shot that helps me cope. This recipe was shared with me on a vegan retreat. I add black pepper which allows for easier absorption of the curcumin of the turmeric. Please note that turmeric interferes with some medication such as blood thinners. Please buy quality organic turmeric, as I found some commercial turmeric powders are mixed with flour.

Turmeric shot recipe

RECIPE BOOK

Ingredients

2 teaspoons organic turmeric powder
A sprinkle of black pepper
1 teaspoon of coconut oil
¼ cup water

Method

Place in a pot and simmer on stove for five minutes. Remove from heat and allow to cool down. Add a drop of honey for taste. Remember not to add honey to hot liquid as it destroys the nutritional value of the honey.

Drink early in the morning before breakfast or as an afternoon shot.

Benefits of breathing

Our bodies need oxygen to properly function, so you do not have to be a genius to figure out that the more oxygen you can get into your body, the better it is for you. Deep breathing helps to release toxins from our body. When you exhale you get rid of toxins as well as carbon dioxide. When we breathe in deeply we take in more oxygen and become calmer. Have you noticed that people who are stressed breathe at a faster pace with shallow breaths? Breathing deeply normalises your heartbeat and makes you more relaxed. Deep breathing also helps to improve your mood by stimulating certain chemicals in the brain.

Deep breathing

Diaphragmatic breathing, or deep breathing, is breathing that is done by contracting the diaphragm, a muscle located at the base of your lungs. Air enters the lungs, the chest does not rise, and the belly expands during this type of breathing. Diaphragmatic breathing (also called "abdominal breathing" or "belly breathing") encourages full oxygen exchange, that is, the beneficial trade of incoming oxygen for outgoing carbon dioxide. Place one hand on your upper chest and the other just below your rib cage. This will allow you to feel your diaphragm move as you breathe.

Recipe for deep breathing

RECIPE BOOK

Lie on your back on a flat surface or on your bed, with your knees bent and your head supported. You can use a pillow under your knees to support your legs. Place one hand on your upper chest and the other just below your rib cage. This will allow you to feel your diaphragm move as you breathe. Breathe in slowly through your nose so that your stomach moves out against your hand. The hand on your chest should remain as still as possible. Tighten your stomach muscles, letting them fall inward as you exhale through your lips. The hand on your upper chest must remain as still as possible. Imagine you have a balloon in your stomach and take in a long breath; as you inhale the air fills the imaginary balloon, and as you exhale the balloon deflates. We are so used to quick and shallow breathing that it may take a long time for you to practice and incorporate this deep breathing into your daily lives. A good idea is to schedule breathing exercises as part of your routine, such as immediately after a shower or once you get to work. You can start with three times a day and gradually increase it. I have a reminder on my watch to do deep breathing throughout the day. When I first got the reminder to breathe deeply for two minutes, I would switch off the reminder and say to myself, I am too busy to breathe properly now. I have since learned that breathing exercises keep me more focused and help me to be more mindful.

Summary

- We all know that exercise is important in our daily lives, but many of us do not know the full extent of those benefits.

- Some of the benefits of exercise are as follows: increases energy levels, improves muscle strength, keeps muscles strong and joints, tendons and ligaments flexible, helps us to maintain a healthy weight, improves brain function, increases blood flow and oxygen levels in the brain, reduces LDL cholesterol (the type that clogs our arteries), increases HDL (the good cholesterol) and reduces blood pressure so it lowers the stress on our hearts.

- Physical inactivity may contribute to anxiety and depression as well as be a risk factor for certain cardiovascular diseases, diabetes, obesity and back aches.

- Research has found that one's positive mood and energy rises in the morning, dips in the afternoon, and rises again in the evening.

- It is recommended by most health professionals to do 30 - 60 minutes of moderate intensity exercise five times a week, 20 - 60 minutes of vigorous-intensity exercise three times a week, or a combination of both types.

- Deep breathing helps to release toxins from our bodies. When we exhale we get rid of toxins as well as carbon dioxide. Diaphragmatic breathing (also called "abdominal breathing" or "belly breathing") encourages full oxygen exchange, that is, the beneficial trade of incoming oxygen for outgoing carbon dioxide.

Chapter 15

Sleep like a baby

I have watched two hours of a series, had some coffee and cake,
I am so full, I shouldn't have eaten dessert, oh what a big mistake!
I feel accomplished having responded to all my emails on my laptop,
I look at the clock, it is getting late maybe it is time to stop.
Hmm, let me support my friends on Facebook before I sleep,
I am sure I will easily drift off when I count a few sheep.
Good night, sweet dreams, nothing is amiss,
Everything is perfect, there is only bliss.
I rest my head on the pillow, count my blessings this night,
I wrote in my gratitude journal so everything is alright.
An hour has passed and still no sleep to report,
Another 8 a.m. meeting, Oops, I simply forgot.
Yawn, I am so tired, what am I to do?
I wish there were sleep techniques that I knew.
Sleep, where art thou my trusting friend?
Really? You chose to abandon me once again.

The above poem illustrates that we often think we are functioning optimally and ticking the boxes by doing the right things, however some of our choices are counterproductive to our sleep patterns. Like all our other behaviours, our beliefs control how we interpret the world and determines what we choose to focus on. We need to work on our beliefs about sleep. We may think that it is obvious that we all close our eyes at night and drift into slumber, however we may have self-limiting beliefs that makes it difficult to sleep.

What did you learn when you were growing up? I know people who love to sleep. They close their eyes and they wake up restful and ready to take on the world. I have a friend, however, who struggles to sleep when she has any problem. Her favourite words are, "How can I sleep when I have this to worry about?" What she is telling her mind is: "Don't you dare sleep when there is so much to think about!"

I know successful executives who see sleep not as a necessity, but a luxury. They sleep for five hours as it gives them more hours in the day to be productive. Then you have the insomniacs who really want to sleep, but can't and are exhausted the next day. The majority of people toss and turn because they just had a marathon of television viewing, had a late meal, or drank lots of coffee.

Here is my story. I have this fear of missing out if I sleep early. The belief that is running my poor sleep habits is that there is so much still to do. I love reading and on any given night I'll have four to six books on my bedside table, usually about nutrition, motivation, spirituality or life skills. This is a pattern that I developed during my childhood. I remember my Dad would come in at night and say, "It is late, you have school tomorrow. Put the book away". I appeared compliant but after my father switched off the light, I would continue reading with a torch. I had a compulsion to finish reading so I could complete the story. Years later my behaviour persisted until I realised the damage I was doing to my body by depriving myself of much-needed sleep. I have since learnt to modify my habits to have a restful sleep. I realised that the quality of my sleep contributes to my energy levels and helps with my overall health.

There is a lot of available research on the damage that poor sleep can have on your body. Firstly, it has negative effects on your hormones and brain functioning. It can also cause weight gain and increase your risk of disease. Many people are adamant that they can easily fall asleep after watching television and drinking coffee in the afternoon. The important thing to know is that whilst you may fall asleep easily, this does not necessarily mean that you are having good quality sleep and that your body is totally relaxed and able to go into deep sleep; it is the deep sleep that is important to your health.

These are some of the sleep ideas I have gathered over the years that have helped me to have a restful state of sleep.

Recipe for sleep

RECIPE BOOK

Dealing with anxiety before you sleep

- If you are stressed about something, speak about the issue with someone so that it does not consume your mind. If it still bothers you, write down on a piece of paper all the things that you are anxious about and leave that paper in another room. Close the door. By writing down your problems, you have removed some of the intensity of the problem. As human beings, when things bother us we tend to exaggerate them in our minds. We often focus on them so much that we dress them up, place them on the centre stage of our minds, and enhance them with special effects. When we write our problem on a piece of paper, we take away the drama and it becomes factual and looks boring. By leaving the paper in another room, you have symbolically placed some distance between your problem and you, allowing you to detach yourself temporarily in order to have a good night's sleep.

- Daily exercise is great for a good night's sleep, however do not exercise too close to bedtime. You can do gentle stretching exercises that relax your body without pumping your body with too much adrenaline. I usually do some yoga poses that are stretching exercises that allow me to relax.

- Keep to a daily sleep schedule of the same bedtime and wake up time, even on the weekends. This helps to regulate your body's clock and could help you fall asleep and stay asleep for the night. You may think that you deserve to sleep in on a weekend, but this just messes with your sleep patterns and will make you more tired the next week.

- Practice a relaxing bedtime ritual. A relaxing, routine activity right before bedtime conducted away from bright lights helps separate your sleep time from activities that can cause excitement, stress or anxiety, which can make it more difficult to fall asleep, get sound and deep sleep, or remain asleep. Some rituals could include having a hot bath, listening to relaxing music, deep breathing, reading a book or visualisation.

- If you have trouble sleeping, avoid naps, especially in the afternoon, as this will make it difficult for you to sleep at night. Sleeping during the day can confuse your internal clock.

- Create a peaceful environment in your room. Your bedroom should be cool – ideally about 22 degrees. Your bedroom should also be free from any light or noise that might disturb your sleep. This includes a bed partner's sleep disruptions such as snoring. This challenge you need to handle on your own though!

- Use light to help manage your circadian rhythms, which are your body's natural sleep patterns. Avoid bright light in the evening and expose yourself to bright sunlight as soon as you get up in the morning. This will keep your circadian rhythms in check. Many of us have gotten into the bad habit of reading on our phones and tablets before we drift off to sleep, however the blue light from electronic devices has been proven to make falling asleep more difficult. Bright light reduces the sleep hormone called melatonin. Our brain secretes more melatonin when it is dark, making us more sleepy, and secretes less melatonin when it is bright, thus keeping us awake. Melatonin is needed to slow down oxidation and is a direct free radical scavenger. It has the ability to directly neutralise a number of free radicals and is efficient as an antioxidant.[112] This means that when you get more sleep, your body produces more melatonin, which helps your body to repair itself. Some insomniacs take melatonin supplements to help them sleep. If you need to work at night, try using glasses that filter out the bright light.

- Avoid alcohol, coffee and heavy meals in the evening, as alcohol and caffeine can disrupt sleep and eating big or spicy meals can cause discomfort from indigestion that can make it hard to sleep. If you can, avoid eating large meals for two to three hours before bedtime. Caffeine is especially bad for sleep as it stimulates your nervous system. It is best to avoid drinking coffee in the afternoon since coffee can stay elevated in your blood for six to eight hours. If you crave coffee, try drinking decaffeinated coffee.

- If you cannot sleep, go into another room and do something relaxing until you feel tired. Your body needs time to shift into sleep mode, so spend the last hour before bed doing a calming activity such as reading.

Reflection exercise
What sleeping habits can you change to improve the quality of your sleep?

summary

- There is a lot of available research on the damage that poor sleep can have on your body.

- Poor sleep has negative effects on your hormones and brain functioning; it can also cause weight gain and increase your risk of disease.

- If you are stressed about something, speak about the issue with someone so that it does not consume your mind.

- Keep to a daily sleep schedule of the same bedtime and wake up time, even on the weekends.

- Practice a relaxing bedtime ritual.

- Avoid bright light in the evening and expose yourself to bright sunlight as soon as you get up in the morning.

- Avoid alcohol, coffee and heavy meals in the evening.

Chapter 16

Mindfulness and play

Just for today, I will not anger.
Just for today, I will let go of worry.
Just for today, I will do my work honestly.
Just for today, I will give thanks for my many blessings.
Just for today, I will be kind to my neighbour and every living thing.
Just for today, I will honour my teachers.[113]

I am a Master Reiki practitioner and the above Reiki principles were taught to me as part of my training. Reiki is a Japanese energy healing technique that when translated means 'universal life energy'. What is beautiful about the principles is that they force one to focus on the present. They teach the discipline of focusing on today as yesterday has passed and tomorrow has not yet come. This is about being in a mindful state. Mindfulness is about being in the moment; not worrying about the past or the future. Meditation is a form of mindfulness. It is letting your thoughts come into the front door and allowing them to leave through the back door without feeling compelled to invite them to stay for tea.

It seems so simple yet each of us struggles to be present. We are physically at a place and yet our minds are engaged elsewhere; we are detached from the moment. I am guilty of this transgression. As I wrote this section, I was in a playground surrounded by the laughter and exuberance of young children as they manoeuvred on the jungle gym. As I watched, my thoughts were suddenly aware of not being present. As I watched my daughter come down a slide, I thought about my book. I put my phone away and I spent the rest of the afternoon focusing on being present in the playground.

It is becoming harder to stay present, especially with the onslaught of technology. We seem to be more dependent on our smartphones than ever before. My friend runs his business on his phone. He can answer emails, access business platforms, check traffic on his security camera at the office, set reminders, and make appointments. For him, it is a blessing that he can do what he needs to without being forced to be at a specific location. The disadvantage is that his mind is always in a high state of alert, and it is more difficult for him to switch off.

Recently I saw a video clip of Tel Aviv, where the government wants to place lights on the road to promote the safety of pedestrians, who are crossing the street looking at their phones and unaware of the cars on the street. It would be a strange sight indeed to walk into a restaurant and see everyone sitting around the table connecting to each other without someone looking at their smartphone or a child playing games on a tablet.

We are so consumed with our obligations and commitments that it is difficult to let go for an instant and enjoy the moment. Schedule playfulness into your life. "It is only possible to live happily ever after on a day to day basis." (Margaret Wander Bonnano[114])

> *Pooh and Piglet are walking together in the snow somewhere in the 100 Acre Wood when Pooh ponders a moment and asks Piglet: "What day is it?" "It's today", squeaked Piglet." My favourite day", said Pooh.*[115]

What a beautiful example of living in the present and being able to open your eyes each morning with a fresh outlook on a new day! Not worrying about the regrets of the past and not focused on the stress of the future. To be able to focus on one day at a time as if it is your favourite day. Have you ever woken up on your birthday feeling special? Now imagine if you felt that same feeling each day. What a wonderful adventure life would be!

We often spend our lives in the future. When I was little, whilst we were busy eating lunch, my mother would ask what we wanted for supper. This was great from a planning ahead perspective, however when you reflect on your life, you realise that so many moments are spent focusing on the future. As a result, we pass through our lives like shadows, constantly waiting for the next train to arrive. Stillness is important when you are learning to be present.

There is a lovely quote by Lily Tomlin that states, "The trouble with the rat race is that even if you win, you are still a rat".[116] This is profound because we are in this vicious cycle of trying to achieve more and more, but we consciously experience less and less. We are jumping from one mountain top to the next and we are unable to pause and reflect on our incredible moments which are truly glorious blessings. We do not savour these moments but tick them off our mental checklist and move on to the next one. Within five seconds we have taken a picture and posted it on Instagram to show the world our accolade. The saddest part of this is that we have robbed ourselves of that moment of joy that will never be replicated by the likes we may get on our social media pages. Since we truly fail to appreciate this moment, it is difficult for us to demonstrate gratitude for the blessings we have received.

We have been doing this for so long that it is difficult for us to disconnect from the expected rituals of the rat race and say, "Carry on, I will catch up later". Sadly we do not do this because we experience an overwhelming feeling of FOMO, or a Fear of Missing Out. Instead we say, "Hang on, I'm coming", as we hop onto the treadmill of life once more. When you realise that you are exactly where you should be at this moment in time in your life, it is a truly liberating experience. It allows you to reflect, relax and watch more sunsets. We so quickly forget that we are human beings and not human doings.

When we have children we tend to replicate this behaviour and we forget to appreciate the fact that our children can teach us about connecting with the present moment. I take my daughter to school in the morning and it has become a daily mantra, "Hurry up, we're going to be late". My four year old looks at me like: "What are you on about now?" and proceeds to ignore me as she continues to practice her different expressions in the mirror with the toothbrush in her mouth. I have since learnt to appreciate that these moments of innocence are so precious and give her those moments to have fun.

The following story is based on an actual incident which helped me cure myself of FOMO.

A few years ago my husband and I went to Bangkok for a holiday. It was a long flight and we were both exhausted. When we landed, at the airport we met our tour guide who took us through our itinerary. Then she mentioned that if we were interested, we could attend a cultural show that was happening on that very evening. (What I need to share with you is my interpretation of a holiday is to fill each hour with every activity and sightseeing tour I can find. I am usually exhausted by the end of the holiday.) So when I heard 'cultural show' I was determined to add it to my itinerary. I really had a bad case of FOMO. My husband, however, suggested that we pass on the experience and go to the hotel and have a relaxing evening. I was so determined not to miss out that I convinced him that it was a great idea. I said that the tour the next day started in the afternoon so we would have plenty of time to relax. He reluctantly caved in, so we stopped at the hotel to drop our luggage and accompanied the tour guide to the cultural show.

I already had images in my head about the beautifully dressed Thai dancers. I was so excited that I barely paid attention to the venue we were going to. Our guide pointed to a building and briefly showed us where to take a taxi back to the hotel. As we approached the building for the first time I noticed the poorly lit venue and a lot of men loitering outside. We walked into a darkened smoke filled room, filled with beautiful Thai women on the stage. To my disappointment my cultural show was in fact a strip club. As we entered the room, we were offered complimentary cooldrink. I will never forget my husband's expression. He said, "Don't you dare drink that cooldrink". Judging by his tone of voice and his expression, I knew I had to do fancy footwork to talk myself out of this escapade. So I reframed the experience and feebly said to my husband, "Well think about it, by their standard it is a cultural show". The evening did not get any better. We struggled to get a taxi. It was a dodgy part of the city. We did not speak the language and it was getting very late. We finally made it safely to our hotel room. It was such a stressful evening that whenever I feel the slightest symptoms of FOMO, I remember that night and all my symptoms magically disappear.

Recipe for mindfulness

By Monsignor Lawrence Luciana[117]

No TIME for God

I knelt to pray but not for long.
I had too much to do.
I had to hurry and get to work
For bills would soon be due.

So I knelt and said a hurried prayer
And jumped up off my knees.
My Christian duty was now done.
My soul could rest at ease.

Now all day long I had no time
To spread a word of cheer.
No time to speak of Christ to friends.
They'd laugh at me I'd fear.

"No time. No time. Too much to do."
That was my constant cry.
No time to give to souls in need.
At last the time to die.

I went before the Lord, I came,
I stood with downcast eyes.
For in his hands God held a book.
It was the book of life.

God looked into his book and said,
"Your name I cannot find.
I once was going to write it down
But never found the time."

I have always loved this poem as it beautifully captures how when we hurry through life and are caught up in the daily busyness, we often lose track of important priorities. To accomplish this state many have spoken of becoming more mindful, and focusing on the one thing that you are doing. Through too much multitasking you rob yourself of the moment which leaves you feeling disassociated. If you are having a meal, enjoy the meal with your friends or family. Give attention to people. Use your cell phone sparingly when in the company of others. Our smartphones are the puppeteers and we are the puppets. As soon as we hear a beep, we have become conditioned to look at our phones. There was a physiologist called Pavlov who did an experiment where he played a sound and then gave his dog food. Over time, when the dog heard the sound he would start to salivate. This famous experiment is often quoted to explain how conditioning occurs. When I think about how we respond to the beeps on our phones, I immediately think how conditioned we have become.

Remember a time when there were no mobile devices and if you went for a picnic you went with just a small group of family or friends and not your entire social network on Instagram, Facebook and Twitter.

#having great fun #just checked in this picnic spot #wish you were here.

It is becoming more difficult to disconnect from the grid. Last year I took a social media sabbatical after my birthday in December. I wished everyone well for the holidays and switched off all social media until late January. It was such a liberating experience to enjoy myself with my family and be present.

Work at feeling engaged in the moment. Forget about eating in front of the television or watching a YouTube clip on your phone; focus on chewing your food and enjoy the flavours. When you are preoccupied with doing other things, you forget to practice mindful eating. Appreciate that you have a meal to eat whilst many children in the world go to bed hungry and would love to exchange places with you.

Thich Nhat Hanh said, "To dwell in the here and now does not mean you never think about the past or plan responsibly for the future. That idea is simply not to allow yourself to get lost in regrets about the past or worries about the future. If you are firmly grounded in the present moment, the past can be an object of inquiry, the object of your mindfulness and concentration. You can attain many insights by looking into the past. But you are still grounded in the present moment".[118]

Try to simplify your life, surrender certain obligations and delegate to others. Stop focusing on making mental checklists. Just be present and enjoy the power of Now. Schedule time to do nothing. It is your life and yet you do not make free time to appreciate you. Have you ever heard the saying, stop to smell the flowers? Sometimes we need to literally stop what we are doing and smell the flowers to remind us that we exist not in our minds, but in a beautiful world whose beauty we are overlooking because we are stuck watching videos of our past or anticipating the work of tomorrow. My daily ritual is watering my vegetable garden every evening. This simple act provides me with me time, but also helps me appreciate nature.

When asked what surprised him about humanity the most, the Dalai Lama replied: "Man. Because he sacrifices his health in order to make money. Then he sacrifices money to recuperate his health. And then he is so anxious about the future that he does not enjoy the present; the result being that he does not live in the present or the future; he lives as if he is never going to die, and then dies having never really lived."[119] This quote is such an accurate reflection of how we rush through our lives, never enjoying the present moment.

Being in a state of flow is an example of mindfulness. Have you ever done something that you were so focused on that you forgot about having your lunch? Where time flew by so quickly? When you watch someone who is passionate about what they do, they are so absorbed in their task that nothing else matters.

Mihaly Csikszentmihalyi is a Hungarian-American psychologist, who from his own adverse experiences as a prisoner during World War II and from witnessing the pain and suffering from many people around him during this time, developed a curiosity about happiness and being content with life.[120]

Through much research, he began to understand that people were most creative, productive, and often, happiest, when they were in this state of flow that determines success. He interviewed athletes, musicians and artists, amongst others, as he wanted to know when they experienced the most optimal performance levels. These investigations have revealed that what makes an experience genuinely satisfying is a state of consciousness called flow – a state of concentration so focused that it amounts to absolute absorption in an activity.

The 8 characteristics of flow

Csikszentmihalyi found that it is not how much time you spend on achieving things, but how much time you spend in a state of flow. He came to the conclusion that a state of flow is a universal experience and described the eight characteristics of flow as follows:

1. Complete concentration on a task where you do not give attention to anything else.

2. You are clear about your goals and rewards, and the process provides immediate feedback. This is knowing what you want to achieve and understanding how well you are progressing in that goal.

3. Time passes much quicker when you are enjoying a task and slower when it is a task you dislike. When you are in a state of flow, time feels as if it accelerates.

4. The experience is intrinsically rewarding; you feel accomplished to be achieving an inner goal. Just the experience itself without any reward is satisfying.

5. Effortlessness and ease refer to the way you manage the task, which comes so naturally that you do not have to think about it.

6. There is a balance between challenge and skills, i.e. you have the right level of skill to deal with the task.

7.   You do not think about your actions, you just do them seamlessly. This is where you are so lost in the activity that you do not think about actually doing it. Have you ever driven your car, only to arrive at your destination and you cannot remember the journey as you were so preoccupied?

8. There is a feeling of control over the task. There is no concern over the future as you feel that you have all the resources to complete the task competently.[121]

When you read through these characteristics, can you think of a time that you experienced a state of flow?

Csikszentmihalyi said that the human nervous system is unable to process more than 110 bytes of information per second. To hear and understand someone your mind uses 60 bytes of information. When you are in a state of flow, you do not have enough attention to focus on other functions such as eating. Some scientists have referred to this as cognitive bandwidth, or how much information you can deal with at any point in time. Think about a time when you enjoyed doing a task such that you completely forgot about everything else. When you watch people play games on their smartphone or watch a child play a game on their PlayStation, you will see examples of flow.

On the one hand, when a challenge is bigger than your skill level, you become anxious and stressed. On the other hand, when your level of skill exceeds the size of the challenge, you become bored and distracted. A state of flow is the optimum balance between your skills and the challenge of the task. It is important for you to understand that if you want to get into a state of flow, you need to be clear about your goals and improve your level of skills. When you are feeling stuck in your career, it could be because you have mastered your skills, you are bored, and the job has stopped providing a sufficient challenge for you. When you are feeling bored you are not energised. Similarly, you could be in a role where you are overwhelmed and feel that you do not have sufficient skills to be successful. In this case, you need to clarify your goals and create an action plan to improve your skills to be able to adequately deal with tasks.

When I am writing this book, I can honestly describe my state as being in flow. I write when it is late at night and I can totally focus whilst my daughter is asleep and after I have prepared for the next day so I have no further distractions. Time seems to pass so quickly because I am totally absorbed in what I am doing.

Recipe for flow

RECIPE BOOK

Here are the key steps to achieving and benefiting from flow:

1. Choose work you love. When you are enjoying things you love doing you are more likely to experience flow. I love writing so I experience flow when I am being creative.

2. Make sure you find tasks of the appropriate level of difficulty. Writing about topics I am still learning about allows me to continue to grow and learn and do what I love.

3. Find a time when you have lots of energy and can concentrate. I can usually focus late at night when there are no disruptions.

4. Clear away all distractions. That means turning off anything that will draw your attention away from the task at hand and interrupt your thoughts. I have to complete my work before I write so I know nothing is going to worry me when I am writing.

5. Learn to focus on that task for as long as possible. I have learnt to schedule time where I can focus uninterrupted.

6. Keep practising. It may take some time, but eventually it will become easier.

Another mindfulness practice is play

Our childish dreams we too quickly forget my friend,
Those joyful adventures that have come to an end.
We turn and walk away from those precious moments of Joy,
'Cos we are told we are getting too big to play with toys.
"Put on your shoes, don't walk barefoot on the grass,
There may be stones or shards of glass."

"Grow up," they say, "and become responsible like me".
What they really saying is, "We envy you being so carefree".
"No time for play only time for your chores,
It is getting dark, say goodbye and come indoors."

"You need to be more serious about life", they claim.
So we reluctantly pack away our toys and our childish games,
But what if they were wrong and we hold onto moments of play?
Will this laughter, merriment transform our tedious day?

When last did you play? When last did you experience going on a playground swing, feeling the sun on your face and the wind in your hair as you soar towards the sky? The absolute exhilaration and your heart pounding. Or simply sitting still and feeling calm and peaceful as you colour in a colouring book. There is a great availability of adult colouring books to help adults cope with the stress of everyday life. Play is all about simplicity and you can choose the activity that best connects you with the feeling of your childhood. One of the greatest gifts I am finding as a parent is that I have a second chance by exploring the world through the innocent eyes of my daughter. I get to play with playdough, have tea parties in the garden, play with sand, colour and pretend to cook. I am reconnecting to my inner child and finding other ways to cope with the daily pressures of life. George Bernard Shaw observed that people do not stop playing because they grow old, they grow old because they stop playing.

You need this when you feel the stress of the world weighing you down. My mother always referred to a game called '3 tins' which I vaguely remember playing as a child, but when she speaks of it the tone of her voice changes and you can hear her excitement as she recalls her childhood memories fondly. Our happiest times are those in our childhood as we are carefree without the responsibility of paying bills.

Positive activities that can reconnect you to your childhood include colouring, playdough, building with LEGO, going for a picnic, playing a game outside, paintballing, going on a rollercoaster, or eating foods you loved as a child (a burger, a gingerbread man, candy floss, red candy apples, a cherry flavoured lollipop, chewing gum, coloured popcorn or simply jelly beans).

There is no age limit to these activities, yet in our minds we associate them with a particular phase in our lives... childhood.

I have shared with you a lot of ideas on how you can optimise your energy, but these ideas will only work if you put them into action. You do not have to do everything – all you have to do is choose the habits that will improve your energy levels and the quality of your life. A good start is to make a list of the things that you are going to stop doing, start doing and continue doing.

Reflection exercise
What is the one habit that you can change that will make you more mindful in your life?

Reflection exercise		
What are you going to stop doing?	What are you going to continue doing?	What are you going to start doing?

Summary

- Mihaly Csikszentmihalyi is a Hungarian-American psychologist who developed a curiosity about happiness and being content with life.

- Csikszentmihalyi came up with the concept of flow, which he described as having eight characteristics:

  1. Complete concentration on a task where you do not give attention to anything else.

  2. You are clear about your goals and rewards, and the process provides immediate feedback.

  3. When you are in a state of flow, time feels as if it accelerates.

  4. The experience is intrinsically rewarding.

  5. Effortlessness and ease refer to the way you manage the task.

  6. There is a balance between challenge and skills.

  7. You do not think about your actions, you just do them seamlessly.

  8. There is a feeling of control over the task.

- Another mindfulness practice is play; you need to play when you feel the stress of the world weighing you down.

Section 5

Realise Your Dreams

- Discover your vision and life purpose

- Create focused goals

- Role models and mentors

- Flourish through feedback

For your entire life, were you sitting on the sideline?
Waiting for life to notice you and show you a sign.
Put away your silliness; pack away your doubts,
Stop allowing your insecurity to lead you about.
No one needs to nudge you, just take a few steps over there,
It is your life, so no one is really going to care.
Just gracefully bow in front of her and ask, "My dear, shall we dance?"
Sometimes you will be pleasantly surprised if you just take a chance.
Gently take her by her hands and lead her to the dance floor,
You will wonder why you did not try this before.
Be present in the moment as you dance along,
As you focus on the rhythm and the beat of the song.
As you sway to the music, you will often find,
Life is right in your arms rather than being left behind...

This section focuses on creating and realising your dreams, however before you start realising your dreams, you need to be committed to make a change to improve the present circumstances of your life. Make the right decision and set a vision and purpose for yourself. Translate that purpose into tangible goals. You can achieve your goals by seeking assistance from mentors and role models. Only when you are willing to seek feedback will you flourish.

Be committed to change

"It takes a deep commitment to change and an even greater commitment to grow." (Ralph Ellison[122])

You must be willing to change; only when you are willing to release all resistance, will you be able to change your behaviour. This is often only a commitment you can make. As soon as someone suggests that you change your behaviour, it could be starting a healthy diet, joining a gym, stop eating junk food or give up smoking, you will naturally come up with excuses because you do not want to change. You will rationalise your behaviour. People do not want to change because their present lifestyle is serving them on some level.

It takes courage to re-evaluate your life and make the necessary changes. People will comment and judge you... let them. It is okay if others do not understand. It will not be easy to withstand the onslaught of criticism whilst others question your motives and ridicule your choices, but you are the only one who has all the facts to make the right decision for you. Remember at night when you lay your head on your pillow that you only stay true to your conscience. Make the right choices and do the things that are right for you. When you make the right choice, do not regret it. Accept the path you have chosen and walk as a strong soldier according to the rhythm of your wisdom.

You are never too old to make a change in your life, but before you make a change, ask yourself what impact the change will have on the people around you. Since we exist in a social system, our choices often do not only affect ourselves, but influence others as well. For example, you could decide to study part-time which will require you to focus on your studies every evening, but this may be the time you usually spend with your kids helping them with their homework and cooking the evening meal. You will therefore need to make alternative arrangements for your other responsibilities. Similarly, you may choose to be healthier and join a gym, but this may mean that you may be late for work. It is important to strive to be the best version of yourself, but always remember that any change in your life will also affect the lives of others in your close circle.

Making the right choices

"The doors we open and close each day decide the lives we live." (Flora Whittemore[123])

The choices that you make determine the quality and the direction of your life. If you reflect on where you are presently, there were specific choices that you made in the past that brought you to this point in time. Therefore, if you want to have a different life then you need to make different choices.

When Steve Jobs faced a big choice, he asked himself: "What would I do if this was the last night of my life?" According to Debbie Ford, within each one of us there is an internal flame that is our life force. Each choice that we make either strengthens our life force or diminishes it. Some of the things that dim our life force are lying to ourselves, judging ourselves and others, living in fear, comparing ourselves to others, trying to be someone we are not and ignoring our inner voice. Some examples of choices that make our heart's flame roar are when we have empathy for others, have fun, rest, eat well, exercise, take time to nurture ourselves, appreciate ourselves, do what we love, forgive, take responsibility and speak our truth. In her book, *The Right Questions*, Ford designed 10 questions that she suggests you ask before you make important life choices.[124]

The right questions

- Will this choice propel me toward an inspiring future, or will it keep me stuck in the past?

- Will this choice bring me long-term fulfilment, or will it bring me short-term gratification?

- Am I standing in my power or am I trying to please another?

- Am I looking for what is right or am I looking for what is wrong?

- Will this choice add to my life force or will it rob me of my energy?

- Will I use this situation as a catalyst to grow and evolve, or will I use it to beat myself up?

- Does this choice empower me or does it disempower me?

- Is this an act of self-love or is it an act of self-sabotage?

- Is this an act of faith or is it an act of fear?

- Am I choosing from my divinity or am I choosing from my humanity?

No matter who you are and what you have done, it is time to forgive yourself, forgive others and make the choice to live a life aligned to your passion and purpose. All it takes is a small change in a direction that will change the trajectory of your life. Mahatma Gandhi said, "The future depends on what we do in the present". You can believe that everything is possible, or you can continue on the path you are travelling and allow your circumstances and other people to push you in different directions.

Chapter 17

Your vision for the future

"Everyone takes the limits of his own vision for the limits of the world."
(Arthur Schopenhauer[125])

People are happy when they have a sense of purpose and meaning in their lives. We engage with the world when we feel needed and that we are contributing to some bigger picture. Eckhart Tolle, in his book, *The Power of Now*[126], suggests that each person's life journey has an inner and outer purpose. The outer purpose is to arrive at one's goal or destination and deal with what one is doing or where one is going, whilst the inner purpose has to do with how one gets there. He stated that life may become meaningless when one focuses primarily on the outer purpose, i.e. the destination, rather than on the inner purpose of one's being. The outer purpose has limitations and cannot provide one with lasting fulfilment. Carl Jung described this best when he said: "Your vision will become clear only when you look into your own heart. Who looks outside, dreams; who looks inside, awakes."[127]

The challenge is that most people do not have a vision or know where they are going in their lives; they have no plans and drift aimlessly from one experience to another. They become frustrated as their lives lack meaning and they are not successful. Therefore, the first step is to understand the direction that you are heading in and then work on your goals, which will give you the how. I believe Tolle was referring to 'how' on a deeper level and the actions that you take. It is important to continually grow and experience joy when we are working towards a goal. When I look back at my life and my achievements, I was happiest when I was striving towards a goal rather than when I achieved it. The striving towards my objective gave me a great sense of purpose and meaning.

If you have not been living your life with a greater purpose, determining your vision may seem overwhelming to you. Stephen Covey, in his book *Seven Habits of Highly Effective People,* provides an exercise that might help

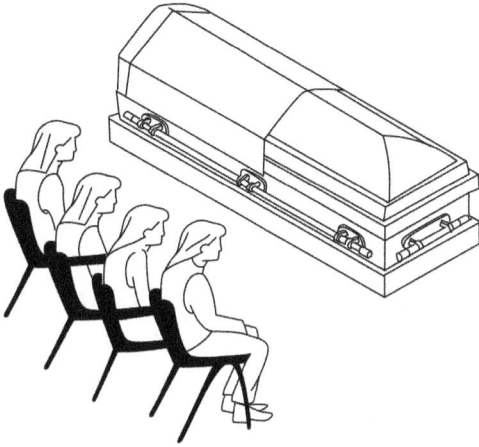

with finding your vision. Covey speaks about imagining that you are at your own funeral.[128] Four people come up to speak. One person is from your family, the second person is your friend, the third person is from your work and the fourth person is someone from the community. Imagine what you would like each of them to say about you. Covey suggests beginning with the end in mind. Then think about the life you want to lead and the vision you have for your life. How would you like others to remember you? Will you be spoken well of? Will others remember you with love and respect?

A century ago, a man looked at the morning newspaper and was shocked to read his name in the obituary column. The newspapers had reported the death of the wrong person by mistake. His first response was horror. When he regained his composure, his second thought was to find out what people had said about him. The obituary read, "Dynamite King Dies" and referred to him as a "merchant of death". This man was the inventor of dynamite and when he read the words "merchant of death", he asked himself a question: "Is this how I want to be remembered?" After great reflection, the man decided that this was not the way he wanted others to remember him. From that day on, he started working toward peace. His name was Alfred Nobel and the world celebrates him today for the Nobel Peace Prize.

Brian Tracy says that when you start to create your vision you should begin by dreaming about what is possible. He suggests that you imagine that you have all the time and money that you need. Imagine that you have all the contacts, resources and opportunities you could want. Now make a dream list; give yourself permission to write down these dreams freely, without interrogating them through a reality lens. You need to ask yourself the question: "What one great thing would I dare to dream if I knew I could not fail?" If you were guaranteed success, what would that be?"[129]

Discovering your life purpose

"When you walk with purpose, you collide with destiny." (Bertice Berry[130])

Everyone is on a constant quest to find a purpose for their life that differentiates them from all others. The questions people ask themselves range from, "Am I living my purpose?" to "What is my overall purpose?" Since we want to be special, we want our purpose to be truly unique. We arrogantly believe that our purpose is something that differentiates us from each other. The Inuits have many words in their language for snow, but in English, we just refer to it as snow. In the same way, the word 'purpose' could similarly be used in different ways based on different perceptions. What if our lives do not comprise a singular purpose but we have multi-purpose roles? We are so busy searching for the one big reason that we negate the million other purposes we have. Our purpose might be leaving meaningful footprints in someone else's life. For example, I would like to think that my purpose is to provide self-awareness to others, which will enable them to grow. However, at the same time, my purpose is to provide love and a stimulating and safe environment for my daughter to develop and flourish into a happy, well-balanced being.

Reflection exercise	
What would your purpose be in each life area?	
Life area	**Your purpose**
Spiritual	
Mental	

Emotional	
Physical	
Social	
Career	
Financial	
Environmental	

There is a beautiful Sufi story about a Mullah who lost his house key.[131] *Mullah was on his knees searching for something in his garden. When his neighbour asked him what he was searching for, he replied that he was looking for his house key. Wanting to help him, his neighbour dropped to his knees as well and joined him. After a while, their search proved unsuccessful. The neighbour asked Mullah where specifically in the garden he had lost his key. "Mullah, do you remember where you dropped it?" Mullah promptly answered: "Of course I do, in my house." "I don't understand Mullah. If you dropped your key in your house why are you looking here?" asked his neighbour, confused. Mullah replied: "Because there is much more light out here than in my house."*

Many of us look for clues about who we really are not through self-exploration, but through other people. We want other people to give us answers and show us the direction that we should travel on our life journey because it is easier. We look to others for validation when what we should be doing is looking for answers within ourselves.

Over the last two decades I have conducted numerous career counselling sessions with people who were feeling stuck in their careers. They hoped that by completing some psychometric assessment tests they would discover the direction their lives should follow. In 80% of the cases, people knew exactly what they needed to do, but they wanted me to provide some external validation that they were on the right track. Most personality and interest questionnaires are self-reporting, which means that the person completes their questionnaire based on their view of the world. For this reason, the results are often an integrated summary of what they themselves responded. When I align feedback with their interests and provide them with career feedback, they are overwhelmed at the accuracy of the tests.

Colin P. Sisson said: "What we vividly imagine, ardently desire, and enthusiastically act upon, must inevitably come to pass."[132] Some people have already found meaning and purpose in their present lives; they have discovered their reason for being. These people are often free from the daily stress that affects us; they live their lives in a state of flow, not allowing the trivial things to cloud their overall happiness. One of the young women I used to mentor was a good example of this. When we discussed her future in the organisation, she said she was perfectly happy in her role. She did not want to climb the career ladder but was content where she was. She viewed her purpose as being a connector, enabling others to be successful whilst she provided the support. She wanted to realise her full potential so that she could fulfil her purpose.

Robert Byrne said that the purpose of life is a life of purpose.[133] Sometimes the most difficult questions have the simplest answers. We tend to struggle as people to look for complex solutions for life challenges. The philosophical questions that each of us grapples with one time or the other are: "Why am I here?" and "What is my purpose?" We do not want obvious simple answers but search for sophisticated answers that make us feel important. This same kind of thinking or paradigm prevented scientists from realising that the earth rotated around the sun. We often extend this same type of thinking to ourselves by placing ourselves at the centre of any story.

I watched a TED talk by Adam Leipzig on *How to know your life purpose in 5 minutes*.[134] The skeptic in me wondered how this person was going to help me figure out something that I had pondered on for the past 10 years, but I am happy to admit that I was wrong. I watched the video, reflected on the questions and was able to articulate answers that are true for me.

Reflection exercise
Questions to determine your life purpose (Adam Leipzig[135])
1. Who are you? (Not your job title)
2. What do you love to do? Write, cook, design? What is the one thing you feel qualified to teach other people? (One word)
3. Who do you do it for? Who do you serve?
4. What do those people want or need?
5. How do people change or transform as a result of what you give them?

These were my answers to these questions.

1. Who are you?

I am a student of life.

2. What do you love to do?

I love to inspire and teach.

3. Who do you do it for?

For ordinary people to realise their potential.

4. What do those people want or need?

They want to live fulfilling lives.

5. How do people change or transform as a result of what you give them?

They connect with their purpose.

My purpose: I inspire people to lead fulfilling lives to realise their potential and connect to their purpose.

In their book Héctor García and Francesc Miralles explained that, "Our ikigai is different for all of us, but one thing we have in common is that we are all searching for meaning. When we spend our days feeling connected to what is meaningful to us, we live more fully; when we lose the connection, we feel despair". They added that, "The happiest people are not the ones who achieve the most. They are the ones who spend more time than others in a state of flow".[136]

Everyone's ikigai is different. It is a reflection and expression of your true inner self. It cannot be forced upon you, but must come from within. As such, when you put your ikigai to work, it should create an affirming mental state in which you feel comfortable and fulfilled.

Dan Buettner, who did the original research on ikigai, suggested the following method to discover your ikigai.[137] He recommends that each person should find a way to express their ikigai in their lives.

Reflection exercise: Discover your ikigai		
What do I love to do?	What am I good at?	What allows me to live my values?
One's ikigai is the central theme amongst all three.		

Ikigai diagram (Marc Winn[138])

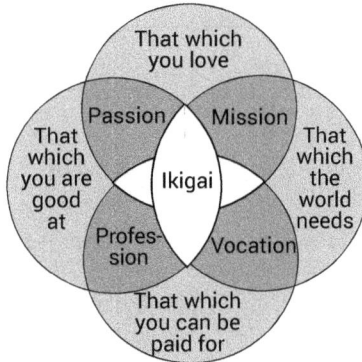

A more thorough and practical equation for ikigai is in the meeting point between four principles, represented by the below questions:

1.   What do you love to do?

2.   What are you good (preferably great) at?

3.   Does the world need it (does it offer value to other people)?

4.   Can you make money doing it?

"Don't worry about what the world needs. Ask what makes you come alive and do that. Because what the world needs is people who have come alive." (Howard Thurman[139])

What is great about this model is that it is practical and considers whether your passion can support your livelihood. We live in a world where we need money to pay for our daily necessities, so it is important to be realistic about how you can survive using your skills.

MY IKIGAI			
Mission	**Passion**	**Vision**	**Profession**
That which you love	That which you are good at	That which the world needs	That which you can be paid for
I love inspiring people	Good at inspiring people	The world needs more positive and inspirational people	Write inspirational books

I am grateful that my organisation allows me to experience my ikigai in my free time. To ensure that there is no conflict of interest with my job, I often use my free time to write or speak at conferences or workshops.

Reflection exercise			
Mission	**Passion**	**Vision**	**Profession**
That which you love	That which you are good at	That which the world needs	That which you can be paid for

Once you understand what your purpose is, you need to understand how that purpose will manifest in the future. What would you like it to be? Where would you like to go with that vision? This requires you to let go of your scepticism and use the opportunity to brainstorm and create what you want your future to be. Be known for your legacy and the contribution you want to make in the world.

summary

- It takes courage to re-evaluate your life and make the necessary changes.
- You are never too old to make a change in your life. Before you make a change, however, you should ask yourself what impact the change will have on the people around you.
- The choices that you make determine the quality and the direction of your life. If you reflect on where you are presently, you made specific choices in the past that brought you to this point in time.
- People are happy when they have a sense of purpose and meaning in their lives. We engage with the world when we feel needed and know that we are contributing to some bigger picture.
- Five questions can determine your life's purpose:

  1. Who are you? (Not your job title)

  2. What do you love to do? Write, cook, design? What is the one thing you feel qualified to teach other people? (One word)

  3. Who do you do it for? Who do you serve?

  4. What do those people want or need?

  5. How do people change or transform as a result of what you give them?

Chapter 18

Create well-formed goals

"Enthusiasm comes with an emotional commitment to a vision, goal, and dream. It comes when you pursue your goals as if your life depends on it, and it does. Understand, your life depends not on your goals, but on your pursuit of these goals, because when you are leading a life with direction and purpose and enthusiasm, you are truly living." (Stedman Graham[140])

Once you complete the vision for your life, finish the purpose exercise and know your highest values, the next step is to formulate your goals for how you are going to get there. What are the goals that will align with your vision for life, your purpose and your governing values? Your goals will become the stepping-stones to you achieving your vision.

As I was writing this book I asked my husband what would be a life lesson he would like to share with our daughter and he said the following: "Assume that everything that you wanted is possible and start with that as a baseline. Next just focus on how you are going to get it." Now, this kind of thinking does not even entertain the words "I can't".

The book *Flight Plan* by Brian Tracy is a great book about how to achieve one's goals. The author suggests that people who are clear about who they are, what they want, and where they want to go will accomplish ten times as much as the average person, and much faster as well. He adds that all people have four common goals: 1) to be fit, healthy, and live a long life; 2) to do work they enjoy and be well paid for it; 3) to be in happy relationships with people they love and respect and who love and respect them in return; and 4) to achieve financial independence so they never have to worry about money again.[141] I can honestly say that I personally subscribe to these four goals in my life.

Brainstorm ideas

If you have never set goals for yourself, it may seem like a difficult task. First, it takes courage to be willing to change your life for the better. The question is, where do you start? Set yourself an hour where you will be not disturbed and start brainstorming in the eight areas of your life about what you would like to achieve. Project yourself ten years into the future and ask yourself what you would like to be, have or do in each of these areas in your life. Once you have a vision of your future, work backward and write down what you would need to achieve to attain that future reality. You will end up with a list of different ideas. Now complete the Integrated Vision and Goals Worksheet in Annexure 2.

Refine your list

Zig Ziglar suggests that if you look at your long list of ideas, you should be able to answer why you want to be, do or have it. If you cannot answer why for one of your ideas, then you need to remove it as a goal from your list.[142]

Ziglar suggests answering the following questions to refine this list:[143]

1. Is it really my goal?

2. Is it morally right and fair to everyone concerned?

3. Will reaching this goal take me closer to or farther from my major objective in life?

4. Can I emotionally commit myself to start and finish this goal?

5. Can I see myself reaching this goal?

Once you have reduced your list of goals, Ziglar suggests asking yourself two further questions:[144]

1. Will reaching this goal make me happier, healthier and more prosperous; win me friends; give me peace of mind; make me more secure; improve my family relationships; and give me hope?

2. Most important, will reaching this goal contribute to more balanced success?

Once you have a short list of goals, categorise them into short-term (one month or less), intermediate (more than a month to a year) and long-term goals (more than a year). Then refine them into SMART goals. You also need to understand the benefits of your goals; knowing these will keep you inspired when you lack self-discipline.

Obstacles and sacrifices to meeting your goals

What are the obstacles that you will have to overcome to achieve each goal? You need to be realistic about the obstacles to achieving your goals; if you know the obstacles, you can properly plan and put in place mitigating actions. You also need to understand the sacrifices that you may have to make to support your goals. Brian Tracy[145] suggests that you must be willing to pay the price for achieving your goals. For example, if you want to pursue a degree part-time whilst you are working and have family commitments, you may have to finish work earlier, sacrifice your holidays to study, and spend less time with your children.

Additional skills to support your goals

It is important to understand if you need further skills or abilities to fulfil your goal. For example, you could have the goal of climbing Mount Kilimanjaro, so you will need to be physically and mentally fit to achieve this goal. Are there other people or groups you could work with who would help you achieve your goal? For example, if you wanted to climb Mount Kilimanjaro, you may need to join a hiking club.

Clarify your goal

These are other questions you can consider when you are goal setting:

- How will you know when you have achieved what you want?
- Under what circumstances, where, when, and with whom, do you want to have this result?
- How will your desired outcome affect your life? What will the potential ripple effect on the important people in your life be should you achieve this goal?

- What is stopping you from having your desired outcome already?

By answering these questions, you will create a list of things that can be an action list.

- What resources will you need to help you create what you want?
- What resources do you already have and what additional resources might you require?
- How are you going to get there and what is the first step to begin to achieve this result?

What specifically do you want? Describe your desired outcome in a positive, sensory-based way that is appropriate. Describe what success will look like when you achieve your goal, what it will feel like, and what feedback will sound like from others when you complete your goal? Is there a standing ovation or a large round of applause?

> *"A dream is just a dream. A goal is a dream with a plan and a deadline."* (Harvey Mackay[146])

It is important to state the goal or outcome in the positive and it must be specific, measurable, achievable, realistic and within a realistic timeframe. Brian Tracy suggests writing your goals in the present, personal and positive tense.[147] For example, "I eat only healthy food" is a better phrase than a negative phrase such as, "I am quitting junk food". There is a different energy in the two statements; the first one is positive and has a compelling pull factor, while the second implies scarcity, as if you are restraining yourself.

SMART	Description	Clarifying questions
Specific	Objectives clearly define what will be achieved. Objectives include both the actions needed and the results expected.	• What do I want to achieve? • Why do I need to achieve it? • How am I going to achieve it?
Measurable	The results of objectives are observable and measurable. Larger objectives may have smaller measures that build up to the full achievement of the objective.	• How will I know when the objective is achieved? What will I experience, see and feel? • How will progress be measured?
Achievable	Objectives must be achievable and realistic according to your capabilities.	• Is the objective achievable? • What are the steps I should take to achieve the objective? • Do I have the knowledge, skills, abilities, authority and resources needed to achieve the objective?
Relevant	Objectives must be relevant to your overall vision in life.	• Is the objective relevant to my highest life purpose? • Is the objective relevant to my short-and long-term priorities?
Time-bound	Objectives include time frames or target dates.	• How long will it take to achieve the objective? • When is the objective due to be completed? • When am I going to work on this objective?

Take action

Make a detailed plan of action towards achieving your goal. You must organise the list of activities in terms of highest priority and sequence. Certain activities must happen before other tasks, for example you may need to secure a student loan before registering with a university to study.

It is important to act to achieve your goal; you can have a great plan and take time to put the plan in place, but without action, it is meaningless. When my husband advises me about doing something I always respond, "I know, I am going to do it". His automatic response is "Realisation is not action". It is important to do something every day that moves you towards your goal.

Winston Churchill said: "It is a mistake to look too far ahead. Only one link in the chain of destiny can be handled at a time."[148] Focus on immediate actions rather than be overwhelmed by the bigger journey.

Accelerate your progress towards meeting your goals

Brian Tracy suggests four techniques to accelerate your progress towards achieving your goals. The first technique is verbalisation, where you write down a clear, specific and measurable goal. Next he suggests visualisation, where you should visualise your goals with as much clarity and vividness as possible. Visualise your goals intensely and create within yourself the same feeling that you would have if you had already achieved your goals. He also suggests visualising your goals frequently; the more you visualise your goals, the more clarity you will get on them. The third technique is emotionalisation, which is about creating feelings within yourself that you would experience if you had already attained the goal. The greater your desire to achieve the goal, the more power and energy you will put into it. The last technique is rationalisation. A rationalisation occurs when you write down all the reasons why you want to achieve this goal and the benefits you will enjoy when you attain it.[149]

He also suggests using your time wisely, arguing that you should only do the habits that move you closer to your goals. When you are clear about your goals and know what you want, you will become increasingly impatient with activities that do not support your goals. To ensure that you stick to your action plans to achieve your goals, Brian Tracy suggests projecting yourself forward in time to when your goal is achieved, and then looking back from the perspective of success to the present time and writing down at least 20 answers to "I achieved this goal because I". Write down the things that made you successful. Tracy suggests taking another paper and completing the sentence: "I failed to achieve my goal because I didn't..."[150] Make another list of answers.

When I completed this exercise on adhering to my action plan, it helped me to stay disciplined and focused on my goal, which was writing a book in an agreed time. Some of the things that could detract me from my goal were procrastination, focusing on other activities, a lack of discipline, being negatively influenced, a lack of confidence, and feeling insecure. My positive list of habits that would help me achieve my goal was planning to write each day, eating healthy food for more energy, allocating a no distraction period, positive affirmations, writing from experience, drawing authentic examples from my life, and committing to my own deadlines. Once you have a goal that you want to achieve, complete Annexure 4, *Worksheet for Goal Setting*, which will help you to include all the important elements. Look at the example I completed in Annexure 3 to guide you with this exercise.

Summary

- Once you complete the vision for your life, finish the purpose exercise and know your highest values, the next step is to formulate your goals on how you are going to get there. What are the goals that will align with your vision for life, to your purpose and your governing values? Once you have a vision, set goals, which become stepping-stones to you achieving your vision.

- Set yourself an hour where you will be not disturbed and start brainstorming in the eight areas of your life that which you would like to achieve. Project yourself ten years into the future and ask yourself what you would like to be, have or do in each of these areas in your life.

- Once you have a short list of goals, categorise them into short-term (one month or less), intermediate (more than a month to a year) and long-term goals (more than a year).

- These goals need to be further refined into SMART goals.

- Make a detailed plan of action towards achieving each goal. You must organise the list of activities in terms of highest priority and sequence.

Chapter 19

Identify role models and mentors

"A mentor is someone who allows you to see the hope inside yourself."
(Oprah Winfrey[151])

I have mentored many people and I have had great mentors in my life. Mentorship is a wonderful, magical experience, which sadly very few people explore. Mentorship is not counselling or therapy, but an opportunity for someone who has walked the path before to provide guidance and share the lessons from their own journey. I do not have all the answers and I am continuously growing and learning. I often reach out to people to help me on my journey. A mentor is not only a person who is older than you are; I have many millennial mentors who help me navigate the complex world of social media. My daughter sometimes plays the role of my mentor by challenging my perceptions. Find yourself a mentor who has journeyed the less travelled path and will help you navigate the road ahead. The right mentor is someone who has overcome obstacles. Find someone you respect and who can teach you new skills or share life lessons.

Read the biographies of great people like Nelson Mandela, Gandhi and Oprah; let their lives be a lesson to you. You need to be prepared to learn from the experiences of others who have travelled the same path as you. Most of the time you will learn that the path to success never runs smoothly, and that these people demonstrated courage and tenacity to overcome the challenges in their lives. Remember, you can learn from everyone. In this way, you do not need to repeat others' mistakes. Sir Isaac Newton said, "If I have seen further, it is by standing on the shoulders of giants".[152]

Decide what kind of a person you want to be. What are some of the positive habits and principles that are important to you? Find someone who exemplifies them. Robin Sharma suggests that one finds positive reference points, which are people who are brilliant at what they do. "Positive reference points will pull you into a new way of seeing things and introduce you to a new set of possibilities. Doors you never even knew existed will begin to open."[153]

I will always remember the moment I identified a role model. I was nine years old and I loved having my hair short. One Saturday afternoon my aunt was cutting my hair and talking with such exuberance as she completed the task. I remember thinking that one day I wished I could display that level of confidence. Over the years, as I grew up I continued to admire her passion for life and effervescence.

Many people who have come before us have walked the same path and have learnt how to avoid the potholes in the road. It is our responsibility to seek out these people with humility and ask them to be our wise guides on our journey ahead. Ask these guides how they achieved what they did and what they learned. Also, ask them about the pitfalls and the obstacles. What would they do differently if they had to take this trip over again? Through social media it has become easier to engage these successful people – we can follow their blogs or pose questions directly to them. It takes courage to approach someone and ask them to show you the way; many people prefer to struggle alone and are too proud to ask for assistance.

An ideal mentor is:

- someone who has experience in the field (they have been there before);
- someone who is interested in developing others;
- someone who is prepared to take another by the hand and guide them through the territory;
- someone who asks questions that the mentee does not ask themselves but ought to;

- someone who is trustworthy and inspires confidence; and

- someone who will be available in times of need.

Since people have varied skills and talents, it is natural to have more than one mentor in your life who can help you to deal with different life challenges.

Choosing role models

"If you do what other successful people do, nothing can stop you from eventually getting the same results they do. And if you don't do what they do, nothing can help you." (Brian Tracy)[154]

Many ordinary people have taken great steps to translate their lives into extraordinary success stories; they defied their own limitations to become successful. These are role models – they demonstrate certain characteristics or talents that you admire. Remember to choose your role models carefully. Everyone has strengths and developmental areas and whilst some role models may demonstrate great strengths, they may also demonstrate some vices or bad habits. Therefore, it is important to view role models holistically. Sometimes you may start to idolise the employee and then unfortunately role model other bad habits.

Summary

- Find someone you respect and who can teach you new skills or share life lessons.

- Many people who have come before us have walked the same path and have learnt how to avoid the potholes in the road.

- It is our responsibility to seek out these people with humility and ask them to be our wise guides on our journey ahead.

An ideal mentor is:

- someone who has experience in the field (they have been there before);

- someone who is interested in developing others;

- someone who is prepared to take another by the hand and guide them through the territory;

- someone who asks questions that the mentee does not ask themselves but ought to;

- someone trustworthy who inspires confidence; and

- someone who will be there in times of need.

Chapter 20

Flourish through feedback

We pack away our schoolbooks. Yippee! School is finally done!
No more homework, no more lessons, just chilling in the sun.
Over time, we find our favourite response to everyone is, "I KNOW",
That is the first sign that you are complacent, and not open to grow.
You stop taking feedback and feel you know best,
You pat yourself on your back, no more silly tests!
Every night before you lay down your head to rest,
You need to ask yourself did you really do your best?
It is time to reflect on what you learnt from the day,
Did you rant and rave or stay calm when things did not go your way?

"Learn as if you were going to live forever. Live as if you were to die tomorrow."
(Mahatma Gandhi[155])

As human beings we are all works in progress and there is always something new to learn. As the world is developing at an accelerated pace, with technological developments changing the global landscape, old knowledge quickly becomes obsolete. Stephen Covey refers to sharpening your sword, i.e. staying relevant, while the Japanese refer to Kaizen, which means 'continuous improvement'.

"By three methods we may learn wisdom: First by reflection, which is the noblest; second by imitation, which is the easiest; and third by experience, which is bitterest." (Confucius[156])

It is important that we are open systems that can receive feedback without judgement and accept the wisdom within. When people tell us their stories and experiences, we can take those and learn from them by looking at the lessons. Whilst experience is a great teacher, it is not only your own experiences that you learn from, but also those of others. Read books and learn from the mistakes of others.

One morning, just after breakfast, I said aloud, "I don't know why Dad used that pan to fry his eggs". My daughter, who loves her father dearly, piped up in his defence. She threw up her hands dramatically and said, "You must understand Mummy, he is still learning". At that moment I thought, for someone so small, she has wisdom beyond her years. Sometimes we are so tough on ourselves and we forget that we are still learning, no matter our age.

Being an open system means being willing to take in feedback from the external environment. Have you ever stubbed your toe on a rock because you were in a rush and did not slow down? Even a stone can be a teacher. I earnestly believe that there are lessons that can be found in everything – you just need to be aware of them. Remember to tap into the wisdom of children; they provide a magic mirror that reveals all your vices.

Understanding our preferred way of learning

In school, we used to sit patiently whilst the teacher explained the lesson for the day. Some students thrived, while others were disengaged to the point of boredom. This is because as human beings, we have different styles of learning. Some of us may be visual and learn better by watching and seeing, whilst others may learn through listening and are auditory in nature. Other people learn through experience and are more kinesthetic. By understanding our preferred style of learning, we can grasp new information and improve our communication skills. I am visual and I need to write down notes in order for me to see the information and retain it. I have tried listening to audio recordings but I lost interest after a while. I would rather read the book.

The visual learner

The visual learner likes to see things in front of them; they generally learn by reading. I studied full time at university when I completed my degree. Years later, I studied a diploma through correspondence. When I compare the two experiences, I enjoyed the full-time lectures where I could see the lecturers and remembered what they said based on their body language, their expressions and their tones of voice. I visually recorded most of the lectures in my mind and used my notes from the lectures to trigger my stored memories. I always go to important meetings with a notebook to record the salient points.

The auditory learner

The auditory learner listens to others and learns through listening; they love listening to audio books and listening to music. I have an auditory husband and he is great at distinguishing tones, even in music. His primary way of learning is through audio tapes. It is horrible when we have a disagreement, as he is able to remember exactly what I said. Being a visual learner, in my personal relationships it would not be practical to carry a notebook, so I often forget discussions unless I place reminders on my phone.

The kinesthetic learner

Kinesthetic learners learn through experience and application; they want to try things out and get bored sitting in a classroom listening to a lecture. They prefer hands-on learning. My mother is an example of a kinesthetic learner. She loves experimenting when she bakes and is only happy when she tries something for herself. These learners love learning by playing games and gamification techniques are great for them to have fun and learn at the same time.

You also get people who are great at a combination of two or three of these learning styles. What type of learner are you? If you would like to identify your learning style, you can complete an online questionnaire at www.educationplanner.org.

The stages of competence

I bought a new car which has been a source of both irritation and entertainment. My previous car had the gears on the right of the steering wheel and the new one has it in the centre where most cars have their gears. When I first started driving the new car, I kept switching the windscreen wipers on. My previous car had an automatic brake so I never had to remember to put the handbrake up. The new car has the handbrake that you physically have to pull up. The other day I drove 200 metres only to realise that I forgot to put the handbrake down. I was grappling with change until I changed my mindset, stopped comparing cars, and focused on learning the functions of the new car.

There are four stages of competence that one goes through when learning a new skill. Often we start learning a new skill but because we are not familiar with it, we give up too easily. It is important that we persevere and understand that learning is often a process we need to go through. It starts off with unconscious incompetence, where you are not aware or not interested in a certain skill. Before I learnt self defence, it did not matter to me that I did not know how to fight, just like I was not concerned that I did not know how to drive like a formula one driver – it was not high on my priority list of skills. The only association I had of the word 'shrimp' was with seafood, yet in self defence it is a technique of moving away. I was okay not knowing how to fight and not understanding the vocabulary. I was **unconsciously incompetent**. Once I realised that it is a life skill that is necessary for women to have, I moved to being **consciously incompetent**. This is where I am right now, which means that I have to consciously think about what I am doing. After a few years of disciplined practice I can move to becoming **consciously competent**. I have no illusions of becoming **unconsciously competent**, where I master the skill and it comes naturally. Remember to persevere when you are learning a new skill. Do not give up as learning is a process.

Unconscious incompetence	Conscious incompetence	Conscious competence	Unconscious competence
You are unaware of a skill and your lack of proficiency.	You are aware of the skill but are not yet proficient.	You are able to use the skill but only with effort.	Performing the skill is automatic.

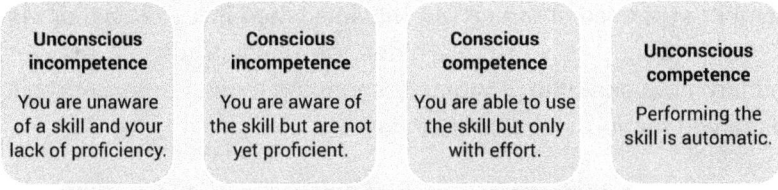

Receiving feedback

Often we deflect any feedback we receive as we consider it to be criticism, but feedback is a brilliant mechanism that we can use to grow. When we shut ourselves off from the perceptions of the world, we construct an unrealistic picture of reality. It is essential to be open-minded when receiving feedback. One morning during the school run, my daughter and I were chatting. She used the word 'following' but pronounced it as 'followring' and I corrected her pronunciation. She refused to change her pronunciation so I explained the importance of growing through feedback. I further explained that she will grow when she learns new things. My daughter is very strong willed and promptly responded, "You are wrong Mummy, the only time you grow is when you have a birthday or when you are sleeping". At just four years old my daughter was rejecting feedback, and I imagined what her life would be if I surrendered my responsibility to give her feedback. When someone offers you their viewpoint, try responding with gratitude. Say "Thank you" and comment that you never considered that before and promise to give it some consideration.

Criticism

"Sticks and stones may break my bones, but words will never hurt me." (Anon)

I remember as a child shouting out this line when I was teased or insulted on the playground. As you grow older, the childish teasing evolves into something more scathing. Imagine responding to your boss with this if he criticised you for your behaviour at work!

We are so used to being defensive that we forget that sometimes there is validity in the criticism. Not all criticism is bad, yet sometimes you may receive constructive feedback in a negative way. I have learned to say "Thank you" to all criticism. Then I take the time to evaluate whether there is any validity in it and if so, assess how I can improve going forward. It takes emotional maturity to accept feedback calmly without retaliating in a destructive way. We are always learning and growing, but to develop effectively into the best version of ourselves, we need to be willing to take feedback from the external world. If we believe that we 'know better', we block opportunities for future growth.

We are works in progress

We are always learning, growing and finding beautiful lessons on the way. There is humility in admitting that you do not always have the answers. I have found that people generally want to share their knowledge and wisdom if they think that you are sincerely looking for guidance. We must be open to the possibility that there will be people on our journey to help us – all we need to do is ask for it.

Alvin Toffler said, "The illiterate of the 21st century will not be those who cannot read and write, but those who cannot learn, unlearn and relearn".[157] When we finish our tertiary education, we often feel that we have spent our years studying and we never have to open another book again. Unfortunately, our education is only the beginning. To truly grow and thrive in this world, we have to continue to learn and adapt. Sometimes we learn through reading or watching, and sometimes we learn through the experiences of others. To differentiate yourself from the ordinary to become extraordinary, you will have to surpass the expectations of others and challenge your own limitations. You also need to create time to reflect on your daily experiences so that you can learn the lessons.

Carol S. Dweck[158] described two different mindsets: a fixed mindset and a growth mindset. People with a fixed mindset believe that their basic qualities are simply fixed traits. They also believe that talent alone creates success without any additional effort. Those with a growth mindset, however, believe that they can develop their most basic abilities through dedication and hard work, and that talent is just the starting point. A growth mindset leads to a focus on learning, increased effort, and a willingness to learn from mistakes.

Many people are transparent in their fixed mindset – just ask them to try new food and they will squish their face in distaste and say unequivocally that they would never eat that! When you are sharing new information with these people, they will interrupt you and say they already know. They will often cut off any suggestions, arguing that they would never work, without bothering to reflect on the situation and evaluating the possibilities.

"It takes a deep commitment to change and an even greater commitment to grow."
(Ralph Ellison[159])

summary

- As the world is developing at an accelerated pace, with technological developments changing the global landscape, knowledge quickly becomes obsolete.

- It is important that we are open systems that can receive feedback without judgement and accept the wisdom within.

- By understanding our preferred style of learning, we can grasp new information and improve our communication skills.

- The visual learner likes to see things in front of them.

- The auditory learner listens to others and learns through listening.

- Kinesthetic learners learn through experience and application.

- There are four stages of competence that one goes through when learning a new skill: unconscious incompetence, conscious incompetence, conscious competence and unconscious competence.

Section 6

Focus on Your True North

- Reinforce relationships and seed out your garden

- Have an abundance mindset

- Resourcefulness, serendipity and resilience

- Discipline and perseverance

This section focuses on the enablers and disablers that will either assist you to reach your dream or prevent you from getting there. Your support networks are important to spur you ahead when you are tired, discouraged and want to give up. There are people in your life who will provide more discouragement than encouragement and you must let them go. The mindset you use to approach your goals is essential.

Embrace the future with an abundance mindset; be optimistic and train your mind to be open to opportunities. Create the habits of self-discipline so that your goals are part of your daily routine. When things do not go as planned, be resilient and bounce back. In addition, pay attention to other lessons you are exposed to through acts of serendipity. You need to persevere to achieve your goals.

Chapter 21

Reinforcing relationships

"Beginning today, treat everyone you meet as if they were going to be dead by midnight. Extend to them all the care, kindness and understanding you can muster, and do it with no thought of any reward. Your life will never be the same again."
(Og Mandino[160])

When I first read this powerful quote and imagined how my day would change knowing that I would not see the same people tomorrow, it physically slowed down time for me. I spent a few moments longer interacting with people, made time to connect with others, and reconnected with friends I had lost touch with. We often take people in our lives for granted – we expect them to always be there. We become emotionally shattered when someone we love passes on, which is why it is necessary to make time for those people who play a significant role in our lives.

As humans we are social beings and need to feel loved and that we belong. When we have healthy relationships with others it helps in all areas of our lives. These relationships are critical in helping us on our journey of life. John Maxwell described the importance of relationships best when he said: "Good relationships are more than icing on the cake in life. They are the cake."[161] Research conducted by the Stanford Research Institute showed that money made in any endeavour is determined by 12.5% knowledge and 87.5% one's ability to deal with people.[162] Many studies have also been done on the impact of social relationships on one's level of physical fitness. People with strong social relationships maintain better health, resist disease better, and deal more successfully with the problems they encounter.[163]

Anthony Robbins listed two of six human needs as a sense of significance and a sense of connection/love. Significance is feeling unique, important, special or needed, while connection/love is a strong feeling of closeness or union with someone or something.[164] We often struggle with getting the right balance – we want to express our own identities and live our lives the way we want to, but still fit in with the needs of others. This is best described in a marriage where each individual wants to optimise their potential, but they need to do it in consultation with the other.

Do not assume that because you come from a big family, a network of friends or work with people that you have effective relationships with them. The very least is that you may know people, but that is no guarantee that these people rate you highly or are willing to forge a meaningful relationship with you. It is therefore important to make a concerted effort to build and reinforce these relationships. To have a meaningful relationship with others, you need to first have a meaningful relationship with yourself. This means that you need to know yourself, like yourself and accept yourself. How are people expected to like you if you do not like yourself? Silence that critical voice inside you that undermines your confidence. Do the necessary work to get to know yourself better. This means that you need to understand the things you truly enjoy, the moments that make you happy, and the activities that bring you joy. Sometimes we are so focused on pleasing others that we sacrifice our likes to fit into a group of friends. Only once you feel that you enjoy your own company will you be confident that others will like you too. If you are a shy and timid person, it does not mean changing who you are to get friends, it just means working on the relationships with people in your inner circle.

RATE YOURSELF IN EACH ROLE

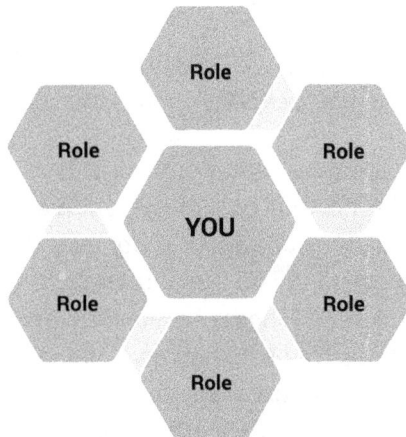

To understand the quality of your relationships, do this exercise by Hyrum Smith[165] where you rate yourself in each of your roles on a scale of one to ten, one being failing and ten being outstanding. In the middle of the circle write your name, and in the outer circles write the different roles that you have in your life. For example, mother, daughter, sister, wife, friend, employee, manager, citizen. For each of the roles give yourself a rating. Also, give yourself an overall rating in the centre as a human being. To get a more accurate score, ask the people in your life to rate you. So, you can ask your mother to rate you as a daughter or you can ask your husband to rate you as a wife. You get the idea.

This exercise will help you understand how much time and attention you have been spending on the significant people in your life. It can also provide feedback on where you have been spending a disproportionate part of your time. For example, if you rated yourself a 9 as an employee and only 2 as a wife and 4 as a mother, you know that that you have spent more time focused on work than on your family. It also clarifies your blind spots. You may think that you are an exceptional wife or husband, only to find that your spouse has rated you poorly. This exercise helps you to reconcile your own perceptions with the views of others, and provides a great compass for where you should focus your time to start reinforcing your relationships. When you do spend time with the significant people in your life, let it be quality time where you focus your attention on them. Sadly this is difficult to do as most people are attached to social media on their smartphones and automatically split their focus.

"I wish I could show you when you are lonely or in darkness the astonishing light of your own being." (Hafiz of Shiraz[166])

This quote expresses the pure sentiment that a true friend brings into our lives. Dave Buettner found that one of the unique things that promotes longevity on the island of Okinawa is a social network. This powerful network is called a 'moai', and is a lifelong circle of friends that supports people well into old age.[167] These social networks lend financial and emotional support in times of need, and give all their members the stress-shedding security of knowing that there is always someone there for them. We often underestimate the influence that our friends have on our lives, and do not spend enough time nurturing these relationships. In stressful times it is comforting to have the caring voice of a friend help you through a rough patch. The television series *Friends* was one of the most popular and successful series on television. People watched it for the great story line and cast, but it also became inspirational for people who longed to have the same bond with their own friends.

"A day without a friend is like a pot without a single drop of honey left inside."
(Winnie the Pooh[168])

The power of acknowledgment

"Compliments are gifts of prosperity." (Louise Hay)[169]

Try to have a positive influence on people within your close network. I phone my mother each day to connect with her. I have been doing it for the past 23 years ever since I left home. I do so not out of obligation, but out of love. Since I stay far away from her, the catch-up phone call in the evening has become part of my daily ritual. Sometimes a small action which may seem insignificant to you has a significant impact on somebody else. Never take for granted your potential to brighten someone else's day by simply greeting them and making them feel visible.

Every morning I look at my Facebook and LinkedIn platforms to check whose birthday it is. I try to acknowledge people by wishing them on a day that they most treasure. Sometimes I miss a few, but I have made it a habit to put a smile on someone else's face.

Be known as being happy for other people's successes. Give selflessly without expecting anything in return. Give others mindful attention and be available to listen to them. Be reliable and punctual. Keep your promises and be known to be trustworthy. Have empathy and compassion for others. Demonstrate a sense of humour about life. These will help you to deal with life's small irritations with joy.

"You can't stay in your corner of the forest waiting for others to come to you.
You have to go to them sometimes." (Piglet from Winnie the Pooh[170])

As human beings we are social and have a need for connection. We need people to talk to, laugh with and share our experiences. Find reasons to share compliments and be authentic when you do it. In this way you are focusing your mind on the positive. Practice showing appreciation and gratitude. Most of us pass at least 50 people on a daily basis. How many of us actually greet, smile or acknowledge these people?

Give others mindful attention

"Treat people as if they were what they ought to be and you help them become what they are capable of being." (Johann Wolfgang von Goethe[171])

Sometimes we talk to people and they are not fully engaged; you can hear it in the responses they give us. Those interactions make us feel like they do not value our time or contribution. When we are learning to connect to people, we need to be fully engaged in our interactions with them; we need to make them feel like they have our full attention. My daughter always tries to get my attention when I am busy with something and she gets upset if I do not give her my full attention. When I say, "I am listening", she says, "No Mummy, you are not listening with your eyes". She insists, "Show me your eyes!" Already my daughter understands the difference between selective attention and full attention. Selective attention is disrespectful to the other person. When you are thanking someone, make the effort to catch their eye and put emotion and appreciation into your voice. We have become so accustomed to multi-tasking that we hold complete conversations whilst we are checking our email or typing on our laptops. We fool ourselves into believing that we are living fulfilled lives, using our time optimally.

Appreciate people for their unique perspectives

We often get frustrated with others for their lack of support and are disappointed when they do not see our dreams the way we envision them. We cannot understand why people look at things so differently from us. We forget an important principle – that we are unique beings. Just like we have different sets of thumbprints, similarly, our outlook on life and how we understand things is unique. There are many people who are shy and quiet and love to blend in with their surroundings. They try not to draw attention to themselves but prefer to remain unnoticed. Make time to engage with these people and you will discover that their shyness masks their beautiful souls.

Express your intent

Always communicate your intent. Most of my disagreements with my husband have arisen because I did not communicate my expectations upfront. I have since learnt that I cannot get upset over something that was my responsibility to communicate. We always judge other people by their behaviour because we do not understand their intent. Instead, we make assumptions and then assign motives to them.

Accept others

"When you go out into the woods and you look at trees, you see all these different trees. And some of them are bent, and some of them are straight, and some of them are evergreens, and some of them are whatever. And you look at the tree and you allow it. You see why it is the way it is. You sort of understand that it didn't get enough light, and so it turned that way. And you don't get all emotional about it. You just allow it. You appreciate the tree. The minute you get near humans, you lose all that. And you are constantly saying 'you are too this', or 'I'm too this.' That judgment mind comes in. And so I practice turning people into trees. Which means appreciating them just the way they are." (Ram Dass[172])

Just as you are a product of your experiences and history, so are other people who have their own challenges to deal with. Try not to interpret the behaviours of others through your own filter; rather listen and understand who other people truly are and not who you think they are. We do not see people as they are, we see them as we are. When we interact with other people we judge them based on our character. We may be suspicious by nature and when someone does a good deed, we start looking for ulterior motives rather than accepting their actions. "In times of crisis the wise build bridges, while the foolish build barriers. We must find a way to look after one another as if we were one single tribe." This is a quote from the movie, *Black Panther*.[173]

Create meaningful connections

We can either have healthy functional relationships with others that bring us joy or dysfunctional relationships that bring us pain and disappointment. When we connect to others we need to connect from our true characters in order to create a meaningful connection. When we try to build relationships by connecting through our false selves or personas, there is no real connection. Imagine that you have to cross a chasm between two mountains. The other person reaches out to you but instead of extending their real hand they hold out a plastic hand instead. Would you be confident holding onto something that appears to be fragile or would you prefer holding onto something more substantial? We often develop these personas as a means of protection in the real world. Gandhi said that people should be the same in their private and public lives. Authenticity is critical to building relationships.

Build trust with others

When you are building relationships with others, it is important to establish yourself as trustworthy. This means that you have a strong character and can be relied on. It is important that when you give your word that you follow through. Do not promise something to get out of a difficult situation; it is difficult to rebuild trust once it is broken. When you are trying to earn trust, live up to the expectations you set and always honour your commitments.

In his book *The Speed of Trust*, Stephen Covey[174] suggests that trust is based on one's character which should be constant. When you trust someone, you look at elements of their credibility which include their integrity, intent, capabilities and track record. Does the person make and keep commitments to you? Intent refers to their motives. Do they have the skills to deliver against their promise? Do they have a good history of reliability and dependability when you need them? One of the things Covey suggests we do is build trust accounts with other people where we make deposits continuously when we nurture our relationships with them. When we need to make withdrawals from this trust account, it is easier because we have built a solid relationship with the other person. When you build trust accounts, it is different for each person as individuals are unique and value different things.

The following story is a good example of building a trust account.

Tshepo looked at the kitchen clock again. It felt like time had not moved. She was helpless. It had been almost an hour since she had received a call from her mother pleading for her to come home, but she did not have the money to pay for a flight. She wanted to go home to see her baby sister, Karabo, who was born with diminished lung capacity and was prone to severe asthma attacks. She had just had another attack and her mother was not sure her sister would pull through.

There was no doubt Tshepo was needed at home. The echoes of her mother's heartbreaking sobs still rang in her ears, but Tshepo had no money. She was at university due to a bursary that paid for her tuition and accommodation. She usually paid for her meals through her part time job, and was in a different province far away from home. She had no rich uncle to call for funds – she was usually the person her family called for funds.

Where was Susan, her roommate, when she needed her? Susan should be back from her evening lecture by now. Just then Tshepo heard the door open and burst into tears as soon as she saw Susan. Tshepo shared with Susan her crisis. She felt better having spoken about her fears. Susan listened, provided comforting words and suggested that Tshepo go to sleep. Tshepo was emotionally drained and easily fell asleep.

Whilst Tshepo slept, Susan instantly contacted their mutual friends by WhatsApp. She explained Tshepo's plight and asked for donations. Within an hour, she had raised the return plane fare as well as extra money for doctors' fees. Each of the girls who donated money told Susan their own story of what Tshepo had done for them. One girl related how Tshepo stayed at her side when she had flu to make sure she was eating and nursed her back to health. Another girl spoke about how Tshepo stood by her when she had failed her exam, giving her hope to continue trying. A third girl told Susan how Tshepo shared her notes and tutored her when she was out of class with the measles. Susan knew that Tshepo was indeed a special person, but she was not aware of all the other amazing deeds she had done for others. The next morning Susan shared her surprise with the grateful Tshepo. With her selfless deeds, Tshepo had unknowingly built a trust account with her friends. In her time of need, her friends did not think twice about offering her assistance.

Stedman Graham lists 11 character traits that inspire trust:[175]

1. Keep your word and follow through on your commitments.

2. Accept people by giving them your full attention.

3. When others require your aid, be available. This means being both physically and emotionally available.

4. Pay what you owe when it is due.

5. Act with honour.

6. Lead an honest life.

7. When others share confidential information you need to protect that information.

8. Provide strength to others in their time of need,

9. Be willing to acknowledge your mistakes.

10. Share your blessings without looking for praise or payment. It is important to do good deeds without expecting any compensation or rewards.

11. Help others to succeed by placing their needs before your own. Be interested in seeing others succeed as much as you would like to see yourself succeed.

Be the lighthouse in somebody else's storm by continuously building trust accounts with all the people in your life. Remember that trust is sacred and once lost, it is very difficult to regain.

Be respectful

"You never forget a person who came to you with a torch in the dark." (M. Rose[176])

Respect those who have held you up in your life. Treat everyone with equal respect, irrespective of their social status, their job title or their wealth. We are all on this journey of life; be respectful of your fellow travellers. Be respectful when you interact with other people. Be respectful of their time. Know that each person has a purpose and no one's purpose is superior to any other purpose. These days it seems fashionable to be obsessed with successful people – people with status, fame and wealth. We follow them on social platforms and even watch their lives through reality series on the television. We are so busy respecting "important" people that we have little time for those who walk silently at our side who go unnoticed. I have learnt to respect all people, irrespective of their station in life, from the lady who cleans the toilet to the petrol attendant. I do not respect people just because they have 'fancy job titles' or positional power. I respect people for their personal power. Personal power is about how you show up as a human being. Are you kind, generous and respectful of others?

In 2002, my father was in hospital again after a five month emotional rollercoaster of hope and despair. He was undergoing a simple medical procedure with no cause for concern, yet when he got out of theatre, my father was forever changed. He had gone into cardiac arrest and stopped breathing, and when they revived him he had lost his long-term memory. Thereafter it was mostly downhill. The doctor called in the immediate family and told us that he had done all that he could do and there was nothing further medical science could do. He suggested that we turn to a spiritual solution, prayer. It was one of the lowest points in my life and a day that will forever be ingrained in my memory. We saw the sands of time passing through the hourglass, and valued every single grain. My father was in the Intensive Care Unit (ICU) and every morning and afternoon we would visit him. We would try to go earlier than visiting hours allowed to be able to stretch the time. The security guard at the hospital was very understanding of our situation and often let us in earlier so we could spend extra time with my Dad. The nurse who was responsible for the ICU was a considerate person who prepared special meals for my Dad that he enjoyed. That was a defining moment in my life, when I really came to understand the importance of respecting everyone, irrespective of their job title. The nurse and security guard were two of the most important people to me and deserved and received my acknowledgement and respect.

Take responsibility for your actions and your behaviour. When we accidentally trespass on other people's values, we need to apologise sincerely. Apologise when you are wrong and be humble when you are right. Always do the right thing, even if it is difficult. Be a person your children will be proud of.

Express your affection

Loneliness is one of the most common causes of depression, so communicate your feelings to others and show the people in your life that you care. When you are feeling lonely, ask a close family member for a hug or give a hug to someone. Remember when we discussed the power of anchors? When someone hugs you, the hug is a trigger that takes you back to earlier memories as a child when you were hugged by your parents; when you felt safe and secure in the world.

- Hugging increases levels of the "love hormone", oxytocin, which is beneficial for reducing stress and improving heart health, amongst others. I once heard a neuropsychologist recommend a dose of seven daily hugs to improve one's level of happiness.

- A 20-second hug reduces the harmful physical effects of stress, including its impact on your blood pressure and heart rate.

- A 10-second hug a day may fight infections, boost your immune system, ease depression and lessen fatigue.

- The giver of a hug receives just as much benefit as the receiver, but some research suggests the healthiest hugs must come from someone you trust (as opposed to a stranger).

Never force your attention on others without first getting permission. Some people like their personal space and are uncomfortable with physical contact with friends.

Weed out your garden

"You are the average of the five people you spend the most time with." (John Rohn[177])

Another popular saying is, "Show me your friends and I will show you your future". What research has found is that all the people in your network have the potential to impact you. If a friend of yours became obese, you are 45% more likely to become obese in the next two to four years. We do not really understand the influence of others in our lives. Growing up, authority figures play a significant role in shaping our personality and character, but we forget that as adults we are just as susceptible to the influence of others.

Your garden is an analogy for your life. The state of your garden is dependent on how much time you spend on ensuring that it is healthy. Most people focus on developing their achievements and grow beautiful beds of flowers, however we forget that a beautiful garden with invasive weeds gets destroyed over time. It is therefore important that whilst you are striving to improve your life, you should ensure that there is nothing draining you. We already spoke about getting rid of the kryptonite in your life which are the bad habits, but toxic people can be just as damaging.

Avoid gossipmongers

This story has been accredited to Socrates, although the original source may have been someone else. Either way, it is a great tale that gives us some helpful hints on how to better deal with those who gossip and how to stop ourselves from spreading rumours as well.

One day, a man came up to the great philosopher. "Socrates, I have just heard some news about one of your friends", he exclaimed.
Socrates responded that the man should stop sharing the news until the man passed Socrates' test.
"What's the test?" the man asked.
"The first test is that of truth. Tell me, do you know that what you're going to tell me is absolutely true?" asked Socrates.
The man looked doubtful. "Uh I am not sure. I actually I heard this news from someone else."
"The second test is that of goodness", Socrates continued. "Is what you're about to tell me something good about the other person?"
"No, actually it's not that great..."
Socrates interrupted the man, "So what you're going to tell me is neither true nor good?"
The man was slightly embarrassed and shrugged his shoulders.
Socrates continued, "There is one final test which is usefulness. Is what you're about to tell me going to be useful?"
"Probably not", the man replied.
"Well, if you're not going to tell me something that's true, good or useful, then why tell me at all?" responded the philosopher.[178]

Connect to authentic people who are willing to stand up for you when you are not present. Many people will flow into your life; some of them will be silently competing with you, wishing for your failure. Learn to weed out false friends and focus on sincere ones. Pay attention to their character. People who are always gossiping about others demonstrate their poor judgement. You never know what they are going to say about you behind your back.

Sometimes you have to walk away from people whose energy drains you. The term 'energy vampire' has grown in popularity over the years because people have seen validity in the term. An energy vampire is someone who you interact with who leaves you drained. I am sure you have come across someone in your life that makes you feel physically weighed down.

Just as you outgrow the clothes that you wear, there may be people in your life that you outgrow. Not all people will be rooting for your success. There may be people close to you who will be envious of your achievements and throw water on the fire of your dreams. You need to stay away from these people.

The power of negative influence

The power of suggestion is one of the reasons that negative people are not a good influence over you. It is usually a flippant remark someone in your close circle makes in reaction to a challenge you may be going through. For example, you could innocently share that you are worried about your health and share your symptoms. A negative person will use the power of suggestion and suggest that they know someone with similar symptoms, and it resulted in serious health problems where they were hospitalised. You hear this story and a seed of doubt is planted in your mind. It is therefore important to guard yourself against the poor influences of other people.

Imagine you decided to take a journey on a beautiful day. You have planned the route you are going to take. You have packed all the things you might need. You are confident that you have enough fuel. Feeling generous, you ask a few people to accompany you. Suddenly your car gives you problems and it starts to overheat. As if that is not bad enough, you suddenly hit a pothole and puncture your tyre. No great crisis, as you have a spare wheel. You have an idea of how to change tyres, so there is no worry. Then as you are on the road changing the tyre, there is a sudden downpour. You still maintain a good mood. You get into the car and the passengers start to complain about their experience. They start to blame you for all the things going wrong on the journey. The passengers in the car start to talk you out of completing your journey. This is what happens in our real lives when we allow false friends to accompany us on our journey. At the first sign of difficulty or resistance, they abandon you to fend for yourself.

Research shows that a deliberate suggestion can influence how well people remember things, how they respond to medical treatments, and even how well they will perform and behave. This means that the way we anticipate our response to a situation influences how we will respond. In other words, once you expect something to happen, your behaviours, thoughts and reactions will contribute to making that expectation occur. If you are new in your job and your colleagues tell you a whole lot of negative information about your boss, you will probably have the same experience as them because you will look for evidence to support their view. Stay away from toxic people who only plant negative thoughts in your garden.

Other research has shown that your mood is affected by the moods of others. This means that someone's negative mood can be spread to you through social contagion. This research is important in illustrating what I have always believed – you need to stay away from people who are chronically negative because their emotional state is contagious. These people can contaminate you and your reputation, as you will be judged by your association with them which will reflect poorly on your judgement. If you are a parent, then this research is especially critical for you to ensure that the networks of friends that your children hang out with are positive.

Have you ever played poker? Each person places their money as ante and they keep raising their bets. This is what I think of when I see a group of people sitting around complaining about a person or an issue. Each one tries to outdo the other by adding more complaints, until the winner is the one who leaves with the total pot. The prize is often melancholy and depression caused by emotional contagion.

So what could they have done differently? They did not intend to come across as negative. They were not even aware of the damage they were doing to their mood. In their minds, they were sharing the things that had been stressing them, it just happened to be the same issue. Their mood did not improve after the interaction. All it did is validate that they were in fact treated unfairly and therefore "they were right" and the person or situation was wrong

False friends

Have you ever been deceived by a rosy red apple? You imagine how juicy it is going to be and really look forward to eating it, only to bite into it and realise that it is rotten at the core. What a disappointment! Similarly, we can look at people and see that they appear to be well groomed with no cares in the world, but inside their true character may be filled with anger, bitterness, jealousy and resentment.

Beware of false friends who will surround you when you have material possessions and status, but ignore you if you do not. Look for genuine people who want to associate with you for the strength of your character rather than the number of your possessions. My favourite quote from Oprah is: "Lots of people want to ride with you in the limo, but what you want is someone who will take the bus with you when the limo breaks down." Look for genuine people whose lives demonstrate integrity and substance.

Here are some ways of determining whether your friends are energy generators or energy vampires. Watch how they interact with other people. Do they treat others with respect and speak well of others? Do they consistently blame others for challenges in their lives? Can you rely on these people in times of stress to show up for you?

If you read this and realise that you may be the weed, then it is not too late to change your behaviour. Do not spend your time gossiping with others. When you speak of others, use your influence to praise rather than criticise. Become a person with integrity. Try to be honourable and always do the right thing. Learn to be sincere when you praise your friends. Be genuine in your feedback; you will start to feel good and like yourself. Try being yourself with others so that people can get to know the real you. Build trust by being trustworthy. That means keeping people's confidences when necessary and being there to provide support. If you start to be the friend you want to have, your real friends will show up. Be a friend of quality.

Discover your true friends

Marcel Proust said, "Let us be grateful to people who make us happy; they are the charming gardeners who make our souls blossom".[179]

Once you have gotten rid of the weeds which are negative people, focus on planting perennial plants that will flourish. On your journey you need the right type of people to inspire you and push you. The right friends hold you accountable; they are constantly trying to improve themselves and their capabilities, and inspire you to do the same. These are the people who will inspire you to always try your best because they want you to succeed. They are the people who will be motivating you and cheering you on every step of your journey, encouraging you to persevere. In the book *5 Day Weekend*, the authors suggest you create a life board, which is your personal board of directors who will help you steer your life, conquer your obstacles, and achieve your goals. They also suggest a social influence ratio as follows: spend 20% of your time mentoring others, which allows you to reinforce the knowledge you have; spend 30% of your time with people who are on the same wave length as you; and spend 50% of your time with people who are more experienced, knowledgeable and successful than you.

The people who fill your life with joy demonstrate gratitude and kindness; they help you reveal your best qualities and light the path for you. These are the people you treasure. They may not be the wealthiest or the most famous, popular or successful, but they are the ones with the greatest capacity to bring joy into your life. The only people who deserve to be in your life are those who treat you with kindness, respect and compassion.

summary

- As humans we are social beings and need to feel loved and that we belong. When we have healthy relationships with others it helps in all other areas of our lives.
- To have a meaningful relationship with others, you need to first have a meaningful relationship with yourself. This means that you need to know yourself, like yourself, and accept yourself.
- We need to spend time nurturing our relationships, especially with the significant people in our lives.
- We need to give acknowledgement of others in our lives by giving them mindful attention.
- Give others full attention when we engage with them so they feel valued.
- Appreciate people for their unique perspectives.
- Always express your intent when dealing with others so that you are never misunderstood.
- Accept others unconditionally without judging them through your belief system.
- Create meaningful connections by expressing your authenticity.
- Build trust with others by starting a trust account.
- Be respectful of all people, irrespective of who they are and what they can do for you.
- Connect to authentic people who are willing to stand up for you when you are not present.
- Stay away from toxic people who only plant negative thoughts in your mind.
- The only people who deserve to be in your life are those who treat you with kindness, respect and compassion.

Chapter 22

An abundance mindset

"The key to abundance is meeting limited circumstances with unlimited thoughts."
(Marianne Williamson[180])

We are here in this life to sow and reap, not to hoard and keep. We live in an abundant universe; the more we share and give, the more we receive. It is often beliefs that shape how we process information – they help us to filter messages from the external environment. For example, if you believe that there are limited resources in the world and when you acquire wealth, giving it away will diminish your ability to get more wealth, your scarcity belief will create feelings of depression with any financial loss. However, if you have an abundant mentality and you see that whatever you give away you will receive tenfold, then when you lose money you are less anxious.

When you read any self-help success book the advice is generally always to live a life of abundance; have an abundance mentality and prosperity will come your way. Abundance may have a different meaning to each of us, however. I have often seen people who were brought up in poor living conditions roll their eyes in disbelief when you say they should have an abundance mentality. Their belief system sees this as esoteric mumbo jumbo and they prefer to see life as having finite resources. Yet what if Marianne Williamson's quote offers a clue to how one should achieve an abundance mentality? What if in looking at our present financial or career situation we begin to entertain possibilities? We may start to think creatively about our circumstances and rather than sit back and accept our poor fortune, we might start to wonder, 'What if?' It may seem like wool-gathering, but what we are actually doing is starting to see outside the box and looking at solutions in innovative ways. Have you ever heard the saying that necessity is the mother of all invention? Something magical happens when you feel blocked in a corner. At that moment you have a choice to surrender to anxiety or to let your creative juices flow.

Wayne Dyer offered another clue to abundance when he said, "Doing what you love is the cornerstone of abundance in your life".[181] Abundance only comes when you are in alignment with what makes your heart sing. When you are happier you resonate at a higher level of energy, which makes it easier to think positively and be creative about what other things can bring this energy into your life. Anthony Robbins reinforced this idea when he stated, "When you are grateful, fear disappears and abundance appears".[182] Gratitude places you in a positive frame of mind where you are able to start from a positive balance.

When our beliefs and expectations influence our behaviour at the subconscious level, we are enacting a self-fulfilling prophecy. So what does a self-fulfilling prophecy have to do with an abundance mentality? There is reputable research in this field that demonstrates the power of one's belief in creating certain circumstances in one's life; that through believing in the possibility of an abundance mentality, by its very nature it will manifest great opportunities in one's life. Brian Tracy suggests that if you have an attitude of abundance, then you will be confident, optimistic, and positive, and continually work confidently in the direction of your dreams.[183]

Everyone equates abundance to financial prosperity, but it is actually an attitude you have about life in general. "True abundance is not based on our net worth, it's based on our self-worth." (Gabrielle Bernstein[184])

When you want to develop an abundance mentality, you need to be clear about how you are going to think about your life in the future. Focus on the blessings you already have in your life and use these as a springboard into what else is possible. Each day nurture your thoughts and guard against negative beliefs. Protect yourself from well-meaning family and friends who look at life as the glass being either half full or half empty. You need to hold the belief that the glass is refillable.

My chili tree

I have a beautiful little chili tree that has been growing for the past few years in my garden. I planted the seeds and ensured that I made the effort to water the plant every day. When I planted the seeds I envisioned I would have an abundance of chilis and my intent was clear.

What I found interesting were the different responses these little trees elicited. When my chili trees was still young and growing, the comments were as follows:

"What is the point of growing chilli when you can get them from a supermarket? Is it really worth the effort?"

"Your plants are growing well now that it is summer, but it is going to die in the winter."

"Why did you plant so many chili plants? What do you plan to do with all those chilis?"

The lesson from my chili tree was that your efforts will always be rewarded. No one notices and comments on your incremental progress. Now that my tree has been bearing beautiful chilis, it is always a source of conversation with visiting family and friends.

"You know what you should do with chilis, chop them up and preserve them in olive oil."

"You should cut all the chilis from your tree. They are going to be wasted."

"Why did you leave some chilis to dry on the tree, you should have cut them off."

Everyone will have an opinion on your successes in life, but you should never forget the reason you chose the journey in the first place. Now that my tree is blossoming with chilis, I feel content and accomplished. It feels great knowing I have access to chilis whenever I need them. I have been through enough few winters now to realise that the root of my chili tree is planted strongly in the soil, and that even if it stops giving me chilis in winter, a new tree will sprout in spring; all the seeds from the dried chili will create new plant shoots. It is the same kind of certainty that enables me to have an abundance mentality about life in general. Be unapologetic about your dreams, be unwavering in your faith, and be uncompromising about what you can achieve.

Being open to opportunities

"When one door closes another door opens, but we so often look so long and so regretfully upon the closed door, that we do not see the ones which open for us."
(Alexander Graham Bell)[185]

I have often heard people complain that nothing good ever happens to them, but when you look closer at what they are doing to prepare themselves for opportunities, they are doing nothing. These people subscribe to a scarcity mentality, where they believe opportunities are limited and always given to other people.

"Luck is what happens when opportunity meets preparation." (Seneca)[186]

Sometimes we are oblivious to the opportunities that present themselves because we are focused internally on our own challenges and insecurities. We are so complacent in our lives that we procrastinate our goals and we are never ready to access opportunities when they present themselves. We get used to complaining about the present state of our lives, but do not make a concerted effort to improve the circumstances of our life. Anne Landers[187] described this phenomenon when she said that opportunities are usually disguised as hard work, which is why people never recognise them. I have seen great opportunities being offered to people who turned them down because they were just not ready. Sometimes it was not about their skill level, but their level of personal mastery that let them down; they could not manage their own emotions properly and their interactions with others were poor. The thing about opportunities is that they do not come around very often, and if you let them slip by, you are not going to get another chance for a very long time.

When opportunities present themselves, grab them with both hands – do not doubt yourself. Two years ago I presented at a talent management conference and received such an overwhelmingly positive response that I was asked to write a book on the topic of succession management. I did not think twice and immediately agreed. I did not allow myself time to talk myself out of it. I did not think about the time commitment or intense focus that was required. Neither did I think about whether I had the requisite skills to write a book. I completed the book, which was published and positively received. Last year I presented at a breakfast session on the topic, "Live, Love, Learn and Leave a Legacy". Again, I was approached and asked whether I would be prepared to write a book on the topic. Here I am, six months later, writing this very book.

Summary

- We live in an abundant universe. The more we share and give, the more we receive.
- Abundance only comes in when you are in alignment with what makes your heart sing.
- Focus on the blessings you already have in your life and use these as a springboard into what else is possible.
- Abundance is actually an attitude you have about life in general.
- Be unapologetic about your dreams, be unwavering in your faith, and be uncompromising about what you can achieve.
- Sometimes we are oblivious to the opportunities that present themselves because we are focused internally on our own challenges and insecurities.
- Train your mind to look for opportunities and you are more likely to find them.

Chapter 23

Resilience

"Life is not about how fast you run or how high you climb, but how well you bounce."
(Vivian Komori)[188]

We will all go through times of challenge in our lives. They may come from an unexpected direction when you feel at peace and in control of the events in your life, and you will suddenly be thrown into circumstances where you will feel helpless. It is at times like this that you will require the greatest resilience.

Resilience is about being able to bounce back and being adaptable to change. The famous scientist, Charles Darwin, explained that it is not the strongest of the species nor the most intelligent that survives. It is the one that is most adaptable to change.[189]

This year I faced one stressful situation after another; it felt like I was being knocked down by a series of waves and as I was struggling to get up, another wave knocked me down. Every day I had to remind myself that I was stronger than this; I said to myself, "This too shall pass". Months later, when I reflect back, I am glad that I kept my optimism and did not choose misery. Nobody likes to attend pity parties. Now I think, what if all that I had been through was merely a test? A test that I know I passed and can share with a smile, knowing that I faced life's challenges head-on by choosing the harder road.

Various studies have been conducted on resilience, with one maintaining that a person has a psychological immune system that allows them to recover after a disappointing event. We are familiar with our physical immune system which we try to build up to protect ourselves from catching diseases, however the notion that we also have a psychological immune system suggests that there are actions we can take to build our levels of resilience.

Recipe for resilience

RECIPE BOOK

When things do not go as planned, do the following:

- Reframe the situation.
- Maintain a positive outlook.
- Keep the situation in perspective.
- Avoid negative thinking.
- Focus on your positive abilities and strengths.
- Do not try to solve the problem with the same thinking that created it. Look at alternative ideas in different life dimensions.
- Depend on your strong social network.
- Manage your emotions with exercises like deep breathing.

Serendipity

The Tapestry Poem[190]

"My life is but a weaving
Between my God and me.
I cannot choose the colours
He weaveth steadily.
Oft' times He weaveth sorrow;
And I in foolish pride
Forget He sees the upper
And I the underside.
Not 'til the loom is silent
And the shuttles cease to fly
Will God unroll the canvas
And reveal the reason why.
The dark threads are as needful
In the weaver's skillful hand
As the threads of gold and silver
In the pattern, He has planned
He knows He loves, He cares;
Nothing this truth can dim.
He gives the very best to those
Who leave the choice to Him."

(Corrie ten Boom[191])

"It is the law that any difficulties that can come to you at any time, must be exactly what you need most at the moment to enable you to take the next step forward by overcoming them. The only real misfortune, the only real tragedy, comes when we suffer without learning the lesson." (Emmet Fox[192])

Sometimes we choose a path but along the way we regret our decision. Remember that you are exactly where you are supposed to be. There are lessons on each difficult path that you may never have gotten on the easier path. We are designed to pay more attention and focus when things are going wrong in our lives.

Have you ever felt that you were in the right place at the right time? Serendipity has been described as "the capacity for making happy discoveries along the road of life" or "accidentally discovering something when you were not looking for it".[193] The word 'serendipity' comes from the fairy tale of the three princes of Serendip. These princes have different adventures which seem at first to be disastrous, but due to their happy discoveries turn into great successes. There are often hidden blessings in our challenges when we start to view life from different perspectives, therefore you must adopt a mindset of positive expectations.

Resourcefulness

"The measure of who we are is what we do with what we have." (Vincent Lombardi)[194]

Merely having resources does not make one resourceful. Being resourceful is about having the ability to find quick and clever ways to overcome difficulties and to veer towards goals. It is an attitude that enables you to keep trying different solutions until you succeed.

To be resourceful, you need to create a habit of generating multiple ideas and generating different outcomes to different life challenges. When you are trying to achieve your goals, there will be obstacles in your path. You need to become resourceful by trying alternative paths to get to your goal rather than changing your goal. Great examples of resourceful people include Walt Disney, whose initial ideas were rejected. Being resourceful means you need to practice your problem-solving skills. Look at the problem, understand the challenge fully, create possible solutions and choose the most appropriate solution. If this does not work, have a back-up plan. Always reflect on what the lesson was so that if in the future you face a similar situation, you know the best approach.

Being resourceful is a general approach to life; you need to be able to be in any situation and problem solve effectively by looking at alternatives. You also need to be emotionally resilient. When something does not go according to plan, you need to be mature enough to quickly bounce back and consider an alternative plan. You need creativity, great problem-solving skills and emotional maturity to be resourceful. When we hold a limited view of the world, we box ourselves in and shut down possibilities. Sometimes you also need great relationships with people and a network you can depend on when you need a Plan B.

summary

- Resilience is about being able to bounce back and being adaptable to change.
- When things do not go as planned, practice skills that make you more resilient, such as reframing the situation or maintaining a positive outlook.
- There are often hidden blessings in our challenges when we start to view life from different perspectives.
- Sometimes what we perceive as mistakes become blessings in disguise.
- Accept that there may be bigger lessons that you are not aware of.

Chapter 24

Self-discipline

Do not tarry, do not delay,
Finish up the tasks you commit to today.
We think, Tomorrow is another day, so we procrastinate,
We lose time when we abdicate.

Do not tarry, do not delay,
Remove all distractions out of our way.
The clock is ticking, you will never find,
Another future with extra time.

Do not tarry, do not delay
Complete what little you can do today.
If you stop with excuses and move your feet,
Before you realise it, your goal is complete.

Often, when we do not have the self-discipline to see things through, we surrender too easily and start preparing excuses about why we did not complete a task. Self-discipline is one of the most difficult yet rewarding skills you can develop in your life. To give your word to yourself and honour that commitment is the greatest gift you can give yourself. When you cannot hold your promises to yourself, what hope is there that you will be true to others? We do not place enough value on ourselves. Every year family and friends boldly announce their new year's resolutions, yet these are soon forgotten. I was one of those people who were guilty of setting too many resolutions that I never kept, so now I make quarterly resolutions in each life dimension.

One of my resolutions was to stop eating processed food, sugar, wheat and dairy for six months to bring my body back into a state of balance. It was not as tough as I thought it would be because I had clarified my intention upfront by thinking to myself, 'What is a commitment I am not prepared to break?', which was my wedding vows. I then made a commitment to eat the correct foods and gave it the same significance as I did to staying loyal to my marriage vows. My weakness is chocolate cake and when any idea of chocolate cake came into my mind, I would quickly squash it.

219

In December we were on holiday and I decided to take a break from my diet. One night I had a piece of chocolate while watching TV. The next morning my three year old woke me up and literally waved the chocolate paper in front of my face. Like an angel of repentance, she asked in a reprimanding tone, "Mummy, have you been eating chocolate when you said it is not healthy for you?" She turned to her father, "Dad did you see that Mummy was eating chocolate?" She wanted to check if my husband condoned my behaviour. She continued to wag the chocolate paper in front of me, saying in a scolding tone, "Naughty Mummy!" I felt shamed by a three year old. I explained that chocolate is still unhealthy, but Mummy felt like eating a piece. I believe that you must be accountable for your actions; if you want to teach a young child self-discipline, you need to be a role model.

Keep to the commitments that you make and always be true to your promises. Think carefully before you give your word since you will have to deliver against your promise. It is also important to keep to time commitments you have made to yourself and others. Be disciplined with how you spend your time; do not waste it on things that dissipate your energy. There are generally two misconceptions about time – the first is that we think we will have more time at some unspecified future date than we have presently, and the second is that we think we can save time. It is this limited thinking that causes us to procrastinate. It is therefore important to be aware of your time and how it is spent. If you do not plan your day by prioritising your highest values, your time will be filled with things of no consequence such as interruptions, conflicting priorities, procrastination or preoccupation. We wonder how some people can be so successful when we struggle to find time to fulfil our responsibilities. All of us have 24 hours each day, but our choices in our life determine how we spend our time. When I was on my diet, I wanted to create a state of health so that I could have a better quality of life and be available for my daughter.

"To stay proactive in a reactive world, you need unyielding self-discipline; because you cannot always control your circumstances, but you can control your response. Because in the end, success isn't the result of circumstance; it's the result of the response to circumstance. And that's the heart of self-discipline." (Patrick Ewers[195])

Recipe for self-discipline

RECIPE BOOK

Create a compelling reason to stay disciplined. You are much more likely to stay disciplined if you have a compelling reason to do so; a clear and motivating picture of what you are working towards. Every year millions of people around the world fast for religious reasons. During this time, they stay committed to observing their fast because of their belief that a higher purpose fuels their discipline.

According to Caroline Webb, there are five steps to channelling self-discipline and beat procrastination:[196]

- Vividly imagine how it will feel to complete the task you are putting off. Researchers found that people were more likely to save for retirement if they were given a digitally aged picture of themselves.

- Visualise the consequences of failing to complete that task. This forces us to evaluate the result and impact of not completing something in the required time.

- Publicly commit to completing it by a clear deadline. Research has found that since people respect their social standing, they do not want to look like they failed.

- Break the goal into small manageable tasks and identify the first step to get started.

- Reward yourself for completing the first step by linking incentives to the task.

Aristotle[197] said that, "We are what we repeatedly do. Excellence, then, is not an act, but a habit". Remember that it is easier to be disciplined if you create a habit that you include as part of your daily routine. Over time it becomes the norm. I was brought up to use different spices to create tantalising meals and succulent desserts and exciting dishes. So, going on any diet was truly challenging since my mind had memories of what tasty food looked like, smelled like and tasted like. I had happy associations with food. My mother is a great cook and when I prepare food, I think about her and the recipes that she has passed on. I needed to scramble my memories and reprogramme my mind to build different associations with food. I tried different techniques but finally this one worked for me. Each time I was tempted to cheat on my diet, I would walk into my kitchen and look at the containers in my pantry, which I had temporarily relabeled to create negative associations. For example the label on the sugar container was Diabetes and the label on the biscuit and pasta containers was Obesity.

"Motivation gets you going, and habit gets you there." (Zig Ziglar[198])

Perseverance

Albert Einstein did not speak until he was four years old. Benjamin Franklin, one of the founding fathers of America, dropped out of school when he was ten years old. Richard Branson has dyslexia and did not cope well in school. Thomas Edison failed more than 1.000 times before he invented the light bulb. Vincent Van Gogh only sold one of his paintings whilst he was alive.[199]

History has many stories of successful people who persevered against great odds before they were successful. Nelson Mandela said, "Do not judge me by my successes, judge me by how many times I fell down and got back up again".[200] There is only joy when we succeed and reach our goals in life. We feel accomplished and believe that anything is possible. We must have perseverance and above all, confidence in ourselves.

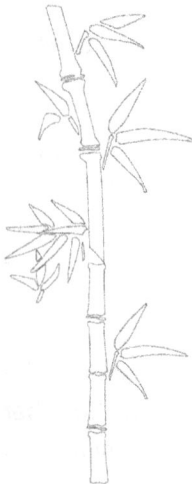

In China, they grow Chinese bamboo trees. This tree grows very differently from most other trees and requires special care and attention. When they sow the seed in the ground and water it, nothing happens in the first year. The gardeners, however, continue to water it and nurture it year after year.

With each year that passes the gardener continues to water, fertilise and take care of the plant. It fails to sprout even after the fourth year. Now, if you were an observer watching the gardener watering a seed that had not germinated for four years, you would be skeptical about whether the plant would ever grow. You might even wonder what the point was if there were not going to be any positive results. Then suddenly in the fifth year, something miraculous and incredible happens. Within five weeks the Chinese bamboo grows up to 90 feet! The question often posed is did it take five years to grow, or did it grow within the five weeks? It is obvious that the five years of nurturing the bamboo shoot was necessary to cultivate the solid root system to support the bamboo tree for the rest of its growth.

This story is often used as an analogy for success in one's life. Sometimes it takes years of continued sacrifice and dedication to a cause, and we often become disheartened when our efforts are not instantly rewarded. However, the years of dedication are important to the long-term success of our projects. The lesson is to persevere even when you do not see immediate results. Take comfort in the fact that you are following your passion and that eventually, you will reap the rewards.

The world seems to be accelerating and everything needs to happen at a quicker pace. There is a greater focus on instant gratification and immediate results, which creates unrealistic pressure on us to want to keep up with this unrealistic rate of progress. There are certain things in life that still take time to achieve. Learn and grow at your own speed. There are certain fundamental lessons in life that cannot be hurried that require learning, failing, relearning and growing. Remember the bamboo tree story the next time you want to give up. Do not get dissuaded from your path and journey by others who do not share your vision. It is not their vision, it is yours.

Recipe for perseverance

RECIPE BOOK

- Remember to set realistic goals that you have the capability to achieve.
- Do not compare your progress with those of others. It creates unnecessary pressure on you.
- Create affirmations around your goals that you repeat to yourself.
- When you feel yourself losing momentum, speak to your support network.
- Motivate yourself with incentives that are aligned to your highest values.

- Remember the previous times when you persevered and achieved your goals.
- Visualise how it will feel when you have achieved your goal.

Summary

- Self-discipline is one of the most difficult yet rewarding skills you can develop in your life.
- Be disciplined with how you spend your time. Do not waste it on things that dissipate your energy.
- We think that we will have more time at some unspecified future date than we have presently.
- We think we can save time so we procrastinate to a later date.
- Create a compelling reason to stay disciplined.
- An idea to stay discipline is publicly committing to complete your action by a specific deadline.
- The lesson is to persevere even when you do not see immediate results. Take comfort in the fact that you are following your passion and that eventually, you will reap the rewards.

Section 7

Your Life as a Message

- Generosity of spirit

- Live with gratitude

- Have no regrets and let your heart sing

- Safeguard your character

It is important to live an authentic life that is aligned to your purpose and to be committed to achieving your dreams. Just as important is the legacy that you contribute to on a daily basis. This section looks at the important characteristics that truly define an individual's success. We live as integrated beings in a social world where our actions impact the lives of others and vice versa. It is important to demonstrate a generosity of spirit through your contribution to the lives of others and the world at large. Live a life of gratitude and service and this will lead to the path of happiness. Once you realise your dreams and consistently follow your heart, there will be no regrets. Let your life be a message to others by inspiring people with your character. This brand of authenticity is the only one you need to differentiate yourself from the rest of the world.

Chapter 25

Generosity of spirit

Your life is a message, what should it convey?
What is the tagline? What should it say?
What would you want your life to teach?
What are the stories that should be shared in your farewell speech?

When we give of our hearts more than our purses,
We start to collect goodwill instead of curses.
Your generosity is worth more than money and time,
It is about surrendering your heart and opening up your mind.

A random act of kindness, oh what is it really worth?
Not much to you, but to the destitute, the Earth.
A cup of hot coffee to a homeless person on the street,
A pair of little shoes to cover dainty blistered feet...

When you reach out a hand to someone in need,
Your life becomes more meaningful with all the good deeds.
It is always you more than the receiver that actually gains,
Once you contribute, you add another link in the Karmic chain...

Mahatma Gandhi was once asked by a reporter, "What is your message to the world?" Gandhi responded by jotting down on a piece of paper: "My life is my message."[201] If your life was a message, what would the message be? Can others learn from your contribution to the world? Not all of us are destined to be world leaders or scientists who come up with breakthrough cures. Our greatness lies in our intention to contribute to the lives of others. You may be a parent, a manager, a big brother or a member of your religious council where you have the opportunity to positively influence lives. It is totally up to you what actions you take. You do not have to try and change the whole world, all you need to do is to touch the heart of one person or make a difference in one life.

Newton said that he saw further by standing on the shoulders of giants. In the same way, we need to be able to learn from those who came before us. This world has seen many examples of brilliant, philanthropic, caring people who all endeavoured to make a difference and leave a legacy. They are testament that anyone can make a significant contribution and shape the destiny of many lives.

Focus on touching one life

Loren Eiseley wrote a beautiful story about starfish which has been adapted over the years.

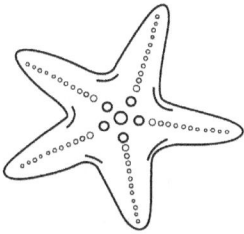

A young man is walking along the ocean and sees a beach upon which thousands and thousands of starfish have washed ashore. Further along he sees an old man, walking slowly and stooping often, picking up one starfish after another and tossing each one gently into the ocean. "Why are you throwing starfish into the ocean?" he asks. "Because the sun is up and the tide is going out and if I don't throw them further in they will die." "But, old man, don't you realize there are miles and miles of beach and starfish all along it! You can't possibly save them all; you can't even save one-tenth of them. In fact, even if you work all day, your efforts won't make any difference at all." The old man listened calmly and then bent down to pick up another starfish and threw it into the sea. "It made a difference to that one."[202]

Create a trigger for continuous change

Sometimes making a difference in one person's life is enough to create a ripple effect in the lives of others. A great example is an apple seed that has the potential of an orchard within it. I was very fortunate to join the Partner for Possibility Initiative six years ago when they first launched the programme in Johannesburg. This programme enables business leaders to partner with principals from disadvantaged schools as part of a two-way leadership journey. One partners with the principal for a duration of a year and works on a project related to improving the lives of the school children. Even though you are partnering with the principal who is one person, by positively influencing his or her leadership style, there is a ripple effect on the teachers, the children in the school, and the community at large. Never

227

underestimate your potential to be a force for good in the world. If each of us does what is necessary to effect positive change, together we can make a huge impact. This sentiment was best described by Johann Wolfgang van Goethe[203], who said, "Let everyone sweep in front of his own door, and the whole world will be clean".

Leave a legacy

Kalu Ndukwe Kalu[204] said, "The things you do for yourself are gone when you are gone, but the things you do for others remain as your legacy". Leave a legacy of value and contribution. A legacy is often misconstrued as something that you leave when you pass on, but you can leave a legacy when you are still alive. You leave a legacy every time you change your social groups, move houses or change jobs. A legacy is not about what you leave behind when you die, it is the character that follows you through all those defining periods in your life when you made choices and lived your life according to your principles. Often, when employees move on to new organisations, the legacies they leave behind in the form of products or processes they developed are still spoken of.

Be responsible for your life and your actions. Live your life aligned with integrity, and start to positively influence the lives around you. To do this you do not need a qualification or a certificate. You do not have to be nominated into an office or have an esteemed job title. All you need is the intention to positively influence change in the areas that you can. Like Gandhi said, "Be the change that you want to see in the world".[205] There is graciousness in living according to your own conscience.

It is important that you create a life of significance, not by accumulating things for yourself, but by contributing to the lives of others. By touching someone else's life you become a gift to them and a blessing in their lives. What a wonderful thing to be, a blessing to someone else. Each of us is special. Our diversity and unique characteristics can help spread joy and happiness to others. Remember, we cannot enlighten others if our own path is draped in darkness, so choose to use your kindness, your attention and your compassion to bring light into someone else's life. Remember the saying, 'Charity begins at home'. It is often glamorous to be seen as a social activist or a philanthropist, but start impacting the lives of your immediate family unit before you start impacting the wider society. "In the end, only three things matter: how much you loved, how gently you lived, and how gracefully you let go of things not meant for you." (Gautama Buddha[206])

Embrace life fully by not settling for second best. When you are living in accordance with your highest values and principles and living towards your potential, you naturally increase the level of your energy. When you have greater energy, you have a more vibrant light to shine in the world. Rather than living a life of pity, choose to live a life of contribution and purpose. All you have to do to change the trajectory of your life is to make different choices about what you spend your time on.

"Service is the virtue that distinguished the great of all times and which they will be remembered by. It places a mark of nobility upon its disciples. It is the dividing line which separates the two great groups of the world—those who help and those who hinder, those who lift and those who lean, those who contribute and those who only consume. How much better it is to give than to receive. Service in any form is comely and beautiful. To give encouragement, to impart sympathy, to show interest, to banish fear, to build self-confidence and awaken hope in the hearts of others. In short—to love them and to show it—is to render the most precious service." (Bryant S. Hinckley[207])

The causes that resonate with you

"Many people have the wrong idea of what constitutes true happiness. It is not attained through self-gratification, but through fidelity to a worthy purpose." (Helen Keller[208]) It is therefore important that you find a cause that you are passionate about. It could be different for each person. I have friends who feel strongly about supporting organisations such as the Society for the Prevention of Cruelty to Animals or the World Wildlife Fund, whilst others focus on orphanages or the protection of children. There are so many worthy charities that require a helping hand, but you need to find a cause that resonates with you. It does not necessarily have to involve financial resources, it can be something as simple as reading a book to a child or spending an afternoon in an old age home. I am a member of the Lightworkers Woman's Organisation which is a group of professional women focused on assisting vulnerable and disadvantaged women and children. "The best way to find yourself is to lose yourself in the service of others." (Mahatma Gandhi[209])

Show love and compassion

"Self-absorption in all its forms kills empathy, let alone compassion. When we focus on ourselves, our world contracts as our problems and preoccupations loom large. But when we focus on others, our world expands. Our own problems drift to the periphery of the mind and so seem smaller, and we increase our capacity for connection – or compassionate action." (Daniel Goleman[210])

Research on altruism demonstrates that altruistic people are less stressed, lead more fulfilled lives and often live longer. Human beings have an overwhelming capacity for love and compassion, yet sometimes we hide these beautiful traits from the world, afraid that we may be exploited. The best time to dance is when you start to hear the music playing. The best time to love is when you feel a human spirit is fractured. Open up your heart and you will discover a boomerang effect; the more you give to others, the more will come back to you through self-fulfillment. Have you ever performed a random act of kindness without expecting anything in return? It is the most fulfilling feeling to surprise someone with kindness; the receiver brightens up with appreciation. Princess Diana[211] believed in this philosophy, noting that one should, "Carry out a random act of kindness, with no expectation of reward, safe in the knowledge that one day someone might do the same for you".

Over the years I have supported many charities and been involved in various community projects. One of the initiatives that most touched my heart was a Youth Day celebration that I was a part of, where I was invited to do a mindfulness session with 100 girls from foster homes. The day was really beautiful; there were girls from the ages of 9 to 17 who were participating in different activities. The most touching part of the day for me was when all the volunteers stood in front of the hall and each one was given an opportunity to give hugs to the girls. As I hugged each girl, I felt so privileged to have friends and family in my life that I can hug any time I want to. To show love and compassion to these beautiful children was not only a gift to them, but a gift to me. The last time I had felt the same level of overwhelming love was when I held my daughter in my hands for the first time.

This was the poem I wrote for the girls to remind them that each one is a special and unique child of God, and that they can keep their inner flame vibrant and bright by loving themselves. The poem was used to anchor the session so that they always remember the message shared with them.

No matter what I do, no matter what I say,
I am a special Child of God, I am special in my own way.
Deep within me is a beautiful light,
No one can touch it, it is locked up safe inside...

I am so unique, there is no one else like me in the world,
No one with my thumbprint, I told you, I am a special girl.
No matter what others tell me, it is simply not true,
I am a precious beautiful child, no matter what I do.

I won't wait for anyone to show me kindness or love,
'Cos deep inside I have more than enough.
No matter what happens, it doesn't matter what they say,
I was born to be unique in every possible way.

You may search the world, you will never find,
Another me, 'cos I am one of a kind.
I don't listen to others, what do they know?
They have not seen my inner beauty, my radiant inner glow.

Do service for the right reasons

The Dalai Lama says, "If you can, help others; if you cannot do that, at least do not harm them".[212]

Service is about how we influence, impact, and elevate the lives of others, and not about elevating our own lives. Unfortunately not all people who do kind deeds have altruistic reasons. There are some people who use their acts of service to build a brand for themselves. Their self-promotion of selflessness is actually selfishness. One of the exercises suggested by Wayne Dyer[213] is to make an attempt to serve others in some way each day and not tell anyone. This is about doing a selfless act and not trying to get praise and recognition for it. I found this exercise very interesting. When I first tried it out it was very difficult not to at least tell my husband of my good deeds. I have become better at this exercise but sometimes I still slip up because I usually get carried away as I become so overwhelmed by the emotion I feel.

Nelson Mandela International Day

"If you want happiness for an hour, take a nap. If you want happiness for a day, go fishing. If you want happiness for a year, inherit a fortune. If you want happiness for a lifetime, help someone else." (Chinese proverb[214])

Nelson Mandela International Day was launched in recognition of Nelson Mandela's birthday on 18 July 2009. It was inspired by a call Nelson Mandela had made a year earlier for the next generation to demonstrate leadership in addressing the world's social injustices, when he said that, "It is in your hands now". Nelson Mandela started making an imprint on the world in 1942 when he first started to campaign for the human rights of every South African. By devoting 67 minutes of your time – one minute for every year of Mandela's public service – you can make a small gesture of unity with humanity. If you have never done anything selfless for anyone, then begin on Mandela Day and join millions around the world to make a difference in the lives of others. Never underestimate the potential of one person to make a difference in the world. The great people we remember and honour are simply individuals who had the courage of their convictions and stood up for what they believed in. They were usually people who stood alone, unrelenting against the winds of fortune.

Just give of yourself

Zig Ziglar[215] said, "You never know when a moment and a few sincere words can have an impact on life". The following story expresses this sentiment.

John and Peter had become good friends. Their doctor appointments coincided and they had a lot in common. They were the same age and often spoke about the teams they both supported. Whilst Peter was an energetic and optimistic person who kept seeing the golden lining, John was depressed and worried about everything. They remained involved in each other's lives over the years through social media.

It had been two years since the boys had met face-to-face. As fate would have it, they were in the same hospital at the same time. Their mothers thought it would be great if they could share a private room. Peter went into the operating theatre first and when he came out he lay in his bed feeling defeated. John tried to cheer him up with stories, which was not really helping. So John started telling Peter about the park outside the window. John's bed was next to the room's only window. The window overlooked a park with a lovely lake. Ducks and swans played on the water as children played in the garden. There was a beautifully manicured garden with lovely colourful flowers. Grand old trees graced the landscape, and birds flew in the sky. John described the beautiful park and the lovely trees that provided shade for the elderly people. As John described all this in exquisite detail, Peter on the other side of the room would close his eyes and imagine the picturesque scene. John knew Peter was a cricket fanatic and described the kids' cricket games in detail.

John's operation was postponed as his blood pressure was too high, so they spent the next few days in each other's company. Whilst Peter lay helpless in his bed, John kept him entertained with exciting stories of the adventures of the park. Peter thought that it was so uncharacteristic of the old John he knew who used to spend his time complaining about everything. Peter looked forward to John's stories which provided a beautiful description of the activities outside. They spoke about their dreams and what they wanted to do when they finished school. Peter wanted to become a surgeon so he could heal other children. John wanted to reach for the stars and do space travel. On the third day John said goodbye to Peter and was wheeled into the operating theatre. The next morning Peter was looking forward to seeing his dear friend again, only to see the nurse pack John's belongings away. "Is John not coming back into this room?' Peter asked. The nurse sadly shook her head. Unfortunately John didn't survive the operation. Peter was in shock and he started to cry for the boy who had become his friend. "Nurse, can you please look through the window and tell me if there are children playing a cricket match today." The nurse looked confused and responded, "Outside the window is a solid wall". "I don't understand", said Peter. "John used to tell me of the cricket games in the park." The nurse replied, "He couldn't have even if there was a park outside, John was almost blind". Peter shook his head in wonder as he realised that even though John was so sick with his own health problems, his friend focused on cheering him up.

This story illustrates the beautiful lesson of the generosity of spirit. John used his resourcefulness and imagination to bring hope to Peter. He gave this gift selflessly and he did not expect anything in return. In today's society, the term *quid quo pro*, which means a favour granted in exchange for something, has become the widely accepted norm. Everyone is so focused on what they can get that the mere thought of doing something for someone with no return on investment seems a ridiculous notion. Sometimes doing a generous act is as simple as giving acknowledgement or attention to people who feel invisible.

Show appreciation and acknowledgement

Everyone wants to be acknowledged, recognised, valued and loved. Show appreciation in words and actions. It is important that others feel acknowledged and seen. You need to acknowledge everyone from the security guard to the petrol attendant to the lady who empties your bin. Your humanity grows when you reach out to others with the intention of sincerity, genuineness and care. Anthony Robbins says he wakes up every morning with the intent of being a blessing in someone's life. Kindness manifests in different ways. You should focus on the little things you can do to bring a smile or joy to someone.[216]

It is important to understand that there are times in our lives when we will all require a helping hand, a willing ear or open arms. Sometimes small gestures to you are phenomenal moments in someone else's life. It does not matter if you hold the door for someone or volunteer in a school – you are giving of yourself to help someone else in need, whether the need is small or large.

Show appreciation for others. It does not have to be a big deal; sometimes all it takes is a smile, a simple gesture or a thank you to make a difference in someone's day. Appreciation makes people feel good about their lives; it is one of the important building blocks of nurturing relationships with other people. It is important that you focus when you are appreciating someone – look them in the eyes or call them when you know that you will have their attention. This thoughtfulness will ensure that you do not do it as an afterthought whilst you are busy doing a hundred other things.

Also, try injecting enthusiasm into your voice. Saying thank you in a bored tone sounds insincere. Steve Jobs used to tell his people to "make a dent in the universe".[217] Isn't that a lovely expression about making an impact on the lives of others? When you appreciate someone, it says that you acknowledge their effort and it has had an impact on you.

> *"The best way to quit being concerned with yourself is to be concerned about others."*
> (Florinda Donner[218])

When you focus on others, your problems seem superficial and less important. Being in the service of someone is one of the key habits of happy people. This was reaffirmed by Wayne Dyer when he said, "When you seek happiness for yourself it will always elude you. When you seek happiness for others you will find it yourself".[219]

Protect the vulnerable

Martin Luther King Jr. explained how important our opinion is to the world when he said, "Our lives begin to end the day we become silent about things that matter".[220]

We cannot always afford to contribute financially, but there are other ways we can contribute – either through time or creating awareness of a cause that requires assistance. Try to mobilise family and friends to support a cause. With the popularity of social media such as Facebook, Twitter and Instagram, you can show support by liking someone's post or tweeting a comment to create awareness. There is a vulnerable group of people in society who require your voice or your influence.

> *"The greatest gift that comes with the privilege of speech is using your voice for those that don't have one."* (Ricky Gervais[221])

The generosity of spirit manifests in different forms. At times it may be about giving your time, while at other times it may be about giving your voice. Sometimes the greatest power you have to give is your compassion.

Summary

- Sometimes making a difference in one person's life is enough to create a ripple effect in the lives of others.

- Never underestimate your potential to be a force for good in the world. If each of us does what is necessary to effect positive change, we can make a great difference together.

- A legacy is not about what you leave behind when you die, but about your character during the defining periods in your life when you make choices and live your life according to your principles.

- It is important that you find a cause that you are passionate about.

- By touching someone else's life you become a gift to them and a blessing in their lives.

- Open up your heart and you will discover that the more you give to others, the more will come back to you through self-fulfillment.

- Your humanity grows when you reach out to others with the intention of sincerity, genuineness and care.

- At times it may be about giving your time and other times it may be about giving your voice or compassion.

Chapter 26

Gratitude

"Some people could be given a field of roses and only see the thorns.
Others could be given a field of the weeds and only see the wildflowers.
Perception is a key component of gratitude. And gratitude is a key component to joy."
(Amy Wetherly[222])

Gratitude is all about perspective. When you compare your little inconveniences in life to the real challenges of others, you begin to appreciate the serenity in your life. Some little child lost her mother today, someone was diagnosed with stage 4 cancer, a breadwinner lost his job and will not be able to feed his family, and children will go hungry another day in their life...

Lao-Tzu's[223] advice is profound. He suggests that we should, "Be content with what you have; rejoice in the way things are. When you realise there is nothing lacking, the whole world belongs to you". We are focused on seeing our cup as half empty because we expect to see it filled with unrealistic things. Yet if we look carefully in our cup and look at the things that matter the most, we will realise that in fact, our cups runneth over. What we focus on will multiply and flow. So if we start counting the blessings in our life then our cup will always be overflowing.

Reframe your experience

Jacque and Jill followed the waiter to their reserved table in the corner of the restaurant. They always chose to sit at this particular table. It is where Jacque first proposed to Jill 15 years ago. Today resembles little of that milestone event. Both Jacque and Jill know that this might be the last time they dine together. They completed their six sessions of marriage counselling and today's dinner is the point at which they will decide whether they should give their marriage another try or separate due to irreparable damage. Over the years, after having kids, they drifted apart. Jacque focused on working harder so that he could support his family, often coming home late at night. Jill tried to hold the fort and between keeping a job and being a mom, there was little time for each other. By the time Jacque got home, Jill was already exhausted and ready to turn in for the night. When she did have time, she was always on social media worrying about catching up with the lives of others instead of working on her life.

Jacque and Jill ordered their drinks whilst they looked at the menu, but they could hardly concentrate thanks to a disturbance at the next table. What a rowdy bunch, Jacque thought. Jill looked at the two women at the other table. One looked six months pregnant and was laughing in a loud and boisterous voice. The other lady was telling a story in a descriptive way, waving her hands around. Jill ignored the noise and continued ordering her meal. "Another one, waiter", requested the pregnant lady at the top of her voice to the waiter on the other side. She sounded intoxicated. The waiter arrived with a transparent liquid. "Jacque, she looks like she is drinking vodka. In her condition, what is she thinking?" Jacque looked over at the three empty glasses on the table in front of the pregnant woman. Jacque and Jill proceeded to place their order and talk about their favourite topic, the kids. There was little else left to say to each other. They could hardly hear each other over the drunken commotion at the next table.

"I think I am going to dance", announced the pregnant woman, and pulled one of the gentlemen from the table. She really looked like she was having a good time. Jill shook her head in astonishment. Jill had experienced difficult pregnancies for both her kids and she was extra cautious. "I wonder what they are celebrating?" she asked Jacque. Jacque, who has become just as curious about his neighbouring table, shrugged. Their food arrived and Jacque and Jill proceeded to eat their meal. It was a foregone conclusion that they would go their separate ways. After dinner, Jacque went out to smoke and found himself standing next to the man from the other table. Jacque was filled with curiosity and asked the man, "It seems like you guys are having a great party. Wow, the ladies are looking like they are enjoying themselves". The man smiled and responded, "Yes, we are celebrating my friend, I am glad the ladies are having fun". Having established a rapport with the stranger, Jacque continued. "Should that lady be having so much vodka in her condition?" The man looked surprised. "She is not drinking vodka, it is only water." "Really? Is she always this lively?"

The man responded, "She is always energetic but today she is extra bubbly". "She deserves to have a good time. She is my sister-in law. Her husband, my brother, died last week after a four month battle with cancer. They got the news the same day she found out she was pregnant. She has been suffering with depression; she has been at his side every day. Today, I forced her to come out and celebrate his life and that is what we are doing." Jacque apologised and conveyed his condolences. The man returned to the restaurant whilst Jacque stood reflecting over what he had just heard. He felt ashamed and remorseful. He thought about Jill and his kids and thought about how grateful he was that he still had his family. Instead of focusing on trying to build their relationship, they were ready to selfishly give up. He imagined if he lost Jill how he would feel and suddenly he knew what he had to do.

He bought a flower from the lady standing outside the restaurant. When he returned to the table, Jill was busy texting. "Who are you talking to?" asked Jacque. "My sister. I'm telling her about the behaviour of the pregnant woman", Jill responded. "Put your phone away, there is something you don't know." Jacque proceeded to relate the story that he heard to Jill, who started to tear up. Jacque handed her his handkerchief and the flower. It seemed that time stood still and in that moment, Jill also realised how fortunate she was to have Jacque in her life. They paid for their meal and walked out more connected than they had in a long time.

The above story illustrates that sometimes we need to reframe our experience. When we see things from one perspective, we rob ourselves of opportunities. We need to be grateful for the relationships we have in our lives and be able to nurture these relationships. Albert Einstein said, "There are only two ways to live your life. One is as though nothing is a miracle. The other is as though everything is a miracle".[224]

This sentiment is further reinforced by Oprah Winfrey who said, "If you look at what you have in life, you'll always have more. If you look at what you don't have in life, you'll never have enough".[225] There are many people who will say that they themselves are struggling, and yet there are many people in this world who are worse off than you.

Many years ago I was on a transformation programme, part of which involved spending an afternoon in the informal settlement of Alexandra.

I had driven past Alexandra many times but I had never actually been into the area. As I walked through the narrow lanes between the homes, I cringed in horror. I could not imagine how thousands of people could live in those cramped conditions. I walked past a house and saw a little girl of maybe two curled up on the step outside the door. I thought about the comfort of my own home and the home that I grew up in and felt so grateful for the little things I had that in comparison seemed like luxuries. I had a comfortable home with electricity, space to play outside when I was a child, and a warm safe home which offered me shelter from the cold and the rain.

According to Amy Morin, these are the benefits of having an attitude of gratitude:[226]

1. Gratitude benefits relationships. Showing appreciation can help you win new friends and build relationships, according to a 2014 study published in *Emotion*. The study found that thanking a new acquaintance makes them more likely to seek an ongoing relationship.

2. Gratitude improves physical health. Grateful people experience fewer aches and pains and report feeling healthier than other people, according to a 2012 study published in *Personality and Individual Differences*.

3. Gratitude improves psychological health. Gratitude reduces a multitude of toxic emotions such as envy, resentment, frustration and regret.

4. Gratitude enhances empathy and reduces aggression. Grateful people are less likely to retaliate against others, even when given negative feedback. They experience more sensitivity and empathy toward other people and a decreased desire to seek revenge.

5. Grateful people sleep better. Writing in a gratitude journal improves sleep; spend just 15 minutes jotting down a few grateful sentiments before bed, and you may sleep better and longer.

6. Gratitude improves self-esteem. Studies have shown that gratitude reduces social comparisons. Rather than becoming resentful toward

people who have more money or better jobs — a major factor in reduced self-esteem — grateful people are able to appreciate other people's accomplishments.

7. Gratitude increases mental strength. For years, research has shown that gratitude not only reduces stress, but it may also play a major role in overcoming trauma. By recognising all that you have to be thankful for — even during the worst times — you foster resilience.

Self-reflection
Acknowledge other people and show gratitude by thanking them. Here are some examples of phrases you can use:

- Your small act of kindness was enough to let me know just how amazing you are as a person and just how fortunate I am.
- Taking the time to help me was a very nice thing for you to do.
- I am grateful for your generosity.
- You are a blessing in my life.

As Winston Churchill said, "We make a living by what we get, but we make a life by what we give".[227]

Recipe for gratitude

1. Gratitude journal

Remember to write down a few things for which you are grateful at the end of each day. You should change the list to include different things that you are happy for. When you start doing this exercise, try being grateful for the obvious things we take for granted in our lives. We can be grateful to significant people in our lives such as parents, family, friends and teachers. We could be grateful for our physical and mental health, our life experiences, our skills, our home, our cars, our job, Mother Nature. There are gratitude journal applications that can be downloaded on a smartphone or tablet, so if you feel restricted a keeping a journal, try completing your gratitude on your phone.

2. **Say Grace**

Saying Grace for everything is a great way to incorporate gratitude in your life. My daughter says Grace and it is the sweetest thing. She thanks God for every ingredient in the salad and everything that she sees in the dining room such as the table and the chairs, amongst others. I have learnt to add an extra ten minutes for dinner time!

3. **Prayer**

When people pray there is usually an acknowledgement and gratitude to a higher power. I incorporate gratitude in my daily prayer for all the blessings I have received in my life.

4. **Remember your victories**

Remembering a difficult journey and how you overcame it enables you to feel grateful that you were victorious.

5. **Gratitude visualisation**

There are always people in our lives who we are grateful for, such as our children, life partners, siblings and parents. Picture in your mind someone for whom you are grateful. Now verbalise out loud or in your mind a few specific reasons for why you are grateful for them. The more specific the better.

6. **Person, pleasure and promise**

Dr Rangan Chatterjee suggests that when you are completing your gratitude, you should focus on person, pleasure and promise.[228] The person is someone you are grateful for, for example it could be a friend who did a favour for you and helped you in a difficult situation. Pleasure is something that has given you a source of pleasure, such as you spent the afternoon watching your child's soccer match. Promise refers to a promise in the future, where you are looking forward to something, for example reading a new book or watching a movie at the cinema.

Summary

- When you compare your little inconveniences in life to the real challenges of others, you begin to appreciate the serenity in your life.

- Gratitude improves psychological and physical health.

- Remember to write down a few items for which you are grateful at the end of each day.

- Saying Grace for everything is a great way to incorporate gratitude in your life.

- There are always people in our lives who we are grateful for, such as our children, life partners, siblings and parents.

Chapter 27

Live with no regrets

My personal regret

*Remember when we were children acting out a scene from a movie and set the curtain
alight? I thought you would restrict our freedom, but you didn't.
What about the time we were secretly building a safe under the bedroom floor? When
you found the chipped concrete I thought we had definitely gone too far and you would
discipline us, but you didn't.
Remember when I showed up at 4am on a school night? I thought you would lecture
me, but you didn't.
Remember when I opened the car door whilst you were reversing out the driveway?
When I saw the mangled door and heard the screeching of metal, I thought you would
shout at me, but you didn't.
And remember the time you were so sick, we took your car out and accidentally
smashed it through the front wall? You just watched calmly. I thought you would be
furious and reprimand us, but you didn't.
There were so many things that you didn't say and things you didn't do, and for that, I
respected you, Dad.
I thought I had enough time to tell you how much I loved and appreciated your
guidance, so I didn't.
There were a lot of things I wanted to tell you when you recovered from your illness,
but you didn't.*

The poem above is based on my real life experience with my father. We
often wait to say all the important things, thinking that there will always be
sufficient time. Time goes by so quickly that we should get into the habit
of appreciating people when they are alive. I am often told by friends to
appreciate my daughter and spend a lot of quality of time with her before
she grows up and we never had time to truly connect. It is important to
remember your highest values and make life choices aligned to those
values.

Live each moment of your life doing things that you want to do. Remember,
if you make life decisions based on your personal map of the world rather
than the maps of others, you will not live with regret. The average life span
is 71.5 years which means that you have 626,340 hours to live your life.

As I was working on this chapter, my daughter interrupted me to show me the bridge she had built. When I went into the lounge I saw my 15 cushions neatly arranged on the floor in front of each other making a bridge from the lounge to the dining room. She has made bridges in her room before with all her pillows on the floor, but it seems she was expanding her play territory. "Do you like my bridge, Mummy?", she asked as she proceeded to walk on the cushions with her dirty shoes.

Usually I would have reacted by giving her one of my "speeches", but as I reflected on this passage I was writing about regrets, I realised that I am so blessed to have an amazing, healthy child with a beautiful spirit. Instead I responded, "Can I walk on your bridge as well?" So I removed my shoes and spent the afternoon crossing the bridge.

"One doesn't recognize the really important moments in one's life until it's too late."
(Agatha Christie[229])

I often regret the things that I did not do, but I have seldom regretted the things that I have done. We lead such busy lives that we forget to slow down and do the things that really bring us joy. The common excuse is that we do not have time as we rush around in our busy lives. One day we will look back when we are old and in poor health, and the people who we treasured will have moved on in their lives.

A week after the cushion adventure my daughter called me into the kitchen to show me her artwork. "Come Mummy", she said. "Look how beautiful the cupboards look, I decorated them with different colours". My daughter had decorated my white kitchen cupboards with different coloured face paint. I was horrified and I asked her why she had decorated the cupboards. Her response: "Look Mummy, I made it beautiful so more people will visit us." I quickly reframed and told myself that it was face paint that would definitely wash out and that no permanent damage was done, so I calmly explained to her that she should not decorate any furniture without asking for permission.

"For of all sad words of tongue or pen, the saddest are these: 'It might have been!'"
(John Greenleaf Whittier[230])

This sentiment was reaffirmed in 2009 by Bronnie Ware, who wrote an online article called *Regrets of the Dying* about her time as a caregiver. She worked with dying people and developed close relationships with them during their last weeks, resulting in conversations about life and death, including what the patients wished they had done differently.

Here are the five most common regrets:

1. **I wish I'd had the courage to live a life true to myself, not the life others expected of me.**

   This was the most common regret of all. It is important that you discover your authenticity and fulfil your purpose.

2. **I wish I hadn't worked so hard.**

   All of the men she nursed deeply regretted spending so much of their lives focused on work instead of their families.

3. **I wish I'd had the courage to express my feelings.**

   Earlier in the book, we looked at managing your emotions so that it does not result in physical and mental challenges in your life.

4. **I wish I had stayed in touch with my friends.**

   Building relationships and reinforcing relationships are critical in leading a fulfilled life. It is important not to live a life of regrets and to express how you feel to the significant others in your life.

5. **I wish that I had let myself be happier.**

   This is a surprisingly common one. Many did not realise until the end that happiness is a choice; they had stayed stuck in old patterns and habits. It is important to make a choice to lead a more fulfilling life.

Robin Sharma says that he has a list of 101 things to do before he dies. He suggests that people ask themselves the following five questions that will help them to live their lives with authenticity, passion and joy:[231]

- *Did I dream richly?*

- *Did I live fully?*

- *Did I learn to let go?*

- *Did I love well?*

- *Did I tread lightly on the earth and leave it better than I found it?*

Let your heart sing

"For a long time, it had seemed to me that life was about to begin – real life. But there was always some obstacle in the way; something to be gotten through first, some unfinished business, time still to be served, and a debt to be paid. Then life would begin. At last, it dawned on me that these obstacles were my life." (Alfred D. Souza[232])

We keep deferring our happiness to some future event which will happen and magically transform our lives. We say we will be happy when we finish school and become an adult. Then we will be happy when we start earning money. Then we will be happy if we get our own car. Then we will be happy when we fall in love and find a life partner. Then we will be happy if we get married. Then we will be happy if we have a child. Then we will be happy when the child grows up and is independent. Then we will be happy when our child gets married. And the list goes on and on. When we are in this state of future anticipation, we miss the beauty of the present moment. Before we know it, we are 85 years old and we cannot remember having savoured the milestones in our life. The great thing about children is that they are able to joyfully give themselves up to the moment. I watch my daughter and she has no perception of time. I will say to her, "You have five minutes until bedtime" and she will innocently ask, "Is five minutes a lot of time Mummy?" Actually, if you think about five minutes, it is an eternity for a child who is drowning or a person going into cardiac arrest waiting for a doctor. We have become so complacent about the routine of our lives that we forget to appreciate the little moments.

One of the Reiki principles, "Just for today, I will not worry", is an easy way, each day, to bring joy into your life. Have you heard people comfort other people saying, "Take one day at a time"? This is what they are referring to. If every day we focus on not worrying, imagine how joyful in the long-term our life will be. Joy and happiness are contagious. Have you ever seen someone laugh and you smile in response? We need to remember what brings us joy and happiness in our lives. We get so busy with our obligations, responsibilities and commitments, which become heavy chains around us, that we forget the little things that bring us a glimpse of joy. A great way is to write down the things that make you joyful. Now try and do at least one joyful thing each day. Build it into your daily ritual. I have many joyful things I do each day, but this one thing gives a great sense of contentment – I love to feed the birds in my garden. I wake up early and just after I pray, I throw rice or bread for the birds. They have come to expect this and are already waiting when I open my kitchen door.

If you want to be a happier human then you need to be doing things that make you happy. This means scheduling these activities since what you make time for actually happens. The year goes by so quickly and before you know it, it is December and you had a miserable year of no fun. You need to get into the habit of putting time in your diary. My husband is a long-term planner whilst I am more spontaneous by nature. At the beginning of each year, he takes out his diary and plans the family holidays. His view is that he does not want to be like most people and only start enjoying life post retirement, so he schedules a quarterly holiday. It gives him something to look forward to as a celebration of working hard during the quarter. Remember to pause and celebrate after achieving a milestone in your life. We move on to quickly too the next challenge. Be kind to yourself and thread a beautiful necklace with beads of happy moments.

This Easter was really exciting for my daughter as she is at an age to ask questions about the Easter bunny, a mythical creature that is based on the 19th century tales of rabbits bringing in new life. At school they were told that the Easter Bunny visited and left Easter eggs for all the children. As evidence there were paw prints in the classroom. My daughter was filled with happiness and joy when I picked her up from school that day. "Mummy, the teacher said the Easter Bunny is going to come to our house and bring Easter eggs. I am so excited, it is going to be so much fun!" she exclaimed, clapping her hands in glee. My daughter's excitement was contagious and I found myself being caught up in the fantasy. I proceeded to perpetuate the myth by placing a trail of paw prints (made from flour and water) from the kitchen to my daughter's room, a trail of Easter eggs and a plate of lettuce and carrots for the Easter Bunny. The next morning my daughter jumped out of bed and rushed into my room, "Mummy did the Easter Bunny come last night?" "I don't know", I replied. "We had no electricity so Mummy could not see but I heard hopping sounds." My daughter rushed into the lounge. "Mummy!" she shouted. "The Easter Bunny did come, look at his paw prints!" The absolute joy and exuberance on my daughter's face was worth every moment of me trying to create paw prints in the dark. The thing about joy is that it has a boomerang effect; I was so focused on creating a memorable experience for my daughter that I didn't realise that the same sense of joy would come back to me. As I observed the absolute joy she experienced I thought about what is lost over time and how disconnected adults have become from the simple pleasures in life.

Numerous research studies have been conducted in the field of happiness. Dr. Martin Seligman created a happiness quiz that you can access on his website, *Pursuit-Of-Happiness.org*. This will provide an overall indicator on your current state of happiness. Studies have shown that there are seven practices associated with happier people. These are healthy relationships, acts of kindness, exercise and physical wellbeing, being in a state of flow, finding meaning in one's life, using your signature strengths and virtues, and having a positive mindset (optimism, mindfulness and gratitude).

If you have at least one close relationship with someone else, you become happier. When you are able to express your feelings to others, you are sharing your concerns. Another practice is cultivating kindness to others. This is about contributing to the lives of others through selfless acts. Exercise has been found to combat depression and is another happiness practice. As discussed previously, creating a state of flow in your life also contributes to happiness. When you find purpose and meaning in life it will add to your level of happiness. The happiest people are those who have discovered their unique strengths (such as creativity) and virtues (such as humanity), and use those strengths and virtues for a purpose that is greater than their own personal goals. Lastly, gratitude, mindfulness and optimism help with one's level of happiness.

What are the things in your life that bring you joy. Is it fishing? Is it going for a walk in your neighbourhood? Do you remember the feeling of walking on the beach and feeling the warm sand under your feet and feeling small against the abundance of the ocean? When last did you watch the sunrise or sunset? Have you ever swung in a hammock and felt a sense of peace and relaxation? When last did you walk barefoot on the grass? We do not make time for the activities that bring us the greatest joy.

Remember to smile each day even if you do not feel like it. Research shows that by putting on a false smile, you start to experience the psychological benefits of smiling. As people, we are more likely to gravitate to someone who is smiling all the time than someone who spends their days complaining and frowning. Be the person who smiles.

Sometimes we can recall happy memories and that brings a sense of joy into our lives. When trying to access your happy memories, remember the details of the joy you felt. Remember the time of day, where you were, what you were doing and what you were thinking. By recalling the details of the moment it makes it more real in your mind and you are able to more easily remember those happy feelings. Remember the anchoring exercise we did earlier on where I asked you to recall moments of happiness and touch your knuckles? You can also recapture feelings of happiness through a collage of pictures that remind you of the times in your life that you were happiest. You can keep this on your desk or on a wall where you are always looking at it.

You also need a happiness list of those things that put you in a positive mood instantly, such as watching a comedy or going for a run. When you are feeling extremely depressed, you can look at your happiness list and do some of the actions. Remember that each person's happiness list is different.

Another thing you can do is to eat foods that boost your serotonin levels. Serotonin is known as the happiness chemical and contributes to your feeling of happiness. Tryptophan is an amino acid that is important for the production of serotonin in the body. It is also key to brain function and has a role in healthy sleep. People cannot make tryptophan in their bodies, so they must obtain it from their diet. The following foods are high in tryptophan: salmon, eggs, nuts, soy products, milk, seeds, turkey and spinach. So when you are feeling depressed, rather than reaching for a packet of potato chips, try some of these foods to provide you with a more balanced meal and a happier mood.

"Happiness grows at our own firesides, and is not to be picked in strangers' gardens."
(Douglas Jerrold[233])

This beautiful quote reminds us to look for intrinsic reasons that make us happy rather than searching for happiness. Remember the story of Mullah who was looking for his keys outside in his garden when he lost them inside his house? He was looking for happiness outside when he had the recipe to make himself happy deep within himself.

"Happiness is when what you think, what you say, and what you do are in harmony."
(Mahatma Gandhi)

This quote highlights that happiness is about being congruent in your thoughts and deeds. It also refers to being authentic. You cannot be happy if you are pretending to be something that you are not. Authentic happiness is about being comfortable in your own skin.

"The happiness of your life depends upon the quality of your thoughts."
(Marcus Aurelius[234])

You cannot be happy if you focus only on the negative conditions in the world. You need to change your beliefs about happiness; start believing that you can be an architect of your own happiness.

Many research studies have been conducted on happiness over the past 50 years. Here are five prerequisites for finding satisfaction or experiencing happiness in life:

1. Human beings need relationships to enjoy optimum well-being and happiness. Simply having good friends who encourage and support you will contribute to your overall feelings of happiness and contentment in life.

2. Being kind to others is essential to finding a sense of personal happiness. Our human brains are wired so that we feel joy when we behave in altruistic ways. Just making plans to do something nice for

252

others — whether it is throwing a party for a friend, volunteering your time for a worthy cause, or planning a monetary donation — will give you a boost and generate a sense of satisfaction and well-being.

3. Acknowledging the abundance of your own life — no matter how austere or extravagant it might be — and experiencing gratitude for how the people, experiences and things in your life positively contribute to your sense of well-being.

4. Finding a sense of meaning and purpose in your pursuits is necessary to your contentment and happiness. Believing that you are contributing to something beyond yourself and being a part of something larger than your individual existence are also necessary to experience a feeling of peace that is a part of happiness.

5. Making healthy lifestyle choices in terms of your basic needs — sleep, nutrition, and exercise — also contribute to your happiness in life.

A recent research study shows that including fresh fruits and vegetables in your diet reduces depression and anxiety.

Happiness practices

People from around the world are rich with diversity so it stands to reason that their approaches to happiness are different. What is acceptable and the norm in society in one group may seem strange to another culture. Here are some examples of wellness practices that are subscribed to by people from different countries.

"To succeed in life you need three things: a wishbone, a backbone and a funny bone."
(Reba McEntire[235])

In India, the practice of laughter yoga was developed in 1995, where you breathe in then start to laugh. Laughing releases endorphins to improve your mood, lowers your blood pressure and helps reduce stress. The idea is to introduce opportunities in your life where you can have more fun and laugh more.

In Japan and Norway, there are similar philosophies to wellness. Shinrin Yoku is a practice in Japan also known as "forest bathing". This is a method of savouring the sights and sounds of the great outdoors to promote well-being. It is about taking a leisurely walk in nature and enjoy its calming, rejuvenating and restorative benefits. In Norway it is referred to as Friluftsliv, which means to "free air life". This Norwegian philosophy suggests we should explore and appreciate nature as a way to promote health and well-being. When you want to minimise the stress in your life, walk outside in nature. This sometimes helps to put things into the correct perspective.

Another practice advocated by the Japanese is Inemuri or Power Naps, which are considered a sign of a hard worker. Inemuri literally means "sleeping while present", and is a widely accepted practice in Japanese culture. The Japanese sleep at work and in public places. You may sometimes see people nap on the trains in Japan and it is an accepted norm.

Tibetan singing bowls have been used for centuries for healing and meditation through sound. The tones created with singing bowls are said to promote healing from pain and depression while reducing stress and disease. They work by training your brain waves to synchronise with the sounds of the bowl, bringing you harmony. I have a Tibetan bowl and it makes the most beautiful sound.

Fika is another practice that is literally a coffee break in Sweden. It is about taking a moment to slow down. Fika is a concept, a state of mind, an attitude and an important part of Swedish culture. Many Swedes consider that it is almost essential to make time for fika every day. It means making time for friends and colleagues to share a cup of coffee (or tea), have a little something to eat and appreciate life. This is a beautiful practice of having a time out. We are often too busy to make time for a break from the pressures of life.

Summary

- Time goes by so quickly that we should get into the habit of appreciating people when they are alive.

- It is important to remember your highest values and make life choices that are aligned to these values.

- We do not recognise the really important moments in our lives until it is too late.

- We lead such busy lives that we forget to slow down and do the things that really bring us joy.

- The common regrets of people who are dying include:

  - I wish I'd had the courage to live a life true to myself, not the life others expected of me.

  - I wish I hadn't worked so hard.

  - I wish I'd had the courage to express my feelings.

  - I wish I had stayed in touch with my friends.

  - I wish that I had let myself be happier.

- We keep deferring our happiness to some future event which will happen and magically transform our lives.

- We get so busy with our obligations, responsibilities and commitments that we forget the little things that bring us a glimpse of joy.

- Try to do at least one joyful thing each day. Include it in your daily ritual.

- You need a happiness list of those things that instantly put you in a positive mood.

- Your happiness list is unique; you cannot use someone else's list.

- Research has shown that there are seven practices that are associated with happier people. These are healthy relationships, acts of kindness, exercise and physical wellbeing, being in a state of flow, finding meaning in one's life, using your signature strengths and virtues, and having a positive mindset (optimism, mindfulness and gratitude).

- Some happiness practices include walking in nature or having coffee with your friends.

Chapter 28

Be a person of character

"Knowledge will give you power, but character, respect." (Bruce Lee[236])

Have you ever heard the saying that small holes sink big ships? Start plugging the holes in your life that are derailing your success. These are the bad habits that sabotage your success. You can be the most accomplished person, but if you do not have a great character, your success will be retarded. These can be habits such as poor punctuality, arrogance towards others, an abrasive personality, an inability to take feedback graciously or a defensive attitude. These are just a few of many things that people do that undermines all their hard work and kills their brand.

Imagine for a moment that all around us there are cameras recording our daily habits, from the time you open your eyes in the morning and start your day. It starts with your kids or your partner or other members of your family observing you. Next, you reverse out of your driveway and you ignore the greeting of your neighbour. You are observing you! I want you to think about this for a moment because it is important that you understand what this means. It means that you are observing your own actions and evaluating whether you are a nice person or not. This feeds into your own view of your self-worth. You start to subconsciously label your behaviour and this determines how you perceive yourself.

Demonstrate integrity

Keep to your word. I have often read the quote that one's promises do not make one a better person, only one's commitment does. It is so easy to distribute promises to everyone you meet — the challenge is remembering to honour those promises. When you fail to keep your word, you start to poke holes in your own character. Once trust is broken it is very difficult to repair the damage.

There is a story of a woman in India who was upset that her son was eating too much sugar. No matter how much she chided him, he continued to satisfy his sweet tooth. Frustrated, she decided to take her son to see his great hero, Mahatma Gandhi. She approached the great leader respectfully and said, "Sir, my son eats too much sugar. It is not good for his health. Would you please advise him to stop eating it?" Gandhi listened to the woman carefully, turned and said to her son, "Go home and come back in two weeks".

The woman looked perplexed and wondered why he had not asked the boy to stop eating sugar. She took the boy by the hand and went home. Two weeks later she returned, the boy in hand. Gandhi motioned for them to come forward. He looked directly at the boy and said, "Boy, you should stop eating sugar. It is not good for your health." The boy nodded and promised he would not continue this habit any longer.

The boy's mother turned to Gandhi and asked, "Why didn't you tell him that two weeks ago when I brought him here to see you?" Gandhi smiled. "Mother, two weeks ago I was still eating sugar myself." Gandhi lived with such integrity that he would not allow himself to give advice unless he was living by it himself.[237]

Demonstrate kindness

"You can easily judge the character of a man by how he treats those who can do nothing for him." (Johann Wolfgang von Goethe[238])

We may have limited resources and may not have been brought up in the lap of luxury, but that does not excuse us from being decent human beings and treating each other with dignity and respect. We need to take the little we have and expand and multiply it. We need to invest in our superpower, which is our compassion. The more we exercise compassion the stronger it becomes.

"Right from the moment of our birth, we are under the care and kindness of our parents. And then later on in our life, when we are oppressed by sickness and become old, we are again dependent on the kindness of others. And since at the beginning and end of our lives we are so dependent on others' kindness, how can it be in the middle that we neglect kindness toward others?" (Dalai Lama)[239]

Do good deeds

*"Take example, all ye that this do hear or see
How they that I loved best do forsake me,
Except my Good Deeds that bideth truly."* (Dalai Lama XIV)[240]

Everyman is a great morality play written in the 15th century which describes the story of Everyman, whose death has come calling. He asks of all his friends and family, wealth which is personified in the play to accompany him on his journey. Everyone promises to accompany him but in the end, everyone forsakes him except for his good deeds. This play illustrates that in the end, it is our character that we are measured on rather than our worldly possessions. We spend so much time accumulating wealth and focusing our attention on things that we forget to love, honour and appreciate the people in our lives. The Dalai Lama XIV best explained this when he said: "People were created to be loved. Things were created to be used. The reason why the world is in chaos is because things are being loved and people are being used."[241]

Demonstrate humility

"Never believe you are above or below anyone. Keep a humble spirit."
(Brendon Burchard[242])

There are many people who remain humble, irrespective of their social stature or success in the world. They remain true to themselves and lead a simple life. They do not look for praise but often make a difference in the lives of others without asking for any glory. When you are full of humility, there is no space for arrogance or pride. Humble people have a fair assessment of their capabilities and focus on being authentic. They do not put their own good above those of others. Humility is developed when you stop focusing on yourself and start focusing on others. Melanie Koulouris said, "Be humble in your confidence, yet courageous in your character".[243] I am grateful to have had role models in my life who were humble people. These individuals had an inner strength in themselves and did not find it necessary to show off their achievements to others.

Nelson Mandela was such an individual; he was a gentle being who captured the hearts of many people in the world by his humility. "As I have said, the first thing is to be honest with yourself. You can never have an impact on society if you have not changed yourself... Great peacemakers are all people of integrity, of honesty, but humility." (Nelson Mandela[244])

Perceptions build your brand

I am always fascinated that people do not realise that their every action is observed by others. When you live in society, you are always being watched. For this reason it is important to be authentic and aware of how your actions are interpreted by others. I have worked for large corporate organisations in my career and I am very aware how the behaviours of employees are observed from the time they enter the building. Your colleagues, clients and managers will have an opinion on you based on your behaviour, the decisions you make and your engagement with them. Are you a positive person who spreads cheer and inspires others, or are you a negative person who spreads the message of doom and gloom? Are you always punctual for appointments or are you disrespectful of the time of others? Do you demonstrate initiative and contribute ideas or are you complacent and do not demonstrate any effort?

Even though you may not be aware of it, you are always selling your brand by showing what value you have to offer. How do we share the gifts we have with others? Creating a brand is not about trying to be something you are not, but rather about accentuating who you really are and making it visible for the world to see. Anne Landers gave the following advice: "Know yourself. Don't accept your dog's admiration as conclusive evidence that you are wonderful." I listened to Stedman Graham speak a few years ago on personal branding and something he said has always stuck with me.[245] "Building a life brand is about who you really are and not who you think people might want you to be." It does not come from a selfish intent but rather an altruistic one that says how the value that you offer can also benefit those around you.

Just as some products with strong brands offer perceived great value, similarly, people in our lives who offer great value also have a brand. Stedman Graham suggested some things to consider when you are building your brand. The first one is that having brand recognition and being famous is not enough; you also need to bring value to your brand. Think about the many Hollywood stars who have maintained their brand and popularity by their philanthropy, rather than just their fame from their movie careers.

Secondly, when you are building your life brand, always associate with other strong brands that can add value and visibility to yours. Even in daily life, the people you associate with have their own brands and you can improve your brand through your association with positively branded people. Similarly, you can damage your brand by associating with negatively branded people.

A strong brand that offers lasting value can weather storms, bounce back from failures, and survive challenges. Everyone goes through a rough patch now and again, but if your brand is strong, it can withstand scrutiny. There are so many examples of people whose brand was tarnished by an incident and they bounced back due to the support they received from others.

Recipe for understanding your character

RECIPE BOOK

We all have a character brand and that is how we are perceived by others. However we may be unaware of what our brand is. The following exercise will assist you to understand your character brand.

Ask three people closest to you – family, friends or work colleagues – what you are great at and what kills your greatness. Choose people who are not afraid of providing you with honest feedback. Look judiciously at the feedback and thank the person genuinely for helping you grow. Do not fall into the trap of defensiveness. For example, if a friend says you have a punctuality problem, you could become extremely defensive and brush it off as it was only one exceptional situation, but if three people are telling you that, you know it is your blind spot.

Consolidate the feedback and understand your brand. If your brand is perceived to be highly negative, try working on yourself. Do not go on a political campaign to show others that you have changed. Einstein said that you cannot solve a challenge at the same level of thinking that created it. Do not work on improving your brand, but rather start at the level of your authenticity. Learn to manage your emotions. Change your limiting beliefs to be the best version of yourself, and start to focus on those qualities that build your character. If these fundamental pillars are in place, your brand will become stronger. Your brand is greater than the sum of all the elements of your character. Who you are, what you believe in, how you behave and how you show up should be congruent. True sustainable change comes from within.

summary

- You can be the most accomplished person but if you do not have a great character, your success will be retarded.

- It is so easy to distribute promises to everyone you meet; the challenge is remembering to honour those promises.

- In the end, it is our character that we are measured on rather than our worldly possessions.

- Humility is developed when you stop focusing on yourself and start focusing on others.

- It is important to always be authentic and be aware of how your actions are interpreted by others.

Conclusion

Life is about learning to dance in the rain,
Reframe your experience, don't focus on the blame.
Put away your umbrella and take out your dancing shoes,
The world is your oyster, the path is yours to choose.
Now is the time to truly celebrate,
Take charge of your future, don't leave it to Fate.
Remember, realisation alone is not an action,
Be purposeful, no time for distractions.
Let go of self-doubt, don't tarry with unnecessary delay.
Design and then create the best version of yourself today.

Thank you for accepting the invitation to read this book. I hope you enjoyed your walk down the road of possibilities. The decision is totally up to you whether you would like to pursue any ideas presented in this book. If there are ideas that have caught your attention, I suggest you do further research and learn more.

There are still occasions when I falter; when I give in to my irritation or frustration. I am not too critical of myself, however, as I am on a journey. It helps to know that I have a great support system of family and friends who care about me enough to gently point out the error of my ways. I am grateful for these teachers in my life. When I fall, I pick myself up, dust myself off, apologise for the mistake, learn my lesson and take another step on my journey. I have gradually lessened the time it takes from making a mistake to learning the lesson. I hope the lessons I have learnt along the way can help you as a guide to your own self development.

Each day for me is a beautiful lesson. As I continue through this magnificent life, I do so with humility and gratitude. I remember I am just a small cog in the bigger machine that is this universe. As Abraham Lincoln[246] said, "In the end, it is not the years in your life that counts but the life in your years".

In order to change your behaviour, you need to take baby steps; each day choose to think positively and act in positive ways. Just remember not to be too hard on yourself. If at first you fall into bad habits, keep on practicing. A child learns to walk by crawling and then standing, holding on for support. Next they fall and get up; there is only nobility in continuing to try. "If you can't fly then run, if you can't run then walk, if you can't walk then crawl, but whatever you do, you have to keep moving forward." (Martin Luther King Jr.[247])

By choosing to change your thoughts, you are changing the direction your life will lead. Break down what you need to do into baby steps and celebrate each milestone as you progress. Remember, just for today, do not worry...

Do not let other people steer your dreams. Take control of the direction you want to be going in. Remember to hold a clear intention of what you want to achieve in your life or you will find yourself aimlessly meandering, never really fitting in or belonging. Take out that crumpled map from your pocket and start to reconnect with your sacred path. Bon voyage! Savour each moment and design the life you were meant to live. There is a beautiful definition of love given by Antoine de Saint Exupery: "Perhaps love is the process of my leading you gently back to yourself." I would like to think that some of the ideas shared in this book will help you find your journey back to yourself.[248]

Some of the recipes I share here are things I have tried in my personal life and I have used when coaching others. The feedback I received from these individuals has been phenomenal. So, if this book inspires you, changes your perspective and touches your life, I would consider this book worth all the time and effort I contributed to it. If you read this book and think of someone else who might benefit, pass it on so that it can influence someone else's life journey.

It is so hard to say goodbye – I feel there is still so much I want to share. As I wrote the last section of this book I started feeling anxious, as if I had not shared all that I wanted to. I reframed my anxiety. I have shared enough information to get you started on your journey. This book is just the first step and provides adequate information to get you started.

My last words for this book are that when you finally meet your true self, take time to celebrate, since it is truly a significant milestone in your life. Remember to treat yourself with gentleness and keep your inner flame burning. Choose to be an inspiration to others and share your life lessons like I have shared mine. The world can only benefit from your gifts. Be unapologetic about what you want out of life. After all, it is your life to manage. Sometimes the battles within are more fierce than the battles outside. Learn to win those inner battles first; they are the most worthy of all your achievements. I would like to put my palms of my hands together and my head slightly bowed forward and greet you Namaste. (A Sanskrit word meaning the divine in me bows down to the divine within you.)

"People are often unreasonable, irrational, and self-centred. Forgive them anyway.
If you are kind, people may accuse you of selfish, ulterior motives. Be kind anyway.
If you are successful, you will win some unfaithful friends and some genuine enemies.
Succeed anyway.
If you are honest and sincere people may deceive you. Be honest and sincere anyway.
What you spend years creating, others could destroy overnight. Create anyway.
If you find serenity and happiness, some may be jealous. Be happy anyway.
The good you do today, will often be forgotten. Do good anyway.
Give the best you have, and it will never be enough. Give your best anyway.
In the final analysis, it is between you and God. It was never between you and them
anyway."
(Mother Theresa[249])

Annexure 1: Life dimensions survey

Wellness is about maintaining a balance between the many different dimensions of our lives. Everyone's optimal wellness will be different and will depend on individual needs, experiences, personality and circumstances.

Emotional wellness

1. I am able to recognise and effectively manage different stressful factors in my life:
    ○ never ○ rarely ○ sometimes ○ often ○ always

2. I able to appropriately express my emotions in different situations:
    ○ never ○ rarely ○ sometimes ○ often ○ always

3. I love and accept myself for who I am:
    ○ never ○ rarely ○ sometimes ○ often ○ always

4. I am able to reflect on and accept critical feedback when necessary:
    ○ never ○ rarely ○ sometimes ○ often ○ always

5. I can easily express joy and happiness in my life:
    ○ never ○ rarely ○ sometimes ○ often ○ always

Physical wellness

1. I get enough sleep to feel rested most nights of the week:
    ○ never ○ rarely ○ sometimes ○ often ○ always

2. I am physically active at least three days a week:
    ○ never ○ rarely ○ sometimes ○ often ○ always

3. I make sure that I do the necessary health checks on a regular basis:
    ○ never ○ rarely ○ sometimes ○ often ○ always

4. I limit my amount of junk food and consumption of alcohol to a minimum:
    ○ never ○ rarely ○ sometimes ○ often ○ always

5. I ensure that I eat the sufficient amount of vegetables to stay: healthy:
    ○ never ○ rarely ○ sometimes ○ often ○ always

Environmental wellness

1. I am consciously aware of the environment around me and strive to live in harmony with it:
    ○ never ○ rarely ○ sometimes ○ often ○ always

2. I am always looking for ways to make a contribution to my community:
    ○ never ○ rarely ○ sometimes ○ often ○ always

3. I try to make the world a better place through my actions:
    ○ never ○ rarely ○ sometimes ○ often ○ always

4. I understand and think about how what I do impacts those around me:
    ○ never ○ rarely ○ sometimes ○ often ○ always

5. I am aware of my responsibility as a citizen to maintain a healthy and clean environment:
    ○ never ○ rarely ○ sometimes ○ often ○ always

Career Wellness

1. I am highly engaged in my work and make a great contribution in my organisation:
    ○ never ○ rarely ○ sometimes ○ often ○ always

2. I seek out new work assignments related to my development and career goals:
    ○ never ○ rarely ○ sometimes ○ often ○ always

3. I reflect on my development gaps to continuously improve:
    ○ never ○ rarely ○ sometimes ○ often ○ always

4. I value increasing my skills, knowledge and abilities:
    ○ never ○ rarely ○ sometimes ○ often ○ always

5. I constantly seek feedback from my managers and my colleagues to improve my performance:
    ○ never ○ rarely ○ sometimes ○ often ○ always

Mental wellness

1. I continuously seek new information and update my perspectives through listening openly to others:
   ○ never ○ rarely ○ sometimes ○ often ○ always

2. I continuously search for new information to increase my knowledge and skills:
   ○ never ○ rarely ○ sometimes ○ often ○ always

3. I understand what factors are within my control and what is beyond my control:
   ○ never ○ rarely ○ sometimes ○ often ○ always

4. I am able to consider the impact of my decisions on situations and people:
   ○ never ○ rarely ○ sometimes ○ often ○ always

5. I am able to think clearly in times of stress:
   ○ never ○ rarely ○ sometimes ○ often ○ always

Social wellness

1. I am respectful, considerate and supportive in all my: relationships:
   ○ never ○ rarely ○ sometimes ○ often ○ always

2. I invest the time and energy to maintain healthy relationships with my friends and loved ones:
   ○ never ○ rarely ○ sometimes ○ often ○ always

3. I create opportunities to regularly meet with my friends and family:
   ○ never ○ rarely ○ sometimes ○ often ○ always

4. I am able to express my beliefs and feelings in a way that is appropriate and respectful of others:
   ○ never ○ rarely ○ sometimes ○ often ○ always

5. I am able to build rapport easily with others and develop friendships:
   ○ never ○ rarely ○ sometimes ○ often ○ always

Spiritual wellness

1. I feel an overall sense of peace and well-being in my life:
   ○ never ○ rarely ○ sometimes ○ often ○ always

2. I engage in regular practices that nurture my sense of purpose:
   ○ never ○ rarely ○ sometimes ○ often ○ always

3. I understand my life purpose and embrace each day with meaning:
   ○ never ○ rarely ○ sometimes ○ often ○ always

4. I understand my core values and beliefs, and respect the values and beliefs of others:
   ○ never ○ rarely ○ sometimes ○ often ○ always

5. I easily demonstrate gratitude in my life:
   ○ never ○ rarely ○ sometimes ○ often ○ always

Financial wellness

1. I have enough money to manage my needs:
   ○ never ○ rarely ○ sometimes ○ often ○ always

2. I have both short- and long-term financial goals:
   ○ never ○ rarely ○ sometimes ○ often ○ always

3. I budget and track my spending each month:
   ○ never ○ rarely ○ sometimes ○ often ○ always

4. I have the knowledge required for how best to live on my income:
   ○ never ○ rarely ○ sometimes ○ often ○ always

5. I do not incur unnecessary debt:
   ○ never ○ rarely ○ sometimes ○ often ○ always

Interpreting your wellness results

Give yourself one point for 'often' and two points for 'always'

Emotional wellness	Physical wellness	Environmental wellness	Career wellness
Score:	Score:	Score:	Score:
Mental wellness	**Social wellness**	**Spiritual wellness**	**Financial wellness**
Score:	Score:	Score:	Score:

You can get a maximum score of 10 in each category. Next, plot your score on the graph below. This will give you a good overview of the areas of your life you need to give attention to.

Life Dimension Graph

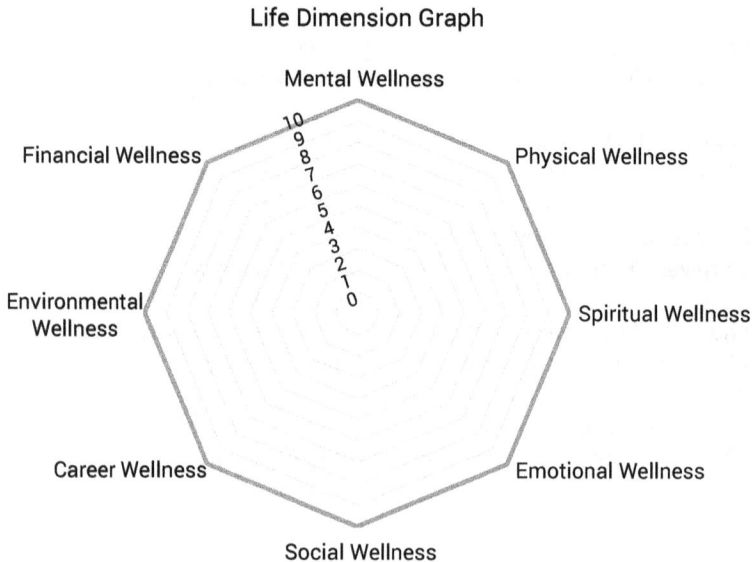

Annexure 2: Worksheet for realising your dreams

Vision			
How would you like to be remembered? What would you like people to say at your funeral? (Write down details from the four perspectives. Your family, your friends, your work or school and your family)			
Your family's view of you	Your friends' view of you	Your work/university/school's view of you	Your community's view of you

Purpose

What is the purpose of your life? Answer the following questions.

1. Who are you? (Not your job title)	
2. What do you love to do? Write, cook, design?	
3. What is the one thing you feel qualified to teach other people? (One word)	

4. Who do you do it for? Who do you serve?

5. What do those people want or need?

6. How do people change or transform as a result of what you give them?

Write down your purpose statement from the above questions

Your dream list

What is your dream list? What one great thing would you dare to dream if you knew you could not fail? If you were guaranteed success, what would that be?

Your dreams for the spiritual area of your life	Your dreams for the mental area of your life	Your dreams for the physical area of your life	Your dreams for the emotional area of your life	Your dreams for the social area of your life	Your dreams for the career area of your life	Your dreams for the financial area of your life	Your dreams for the environmental area of your life

Annexure 3: Goal worksheet

Immediate goal/Short-term goal/Long-term goal	Short term

Goal:

Benefits of goal:		**How are you going to celebrate achieving your goal?**	
Goal in .... life dimension (mental, spiritual, emotional, physical, career, environmental, social, financial)			
Priority actions		**Frequency**	
		Time commitment	
		Preferable day of week	
Obstacles to reaching your goal		**Scheduled time**	
People who will be affected by this action (we need to manage their expectations)		**Resources required**	

Skills or abilities needed		Success measures	
Support network (people who will support your goal)		People who will discourage you	
Supportive action		Sensory measures	
I failed to achieve my objective because I...		Things that made me successful	

Example: Goal worksheet	
Immediate goal/Short-term goal/Long-term goal:	**Short-term**

Goal:	Write a personal mastery book

Benefits of goal:	Share my knowledge and tools with others	**How are you going to celebrate achieving your goal?**	I am going to spend the weekend away with my family
	Outlet for creativity		
	Mental stimulation		
	My personal growth		

Goal in …………. life dimension (mental, spiritual, emotional, physical, career, environmental, social, financial)

Priority actions	Draft book proposal	**Frequency**	Daily
	Contract timelines with publisher		
	Schedule time in diary		
	Contract with my family		
	Research topics	**Time commitment**	4 hours on weekdays
	Brainstorm ideas		12 hours on weekends
	Collate into a framework		
	Write chapters for book	**Preferable day of week**	Daily
	Hand over book to publisher for review		

Obstacles to reaching your goal	Writer's block, work commitments, fatigue, no creative ideas, family commitments	**Scheduled time**	8pm to 12pm

People who will be affected by this action (we need to manage their expectations)	My family and friends	Resources required	Time, books and research
Skills or abilities needed	Referencing skills	Success measures	A published book
Support network (people who will support your goal)	My husband	People who will discourage you	No one
Supportive action	The availability of helper	Sensory measures	I will feel accomplished
	The availability of my husband		I will feel fulfilled
	The availability of my friend to proofread		I will see a completed book
I failed to achieve my objective because I...	Procrastinated	Things that made me successful	Eating correct foods for energy
	Did not plan my time properly		Sticking to my timetable
	Lack of discipline		Leaning on my support system
	Self-doubts		Being open to negative feedback
	Being negatively influenced		Asking for assistance

Endnotes

1   Goodreads.com. (2019). *A quote by Aristotle*. Available at: https://www.goodreads.com/quotes/20103-the-whole-is-greater-than-the-sum-of-its-parts [Accessed 30 March 2019].

2   BrainyQuote. (2019). *Pierre Teilhard de Chardin Quotes*. Available at: https://www.brainyquote.com/quotes/pierre_teilhard_de_chardi_160888 [Accessed 30 March 2019].

3   BrainyQuote. (2019). *Albert Einstein Quotes*. Available at: https://www.brainyquote.com/quotes/albert_einstein_121993 [Accessed 31 March 2019].

4   Sharma, R. (1997). *The monk who sold his Ferrari*. London: Harper Collins Publishing Ltd, p41.

5   Knott-Craig, A. (2018). *13 Rules for being an entrepreneur*. Cape Town: Alan Knott-Craig.

6   Smith, D.P.J. (2007). *The PiPL Perspective. Module1, Personal Leadership A*. Johannesburg: University of Johannesburg.

7   Goodreads. (2019). *A quote from the 7 Habits of Highly Effective People*. Available at: https://www.goodreads.com/quotes/295715-we-see-the-world-not-as-it-is-but-as [Accessed 30 March 2019].

8   BrainyQuote. (2019). *Marcus Aurelius Quotes*. Available at: https://www.brainyquote.com/quotes/marcus_aurelius_148747 [Accessed 30 March 2019].

9   BrainyQuote. (2019). *Khalil Gibran Quotes*. Available at: https://www.brainyquote.com/quotes/khalil_gibran_119996 [Accessed 31 March 2019].

10   Tracy, B. (2006). *Create your own future*. New York: John Wiley and Sons, p10.

11   Gordon, A. (2019). *You Are The Books You Read*. Available at: https://themindsjournal.com/you-are-the-books-you-read/ [Accessed 30 March 2019].

12   Smith, H.W. (1994). *The 10 Natural Laws of Successful Time and Life Management*. New York: Warner Books, p182.

13   Demartini, J. (2019). *What are Values?* Available at: https://drdemartini.com/what-are-values/ [Accessed 31 March 2019].

14   Tracy, B. (2006). *Create your own future*. New York: John Wiley and Sons, p11.

15   Sharma, R. (2006). *The Greatness Guide*. London: Harper Element, p64.

16   BrainyQuote. (2019). *Walter Scott Quotes*. Available at: https://www.brainyquote.com/quotes/walter_scott_118003 [Accessed 31 March 2019].

17   AZ Quotes. (2019). *Charles Darwin Quote*. Available at: https://www.azquotes.com/quote/520404 [Accessed 31 March 2019].

18   QuoteFancy. (2019). *Stephen R Covey Quotes*. Available at: https://quotefancy.com/quote/909734/Stephen-R-Covey-It-is-futile-to-put-personality-ahead-of-character-to-try-to-improve [Accessed 5 May 2019].

19   Cashman, K. (1998). *Leadership from the Inside Out: Becoming a Leader for Life*. Provo, Utah: Executive Excellence Publishing.

20   AZ Quotes. (2019). *Ernest Hemingway Quotes*. Available at: https://www.azquotes.com/quote/1176156 [Accessed 31 March 2019].

21   AZ Quotes. (2019). *Florinda Donner Quotes*. Available at: https://www.azquotes.com/author/39221-Florinda_Donner Way [Accessed 13 April 2019].

22   PlayShakespeare.com. (n.d.). *Hamlet: Act-1, Scene-III*. Available at: https://www.playshakespeare.com/hamlet/scenes/17-act-i-scene-3 [Accessed 31 March 2019].

23   BrainyQuote. (2019). *Herman Melville Quotes*. Available at: https://www.brainyquote.com/quotes/herman_melville_121186 [Accessed 31 March 2019].

24   QuoteFancy. (2019). *Ernest Hemingway Quotes*. Available at: https://quotefancy.com/quote/2460/Ernest-Hemingway-There-is-nothing-noble-in-being-superior-to-your-fellow-man-true [Accessed 31 March 2019].

25   Deri, S., Davidai, S., & Gilovich, T. (2017). *Home Alone. Why people believe others' social lives are richer than their own.* Available at: https://psycnet.apa.org/doiLanding?doi=10.1037%2Fpspa0000105 [Accessed 31 March 2019].

26   Joseph, S. (2016). *7 Qualities of Truly Authentic People.* Available at: https://www.psychologytoday.com/us/blog/what-doesnt-kill-us/201608/7-qualities-truly-authentic-people [Accessed 31 March 2019].

27   Goodreads. (2019). *Aristotle Quotes.* Available at: https://www.goodreads.com/book/show/39177.You_re_Born_an_Original_Don_t_Die_a_Copy_ [Accessed 30 March 2019].

28   Bascaglia, L. (1982). *Living, Loving and Learning.* New York: Ballantine Books, p247.

29   Sturm, M. (2018). *Wabi-Sabi: Beyond Minimalism, and into a Unique Mode of Mindful Simplicity.* Available at: https://betterhumans.coach.me/wabi-sabi-on-the-perfection-of-imperfection-and-the-understated-benefits-of-acceptance-f7d468d4a9fd?%24Ga=true [Accessed 6 April 2019].

30   Hay, L. (1984). *You Can Heal Your Life.* Santa Monica, CA: Hay House.

31   Goodreads. (2019). *Louise L. Hay Quotes.* Available at: https://www.goodreads.com/quotes/9650-remember-you-have-been-criticizing-yourself-for-years-and-it [Accessed 31 March 2019].

32   Ackerman, C. (2018). *Self-Fulfilling Prophecy in Psychology: 10 Examples and Definition.* Available at: https://positivepsychologyprogram.com/self-fulfilling-prophecy/ [Accessed 31 March 2019].

33   Ruiz, M. (1997). *The Four Agreements.* San Rafael, California: Amber-Allen Publishing, p99.

34   Ackerman, C. (2018). *Self-Fulfilling Prophecy in Psychology: 10 Examples and Definition.* Available at: https://positivepsychologyprogram.com/self-fulfilling-prophecy/ [Accessed 31 March 2019].

35   Ackerman, C. (2018). *Self-Fulfilling Prophecy in Psychology: 10 Examples and Definition.* Available at: https://positivepsychology.com/self-fulfilling-prophecy/ [Accessed 6 April 2019].

36   Kwok, R. (2012). *Monkey's Mistake Detector.* Available at: https://www.sciencenewsforstudents.org/article/monkeys%E2%80%99-mistake-detector [Accessed 6 April 2019].

37   Vilhauer, J. (2016). *4 Ways to Stop Beating Yourself Up, Once and For All.* Available at: https://www.psychologytoday.com/us/blog/living-forward/201603/4-ways-stop-beating-yourself-once-and-all [Accessed 6 April 2019].

38   Vilhauer, J. (2015). *One Exercise Sure to Make You Feel Better About Yourself.* Available at: https://www.psychologytoday.com/us/blog/living-forward/201501/one-exercise-sure-make-you-feel-better-about-yourself [Accessed 17 January 2015].

39   Spark Notes. (2019). *Hamlet Translation by William Shakespeare.* Available at: https://www.sparknotes.com/nofear/shakespeare/hamlet/page_106/ [Accessed 6 April 2019].

40   Emoto, M. (2004). *The Healing Power of Water.* Vancouver: Hay House.

41   Hunt, R. (2019). *Building Resilience In A World Of Uncertainty.* Available at: https://www.slideshare.net/RosannaHunt/building-resilience-in-a-world-of-uncertainty [Accessed 6 April 2019].

42   BrainyQuote. (n.d.). *Wayne Dyer Quote.* Available at: https://www.brainyquote.com/quotes/wayne_dyer_384143 [Accessed 7 April 2019].

43   Tracy, B. (2006). *Create your own future*. New York: John Wiley and Sons.

44   Katie, B. (2019). T*he Work is a Practice*. Available at: http://thework.com/instruction-the-work-byron-katie/ [Accessed 6 April 2019].

45   Goal Cast. (2019). *25 Powerful Zig Ziglar Quotes to Boost Your Willpower*. Available at: https://www.goalcast.com/2018/01/16/most-inspiring-zig-ziglar-quotes/ [Accessed 19 April 2019].

46   Covey, S.R. (1994). *The 7 habits of highly effective people*. New York: Simon & Schuster, p70.

47   Goodreads. (2019). *Henry David Thoreau Quote*. Available at: https://www.goodreads.com/quotes/1335615-a-single-footstep-will-not-make-a-path-on-the [Accessed 7 April 2019].

48   Tracy, B. (2006). *Create your own future*. New York: John Wiley and Sons, p102.

49   Cohen G.L., & Sherman D.K. (2014). The psychology of change: self-affirmation and social psychological intervention. *Annual Review of Psychology*, 65, 333–71.

50   Covey, S.R. (1994). *The 7 habits of highly effective people*. New York: Simon & Schuster, p133.

51   Steimle, J. (2019). *7 Reasons Why Positive Affirmations Aren't Working for You*. Available at: https://www.joshsteimle.com/influencer/7-reasons-why-positive-affirmations-dont-work.html: [Accessed 6 April 2019].

52   Alexander, R. (2011). *5 Steps to Make Affirmations Work for You*. Available at: https://www.psychologytoday.com/us/blog/the-wise-open-mind/201108/5-steps-make-affirmations-work-you [Accessed 6 April 2019].

53   Tracy, B. (2006). *Create your own future*. New York: John Wiley and Sons, p20.

54   Goal Cast. (2019). *25 Powerful Zig Ziglar Quotes to Boost Your Willpower*. Available at: https://www.goalcast.com/2018/01/16/most-inspiring-zig-ziglar-quotes/ [Accessed 19 April 2019].

55   Covey, S.R. (1994). *The 7 habits of highly effective people*. New York: Simon & Schuster.

56   The Motivation Mindset. (2017). *How to Be Resilient With An Internal Locus of Control*. Available at: https://themotivationmindset.com/internal-locus-of-control/ [Accessed 6 April 2019].

57   Goodreads. (2019). *Lao Tzu Quote*. Available at: https://www.goodreads.com/quotes/8203490-watch-your-thoughts-they-become-your-words-watch-your-words [Accessed 6 April 2019].

58   QuoteFancy. (2019). *Alain de Botton Quotes*. Available at: https://quotefancy.com/quote/1033905/Alain-de-Botton-You-normally-have-to-be-bashed-about-a-bit-by-life-to-see-the-point-of [Accessed 13 April 2019].

59   Houstan, E. (2019). *What Are Attributional and Explanatory Styles in Psychology?* Available at: https://positivepsychology.com/explanatory-styles-optimism/[Accessed 5 May 2019].

60   BrainyQuote. (n.d.). *Beck Quotes*. Available at: https://www.brainyquote.com/authors/beck-quotes [Accessed 5 May 2019].

61   Economy, P. (2018). *17 Wise Winnie-the-Pooh Quotes About the Remarkable Power of Kindness, Love, and Acceptance*. Available at: https://www.inc.com/peter-economy/17-inspiring-winnie-the-pooh-quotes-about-love-kindness-acceptance.html [Accessed 5 May 2019].

62   Goodreads. (2019). *Erin Hanson Quote*. Available at: https://www.goodreads.com/author/quotes/7802403.Erin_Hanson [Accessed 13 April 2019].

63 Wikipedia. (2019). *Achilles' heel*. Available at: https://en.wikipedia.org/wiki/ Achilles%27_heel [Accessed 6 April 2019].

64 Wealthy Gorilla. (2019). *Charles Darwin Quotes*. Available at: https://wealthygorilla. com/charles-darwin-quotes/ [Accessed 6 April 2019].

65 Quotes Archive. (2019). *Tiny Buddha Quotes*. Available at: https://tinybuddha.com/ wisdom-quotes/be-the-person-who-breaks-the-cycle/[Accessed 13 April 2019].

66 Yeong, D. (2019). *The Fight of Two Wolves Within You*. Available at: https://deanyeong. com/fight-two-wolves-inside/. [Accessed 13 April 2019].

67 BrainyQuote. (2019). *Epictetus Quotes*. Available at: https://www.brainyquote.com/ quotes/epictetus_104206 [Accessed 13 April 2019].

68 Barker, E. (2019). *Barking Up the Wrong Tree*. Available at: https://www.bakadesuyo. com/2015/04/frustrated/ [Accessed 6 April 2019]

69 Famous Quotes. (2019). *Ann Landers Quotes*. Available at: http://famousquotefrom. com/ann-landers/ [Accessed 13 April 2019].

70 BrainyQuote. (2019). *Buddha Quotes*. Available at: https://www.brainyquote.com/ quotes/buddha_104025 [Accessed 21 April 2019].

71 Wikiquote. (2019). *Eleanor Roosevelt Quotes*. Available at: https://simple.wikiquote.org/ wiki/Eleanor_Roosevelt [Accessed 22 April 2019].

72 Quote Load. (2019). *Ambrose Bierce Quotes*. Available at: https://www.quoteload.com/ quotes/authors/ambrose-bierce/8243-speak-when-you-are-angry-and-you-will-make- the-best-speech-you-will-ever-regret [Accessed 22 April 2019].

73 Ziglar, Z. (2019). *The Responsibility is Yours*. Available at: https://www.ziglar.com/ motivation/the-responsibility-is-yours/ [Accessed 6 April 2019].

74 Goodreads. (2019). *Gillian Duce Quotes*. Available at: https://www.goodreads.com/ quotes/7337278-we-don-t-blame-your-shadow-for-the-shape-of-your [Accessed 6 April 2019].

75 Dyer, W. (1995). *Your Sacred Self*. New York: Harper Collins Publishers, p58.

76 Wikisource. (2019). *A prayer of St. Francis of Assisi*. Available at: https://en.wikisource. org/wiki/A_prayer_of_St._Francis_of_Assisi [Accessed 6 April 2019].

77 The Minds Journal. (2018). *Chinese proverb*. Available at: https://themindsjournal.com/ blames-others-long-way-go-journey/ [Accessed 6 April 2019].

78 Tracy, B. (2005). *Change Your Thinking Change Your Life*. New Jersey: John Wiley & Sons, p33.

79 Ziglar, Z. (2002). *Raising Positive Kids in a Negative World*. Nashville, TN: Thomas Nelson.

80 Beliefnet. (2019). *The Lord's Prayer*. Available at: https://www.beliefnet.com/prayers/ catholic/childrens-prayers/the-lords-prayer.aspx#vbu5bvfo3r5lvzDT.99 [Accessed 6 April 2019].

81 Quodid. (2019). *Nelson Mandela Quote*. Available at: http://quodid.com/quotes/722/ nelson-mandela/as-i-walked-out-the-door-toward-the [Accessed 26 April 2019].

82 BrainyQuote. (2019). *Nelson Mandela Quote*. Available at: https://www.brainyquote. com/quotes/nelson_mandela_447223 [Accessed 6 April 2019].

83 Quote Fancy. (2019). *Nelson Mandela Quote*. Available at: https://quotefancy.com/ quote/874257/Nelson-Mandela-Forgiveness-liberates-the-soul-It-removes-fear-That-is- why-it-is-such-a [Accessed 6 April 2019].

84 BrainyQuote. (n.d.). *Lewis B. Smedes Quote*. Available at: https://www.brainyquote. com/quotes/lewis_b_smedes_135524 [Accessed 27 April 2015.

85   Goodreads. (2019). *Steve Maraboli Quote*. Available at: https://www.goodreads.com/ author/quotes/4491185.Steve_Maraboli [Accessed 26 April 2019].

86   Anderson, A.R. (2019). *Resentment Is Like Taking Poison and Waiting for The Other Person to Die*. Available at: https://www.forbes.com/sites/amyanderson/2015/04/07/ resentment-is-like-taking-poison-and-waiting-for-the-other-person-to- die/#27fdf3c2446c [Accessed 27 April 2015.

87   Powers, J. (2016). *Forgiveness Is the Answer to (Almost) All of Our Ills*. Available at: https://www.psychologytoday.com/us/blog/beyond-abstinence/201611/forgiveness- is-the-answer-almost-all-our-ills [Accessed 6 April 2019].

88   Tracy, B. (2005). *Change Your Thinking Change Your Life*. New Jersey: John Wiley & Sons, p33-34.

89   Ibid.

90   Quote Investigator. (2013). *Forgiveness Is the Fragrance the Violet Sheds on the Heel That Has Crushed It*. Available at: https://quoteinvestigator.com/2013/09/30/violet-forgive/ [Accessed 27 April 2019].

91   Goal Cast. (2018). *19 Powerful Winnie the Pooh Quotes to Guide You at Every Stage of Life*. Available at: https://www.goalcast.com/2018/07/10/winnie-the-pooh-quotes/ [Accessed 28 April 2019].

92   BrainyQuote. (2019). *Wayne Dyer Quotes*. Available at: https://www.brainyquote.com/ quotes/wayne_dyer_173498 [Accessed 27 April 2019].

93   Csikszentmihalyi, M. (2004). *Flow, the Secret to Happiness*. Available at: https://www. ted.com/talks/mihaly_csikszentmihalyi_on_flow/transcript?language=en [Accessed 27 April 2019].

94   Healthline. (2019). *What Are the Benefits and Risks of Alternate Nostril Breathing?* Available at: https://www.healthline.com/health/alternate-nostril-breathing [Accessed 27 April 2019].

95   Goodreads. (2019). *Steve Maraboli Quote*. Available at: https://www.goodreads.com/ author/quotes/4491185.Steve_Maraboli [Accessed 26 April 2019].

96   Walansky, A. (2019). *Anne Hathaway Reveals the Fiery Way She Copes with Anxiety and Stress*. Available at: https://www.goalcast.com/2019/01/10/anne-hathaway-stress- method/ [Accessed 13 April 2019].

97   Crosswalk Editorial Staff. (2017). *Serenity Prayer – Applying 3 Truths from the Bible*. Available at: https://www.crosswalk.com/faith/prayer/serenity-prayer-applying-3- truths-from-the-bible.html [Accessed 13 April 2019].

98   Wisdom Quotes. (2019). *440 Time quotes that will inspire you deeply*. Available at: (http://wisdomquotes.com/time-quotes/) [Accessed 13 April 2019].

99   Ibid.

100   AZ Quotes. (2019). *Josh Billings Quote*. Available at: https://www.azquotes.com/ quote/524402 [Accessed 13 April 2019].

101   Tiny Buddha. (2019). *Wayne Fields Quote*. Available at: https://tinybuddha.com/ wisdom-quotes/six-best-doctors-sunshine-water-rest-air-exercise-diet/ [Accessed 14 April 2019].

102   Goodreads. (2019). *Ann Wigmore Quote*. Available at: https://www.goodreads.com/ quotes/563016-the-food-you-eat-can-be-either-the-safest-and [Accessed 13 April 2019].

103   Hay, L. (1984). *You Can Heal Your Life*. Santa Monica, CA: Hay House, p45.

104 García, H., & Miralles, F. (2017). *Ikigai: The Japanese Secret to a Long and Happy life.* New York: Penguin Random House, p125.

105 Healthline. (2019). *Is Raw Food Healthier Than Cooked Food?* Available at: from https://www.healthline.com/nutrition/raw-food-vs-cooked-food [Accessed 13 April 2019].

106 Bracht, P., cited in Emoto, M. (2004). *The Healing Power of Water.* Vancouver: Hay House, p118.

107 García, H., & Miralles, F. (2017). *Ikigai. The Japanese Secret to a Long and Happy life.* New York: Penguin Random House, p123-132.

108 Huffpost. (2016). *Exercise is Not Punishment.* Available at: https://www.huffpost.com/entry/exercise-is-not-punishment_b_579284bfe4b0e002a31335f8 [Accessed 13 April 2019].

109 Weaver, L. (2015). *Exhausted to Energized.* London: Hay House, p18.

110 Gaia. (2009). *Donna Eden on Energy Medicine.* Available at: https://www.gaia.com/video/donna-eden-energy-medicine [Accessed 13 April 2019].

111 Pink, D.H. (2018). *When.* New York: Riverhead Books, p77-78.

112 Reiter, R.J., Tan, D.X., Osuna, C., & Gitto, E. (2002). *Actions of melatonin in the reduction of oxidative stress. A review.* Available at: https://www.ncbi.nlm.nih.gov/pubmed/11060493. [Accessed 13 April 2019].

113 Bacon, E. (2000). *The Halls of Reiki.* Available at: http://hallsofreiki.com/reikiprinciples.html [Accessed 13 April 2019].

114 Goodreads. (2019). *Margaret Bonanno Quote.* Available at: https://www.goodreads.com/quotes/418548-it-is-only-possible-to-live-happily-ever-after-on [Accessed 13 April 2019].

115 Classic Pooh Prints. (2015). *Prints with Quotes: What day is it?* Available at: https://classicpoohprints.com/product/what-day-is-it/ [Accessed 13 April 2019].

116 BrainyQuote. (2019). *Lily Tomlin Quote.* Available at: https://www.brainyquote.com/authors/lily_tomlin [Accessed 13 April 2019].

117 Monsignor, L.L. (2018). *No Time for Pray.* Available at: https://www.ellenbailey.com/poems/ellen_345.htm [Accessed 13 April 2019].

118 Goodreads. (2019). *Thich Nhat Hanh Quote.* Available at: https://www.goodreads.com/quotes/142660-to-dwell-in-the-here-and-now-does-not-mean [Accessed 14 April 2019].

119 Live, Love, Simple. (2019). *He Sacrifices His Health In Order to Make Money.* Available at: http://livelovesimple.com/sacrifice-health-make-money/ [Accessed 14 April 2019].

120 Oppland,M.(2016). *8 Ways To Create Flow According to Mihaly Csikszentmihalyi.* Available at: https://positivepsychology.com/mihaly-csikszentmihalyi-father-of-flow/[Accessed 13 April 2019].

121 Ibid.

122 AZ Quotes. (2019). *Ralph Ellison Quotes.* Available at: https://www.azquotes.com/author/4468-Ralph_Ellison [Accessed 13 April 2019].

123 PassItOn. (2019). *Flora Whittemore Quote.* Available at: https://www.passiton.com/inspirational-quotes/5917-the-doors-we-open-and-close-each-day-decide-the [Accessed 13 April 2019].

124 Ford, D. (2004). *The Right Questions.* New York: Harper Collins, p7-8.

125 Goodreads. (n.d.). *Arthur Schopenhauer Quote.* Available at: https://www.goodreads.com/quotes/695334-everyone-takes-the-limits-of-his-own-vision-for-the [Accessed 13 April 2019].

126 Tolle, E. (2005). *The Power of Now.* Novato, California: New World Library, p73.

127 BrainyQuote. (2019). *Carl Jung Quote.* Available at: https://www.brainyquote.com/quotes/carl_jung_146686 [Accessed 13 April 2019].

128 Covey, S.R. 1994. *The 7 habits of highly effective people.* New York: Simon & Schuster, p96-97.

129 Tracy, B. (2008). *Flight Plan.* San Francisco: Berret-Koehler Publishers, p10.

130 Quote Fancy. (2019). *Bertice Berry Quote.* Available at: https://quotefancy.com/quote/1718778/Bertice-Berry-When-you-walk-with-purpose-you-collide-with-destiny [Accessed 13 April 2019].

131 Deep Spirits. (2019). *The Lost Key Sufi Stories.* Available at: http://www.deepspirits.com/words-of-wisdom/sufi/sufi-story5.php [Accessed 27 April 2019].

132 Goodreads. (2019). *Colin P Sisson Quote.* Available at: https://www.goodreads.com/quotes/57694-what-we-vividly-imagine-ardently-desire-enthusiastically-act-upon-must [Accessed 14 April 2019].

133 BrainyQuote. (2019). *Robert Byrne Quote.* Available at: https://www.brainyquote.com/quotes/robert_byrne_101054 [Accessed 14 April 2019].

134 Leipzig, A. (2013). *How to know your life purpose in 5 minutes.* TED TALK video. Available at: https://www.youtube.com/watch?v=vVsXO9brK7M [Accessed 14 April 2019].

135 Leipzig, A. (2019). *5 Questions to know your life purpose.* Available at: http://mariogiancini.com/5-questions-to-know-your-life-purpose/ [Accessed 28 April 2019].

136 García, H., & Miralles, F. (2017). *Ikigai. The Japanese Secret to a Long and Happy life.* New York: Penguin Random House, p86.

137 Kenny, S. (2019). *Is Ikigai the secret to a longer, happier life? The science says yes.* Available at: https://www.redbull.com/za-en/ikigai-japanese-concept-secrets [Accessed 28 April 2019].

138 Winn, M. (2019). *Ikigai Diagram.* Available at: https://informationisbeautiful.net/visualizations/ikigai-japanese-concept-to-enhance-work-life-sense-of-worth/ [Accessed 14 April 2019].

139 Goodreads. (2019). *Howard Thurman Quote.* Available at: https://www.goodreads.com/quotes/6273-don-t-ask-what-the-world-needs-ask-what-makes-you [Accessed 27 April 2019].

140 Graham, S. (1998). *You Can Make It Happen.* New York: First Fireside Edition, p66.

141 Tracy, B. (2008). *Flight Plan.* San Francisco: Berret-Koehler Publishers, Inc., p8.

142 Ziglar,Z. (1997). *Over the Top.* Nashville, TN: The Zig Ziglar Corporation, p219.

143 Ibid., p220.

144 Ibid., p221.

145 Tracy, B. (2008). *Flight Plan.* San Francisco: Berret-Koehler Publishers, Inc., p40.

146 Quote Fancy. (2019). *Harvey MacKay Quote.* Available at: https://quotefancy.com/quote/822501/Harvey-MacKay-A-dream-is-just-a-dream-A-goal-is-a-dream-with-a-plan-and-a-deadline [Accessed 27 April 2019].

147 Tracy, B. (2008). *Flight Plan.* San Francisco: Berret-Koehler Publishers, Inc., p40.

148 BrainyQuote. (2019). *Winston Churchill Quotes.* Available at: https://www.brainyquote.com/search_results?q=only+one+link+ [Accessed 20 April 2019].

149 Tracy, B. (2008). *Flight Plan.* San Francisco: Berret-Koehler Publishers, Inc., p16.

150 Ibid., p44.

151 Everwise. (2015). *From Oprah to Churchill: 20 Inspiring Mentoring Quotes.* Available at: https://www.geteverwise.com/mentoring/20-inspiring-mentorship-quotes/ [Accessed 27 April 2019].

152 Aerospaceweb. (2019). *On the Shoulders of Giants*. Available at: http://www.aerospaceweb.org/question/history/q0162b.shtml [Accessed 27 April 2019].

153 Sharma, R. (2006). *The Greatness Guide*. London: Harper Element, p22.

154 Tracy, B. (2008). *Flight Plan*. San Francisco: Berret-Koehler Publishers, Inc.

155 Goodreads. (2019). *Mahatma Gandhi Quote*. Available at: https://www.goodreads.com/quotes/2253-live-as-if-you-were-to-die-tomorrow-learn-as [Accessed 14 April 2019].

156 BrainyQuote. (2019). *Confucius Quotes*. Available at: https://www.brainyquote.com/quotes/confucius_131984 [Accessed 20 April 2019].

157 Goodreads. (2019). *Alvin Toffler Quotes*. Available at: https://www.goodreads.com/author/quotes/3030.Alvin_Toffler [Accessed 21 April 2019].

158 Popova, P. (n.a). *Fixed vs. Growth: The Two Basic Mindsets That Shape Our Lives*. Available at: https://www.brainpickings.org/2014/01/29/carol-dweck-mindset/ [Accessed 20 April 2019].

159 AZQuotes. (2019). *Ralph Ellison Quotes*. Available at: https://www.azquotes.com/quote/591459 [Accessed 21 April 2019].

160 BrainyQuote. (2019). *Og Mandino Quote*. Available at: https://www.brainyquote.com/quotes/og_mandino_106300 [Accessed 21 April 2019].

161 Maxwell, J.C. (2004). *Winning with People*. Nashville, TN: Thomas Nelson, p17.

162 Maxwell, J.C. (1995). *The Winning Attitude*. Nashville, TN: Thomas Nelson, p30.

163 Karen, K.J., Hafen, B.Q., Frandsen, K.J., & Smith, M.L. (2006). *Mind/Body Health*. San Francisco: Pearson.

164 Robbins, T. (2019). *The six human needs*. Available at: https://www.tonyrobbins.com/mind-meaning/do-you-need-to-feel-significant/ [Accessed 22 April 2019].

165 Smith, H.W. (1994). *The 10 Natural Laws of Successful Time and Life Management*. New York: Warner Books, p182.

166 Goodreads. (2019). *Hafiz of Shiraz Quote*. Available at: https://www.goodreads.com/quotes/22783-i-wish-i-could-show-you-when-you-are-lonely [Accessed 21 April 2019].

167 Blue Zones. (n.d.). *Okinawa, Japan: Secrets of the world's longest-living women*. Available at: https://www.bluezones.com/exploration/okinawa-japan/ [Accessed 28 April 2019].

168 Milne, A.A. (n.d.). *19 Powerful Winnie the Pooh Quotes to Guide You at Every Stage of Life*. Available at: https://www.goalcast.com/2018/07/10/winnie-the-pooh-quotes/ [Accessed 28 April 2019].

169 Hay, L. (1984). *You Can Heal Your Life*. Santa Monica, CA: Hay House.

170 Ibid.

171 Goodreads. (2019). *Johann Wolfgang von Goethe Quote*. Available at: https://www.goodreads.com/quotes/419209-treat-people-as-if-they-were-what-they-ought-to [Accessed 21 April 2019].

172 Goodreads. (2019). *Ram Dass Quotes*. Available at: https://www.goodreads.com/quotes/7711916-when-you-go-out-into-the-woods-and-you-look [Accessed 21 April 2019].

173 Wikipedia. (2018). *Black Panther Film*. Available at: https://en.wikipedia.org/wiki/Black_Panther_(film) [Accessed 22 April 2019].

174 Covey, S. (2008). *The Speed of Trust: The One Thing that Changes Everything*. New York: Free Press.

175 Graham, S. (1998). *You Can Make It Happen*. New York: First Fireside Edition, p200-204.

176 Hendry, V.A. (n.d.). *Quote on Pinterest.com*. Available at: https://za.pinterest.com/pin/519321400776662987/?lp=true [Accessed 22 April 2019].

177   Burkus, D. (2018). *You are not the average of the five people you surround yourself with.* Available at: https://medium.com/the-mission/youre-not-the-average-of-the-five-people-you-surround-yourself-with-f21b817f6e69 [Accessed 21 April 2019].

178   Better Life Coaching Blog. (2010). *The Triple Filter Test – A Story About Gossip.* Available at: https://betterlifecoachingblog.com/2010/09/10/the-triple-filter-test-a-story-about-gossip/ [Accessed 27 April 2019].

179   BrainyQuote. (2019). *Marcel Proust Quotes.* Available at: https://www.brainyquote.com/search_results?q=marcel+proust+ [Accessed 27 April 2019].

180   BrainyQuote. (2019). *Marianne Williamson Quotes.* Available at: https://www.brainyquote.com/quotes/marianne_williamson_635491 [Accessed 28 April 2019].

181   BrainyQuote. (2019). Wayne Dyer Quote. Available at: https://www.brainyquote.com/quotes/wayne_dyer_173497 [Accessed 27 April 2019].

182   Heart Talk Now. (2019). *Robbins-abundance-quotes-fear-quotes.* Available at: https://www.hearttalknow.com/practice-attitude-of-gratitude/robbins-abundance-quotes-fear-quotes/ [Accessed 27 April 2019].

183   Tracy, B. (2008). *Flight Plan.* San Francisco: Berret-Koehler Publishers, Inc.

184   Middleton, Y. (2016). *46 Extraordinary Gabrielle Bernstein Quotes.* Available at: https://addicted2success.com/quotes/46-extraordinary-gabrielle-bernstein-quotes/ [Accessed 22 April 2019].

185   BrainyQuote. (2019). *Alexander Bell Quote.* Available at: https://www.brainyquote.com/search_results?q=alexander+bell [Accessed 27 April 2019].

186   BrainyQuote. (n.d.). *Seneca Quote.* Available at: https://www.brainyquote.com/quotes/seneca_377999 [Accessed 28 April 2019].

187   Landers, A. (1997). *Best of Ann Landers: Her Favorite Letters of All Time.* New York: Ballantine Books.

188   Fav it. (n.d.). *Vivian Komori Quote.* Available at: https://favqs.com/quotes/vivian-komori/61876-life-is-not-a- [Accessed 28 April 2019].

189   Quote Investigator. (n.d.). Charles Darwin Quote. Available at: https://quoteinvestigator.com/2014/05/04/adapt/ [Accessed 28 April 2019].

190   Ten Boom, C. (2019). *My Life Is but A Weaving Poem.* Available at: https://www.goodreads.com/quotes/741391-life-is-but-a-weaving-the-tapestry-poem-my-life [Accessed 28 April 2019].

191   Ibid.

192   Fox, E. (2019). *Living Life Fully.* Available at: http://www.livinglifefully.com/thinkersfox.htm [Accessed 28 April 2019].

193   Anderson, A. R. (2016). *If you believe in the magic of serendipity, you will have serendipitous experiences!* Available at: http://www.amyreesanderson.com/blog/if-you-believe-in-the-magic-of-serendipity-you-will-have-serendipitous-experiences/#.XUvsCOgzY2w. [Accessed 28 April 2019].

194   BrainyQuote. (n.d.). *Vince Lombardi Quote.* Available at: https://www.brainyquote.com/quotes/vince_lombardi_382625 [Accessed 19 April 2019].

195   Ewers, P. (2018). *The Definitive Guide to Understanding Proactivity and Becoming a Proactive Entrepreneur.* Available at: https://betterhumans.coach.me/the-definitive-guide-to-understanding-proactivity-and-becoming-a-proactive-entrepreneur-558ecf3a755d [Accessed 19 April 2019].

196 Webb, C. (2016). *How to beat procrastination*. Available at: https://hbr.org/2016/07/how-to-beat-procrastination [Accessed 13 April 2019].

197 Goodreads. (2019). *Aristotle Quotes*. Available at: https://www.goodreads.com/quotes/1003359-we-are-what-we-repeatedly-do-excellence-then-is-not [Accessed 19 April 2019].

198 Goal Cast. (2019). *25 Powerful Zig Ziglar Quotes to Boost Your Willpower*. Available at: https://www.goalcast.com/2018/01/16/most-inspiring-zig-ziglar-quotes/ [Accessed 19 April 2019].

199 LIFE. (2017). *16 Wildly Successful People Who Overcame huge obstacles to get there*. Available at: https://www.huffpost.com/entry/successful-people-obstacles_n_3964459. [Accessed 28 April 2019].

200 Goodreads. (n.d.). *Nelson Mandela Quote*. Available at: https://www.goodreads.com/quotes/270163-do-not-judge-me-by-my-successes-judge-me-by [Accessed 28 April 2019].

201 Weil, Z. 2019. *Your Life is Your Message: Why integrity matters if you want to create positive change*. Available at: https://www.psychologytoday.com/za/blog/becoming-solutionary/201904/your-life-is-your-message [Accessed 28 April 2019].

202 Teachers Pay Teachers. (n.a.). *The Starfish Story*. Available at: https://www.teacherspayteachers.com/Product/The-Starfish-Story-2730170 [Accessed 28 April 2019].

203 BrainyQuote. (2019). *Johann Wolfgang von Goethe Quote*. Available at: https://www.brainyquote.com/quotes/johann_wolfgang_von_goeth_133629 [Accessed 28 April 2019].

204 Goodreads. (2019). *Kalu Ndukwe Kalu Quote*. Available at: https://www.goodreads.com/quotes/56602-the-things-you-do-for-yourself-are-gone-when-you [Accessed 28 April 2019].

205 Goodreads. (n.d.). *Mahatma Gandhi Quote*. Available at: https://www.goodreads.com/quotes/24499-be-the-change-that-you-wish-to-see-in-the [Accessed 28 April 2019].

206 Goodreads. (2019). *Gautama Buddha Quote*. Available at: https://www.goodreads.com/quotes/3181192-in-the-end-only-three-things-matter-how-much-you [Accessed 21 April 2019].

207 Goodreads. (2019). *Bryant S. Hinckley Quote*. Available at: https://www.goodreads.com/quotes/798213-service-is-the-virtue-that-distinguished-the-great-of-all [Accessed 28 April 2019].

208 BrainyQuote. (2019). *Hellen Keller Quote*. Available at: https://www.brainyquote.com/quotes/helen_keller_121539 [Accessed 28 April 2019].

209 E Notes. (2019). *Mahatma Gandhi Quote*. Available at: https://www.enotes.com/homework-help/define-this-quote-405335 [Accessed 19 April 2019].

210 Goleman, D. (2015). *Want a Loyal Team? Choose Kindness Over Toughness*. Available at: https://www.ramdass.org/daniel-goleman/ [Accessed 22 April 2019].

211 The Telegraph. (2019). *Princess Diana's 15 Powerful Inspirational Quotes*. Available at: https://www.telegraph.co.uk/women/life/princess-dianas-15-powerful-inspirational-quotes/carry-random-act-kindness-no-expectation-reward-safe-knowledge/ [Accessed 22 April 2019].

212 BrainyQuote. (2019). *Dalai Lama Quote*. Available at: https://www.brainyquote.com/quotes/dalai_lama_384423 [Accessed 28 April 2019].

213 Dyer, W. (1995). *Your Sacred Self*. New York: Harper Collins Publishers, p58.

214 Keep Inspiring Me. (2019). *138 Feel-Good Quotes About Happiness*. Available at: https://www.keepinspiring.me/quotes-about-happiness/ [Accessed 20 April 2019].

215 Goal Cast. (2019). *25 Powerful Zig Ziglar Quotes to Boost Your Willpower*. Available at: https://www.goalcast.com/2018/01/16/most-inspiring-zig-ziglar-quotes/ [Accessed 19 April 2019].

216 Robbins, T. (2019). *The six human needs*. Available at: https://www.tonyrobbins.com/mind-meaning/do-you-need-to-feel-significant/ [Accessed 22 April 2019].

217 Curtin, M. (2019). *33 Steve Jobs Quotes That Will Inspire You to Success*. Availabe at: https://www.inc.com/melanie-curtin/33-steve-jobs-quotes-that-will-inspire-you-to-achieve-massive-success.html [Accessed 19 April 2019].

218 AZ Quotes. (2019). *Florinda Donner Quotes*. Available at: https://www.azquotes.com/author/39221-Florinda_Donner Way [Accessed 19 April 2019].

219 Dyer, W. 1995. *Your Sacred Self*. New York: Harper Collins Publishers.

220 Goodreads. (2019). *Martin Luther King Quote*. Available at: https://www.goodreads.com/quotes/search?utf8=%E2%9C%93&q=martin+luther+king&commit=Search [Accessed 5 May 2019].

221 Gervais, R. (2019). *The greatest privilege that comes with freedom of speech is using your voice for those who don't have one*. [Accessed 19 April 2019]. Available at: https://twitter.com/rickygervais/status/689084695326384128?lang=en [Accessed 28 April 2019].

222 Wetherly, A. (2019). *Amy Wetherly*. Available at: https://www.facebook.com/pg/mrsamyweatherly/photos/?ref=page_internal [Accessed 28 April 2019].

223 BrainyQuote. (2019). *Lao Tzu Quote*. Available at: https://www.brainyquote.com/quotes/lao_tzu_393061 [Accessed 22 April 2019].

224 Goodreads. (2019). *Albert Einstein Quote*. Available at: https://www.goodreads.com/quotes/987-there-are-only-two-ways-to-live-your-life-one [Accessed 22 April 2019].

225 Quotes.net. (2019). *Oprah Winfrey Quotes*. Available at: https://www.quotes.net/quote/19128 [Accessed 13 April 2019].

226 Morin, A. (2015). *7 Scientifically Proven Benefits of Gratitude*. Available at: https://www.psychologytoday.com/intl/blog/what-mentally-strong-people-dont-do/201504/7-scientifically-proven-benefits-gratitude [Accessed 13 April 2019].

227 Pass It On. (2019). *Pass it on quotes*. Available at: https://www.passiton.com/inspirational-quotes/7240-we-make-a-living-by-what-we-get-we-make-a-life . [Accessed 22 April 2019].

228 Chatterjee, R. (2018). *The Stress Solution*. London: Penguin Random House.

229 Wise Old Sayings. (2019). *Regret Sayings and Quotes*. Available at: http://www.wiseoldsayings.com/regret-quotes/ [Accessed 22 April 2019].

230 Ibid.

231 Sharma, R. (2006). *The Greatness Guide*. London: Harper Element, p52.

232 Pass It On. (2019). *Pass it on quotes*. Available at: https://www.passiton.com/inspirational-quotes/5094-for-a-long-time-it-had-seemed-to-me-that-life [Accessed 22 April 2019].

233 Seale, Q. (2019). *138 Feel-Good Quotes About Happiness*. Available at: https://www.keepinspiring.me/quotes-about-happiness/ [Accessed 22 April 2019].

234 Ibid.

235 BrainyQuote. (2019). *Funny Quotes*. Available at: https://www.brainyquote.com/topics/funny [Accessed 21 April 2019].

236   BrainyQuote. (2019). *Bruce Lee Quotes*. Available at: https://www.brainyquote.com/quotes/bruce_lee_378322 [Accessed 21 April 2019].

237   Reilly, P. (2019). *Gandhi Story*. Available at: https://preilly.wordpress.com/2008/07/19/gandhi-story/ [Accessed 21 April 2019].

238   Goalcast. (2019). *Johann Wolfgang von Goethe Quotes*. Available at: https://www.goalcast.com/2019/04/02/johann-wolfgang-von-goethe-quotes/ [Accessed 13 April 2019].

239   Lama, D.(2010). *Dalai Lama*. Available at: https://www.facebook.com/DalaiLama/posts/right-from-the-moment-of-our-birth-we-are-under-the-care-and-kindness-of-our-par/104715156228095/ [Accessed 21 April 2019].

240   Gradesaver. (2019) *Everyman, Morality Play*. Available at: https://www.gradesaver.com/everyman-and-other-miracle-and-morality-plays/study-guide/summary [Accessed 21 April 2019].

241   Goodreads. (2019). *Dalai Lama XIV Quotes*. Available at: https://www.goodreads.com/quotes/8555471-people-were-created-to-be-loved-things-were-created-to [Accessed 21 April 2019].

242   Eminently Quotable. (2019). *Brendon Burchard Quote*. Available at: http://www.eminentlyquotable.com/never-believe-you-are-above-or-below-anyone/ [Accessed 21 April 2019].

243   Pass It On. (2019). *Melanie Koulouris Quote*. Available at: https://www.passiton.com/inspirational-quotes/7921-be-humble-in-your-confidence-yet-courageous-in [Accessed 21 April 2019].

244   AZ Quotes. (2019). *Nelson Mandela Quote*. Available at: https://www.azquotes.com/author/9365-Nelson_Mandela/tag/humility [Accessed 21 April 2019].

245   Graham, S.(2004). *You Can Make It Happen*. Book Launch. Nedbank Corporate Office. Sandton.

246   Goodreads. (2019). *Abraham Lincoln Quote*. Available at: https://www.goodreads.com/quotes/5851097-and-in-the-end-it-s-not-the-years-in-your [Accessed 5 May 2019].

247   Goodreads. (2019). *Martin Luther King Quotes*. Available at: https://www.goodreads.com/quotes/search?utf8=%E2%9C%93&q=martin+luther+king&commit=Search [Accessed 28 April 2019].

248   QuotesCover. (2019). *Antoine de Saint-Exupery Quotes*. Available at: https://quotescover.com/antoine-de-saint-exupery-quote-about-love [Accessed 5 May 2019].

249   Goodreads. (2019). *Mother Teresa Quote*. [Accessed 5 May 2019]. Available at: https://www.goodreads.com/quotes/1139478-people-are-often-unreasonable-irrational-and-self-centered-forgive-them-anyway [Accessed 5 May 2019].

Index